Preparing Students for College and Careers

D1592722

Preparing Students for College and Careers addresses measurement and research issues related to college and career readiness. Educational reform efforts across the United States have increasingly taken aim at measuring and improving postsecondary readiness. These initiatives include developing new content standards, redesigning assessments and performance levels, legislating new developmental education policy for colleges and universities, and highlighting gaps between graduates' skills and employers' needs.

In this comprehensive book, scholarship from leading experts on each of these topics is collected for assessment professionals and for education researchers interested in this new area of focus. Cross-disciplinary chapters cover the current state of research, best practices, leading interventions, and a variety of measurement concepts, including construct definitions, assessments, performance levels, score interpretations, and test uses.

Katie Larsen McClarty is Chief Assessment Officer at Questar Assessments. She oversees item and test development, publishing, psychometrics, and research. Her own research centers on assessment design, college readiness, standard setting, and gifted education.

Krista D. Mattern is a Director of ACT's Statistical and Applied Research Department. Her research focuses on evaluating the validity and fairness of both cognitive and noncognitive measures for predicting student success. She is also interested in higher education issues such as college choice, major selection, and college completion.

Matthew N. Gaertner is Principal Research Scientist at SRI International's Center for Education Policy. His research focuses on college and career readiness and the effects of educational policies and reforms on disadvantaged students' access, persistence, and achievement.

Technology and Testing
Improving Educational and Psychological Measurement
Edited by Fritz Drasgow

Meeting the Challenges to Measurement in an Era of Accountability
Edited by Henry Braun

Fairness in Educational Assessment and Measurement
Edited by Neil J. Dorans and Linda L. Cook

Testing in the Professions
Credentialing Policies and Practice
Edited by Susan Davis-Becker and Chad W. Buckendahl

Validation of Score Meaning for the Next Generation of Assessments
The Use of Response Processes
Edited by Kadriye Ercikan and James W. Pellegrino

Preparing Students for College and Careers
Theory, Measurement, and Educational Practice
Edited by Katie Larsen McClarty, Krista D. Mattern, and Matthew N. Gaertner

Preparing Students for College and Careers

Theory, Measurement, and Educational Practice

Edited by
Katie Larsen McClarty, Krista D. Mattern,
and Matthew N. Gaertner

 Routledge
Taylor & Francis Group

NEW YORK AND LONDON

First published 2018
by Routledge
711 Third Avenue, New York, NY 10017

and by Routledge
2 Park Square, Milton Park, Abingdon, Oxon, OX14 4RN

Routledge is an imprint of the Taylor & Francis Group, an informa business

Library of Congress Cataloging-in-Publication Data
A catalog record for this book has been requested

ISBN: 978-1-138-65630-7 (hbk)
ISBN: 978-1-138-65628-4 (pbk)
ISBN: 978-1-315-62197-5 (ebk)

Typeset in Minion Pro
by codeMantra

For his devotion to public service, his steadfast commitment to equal educational opportunity, and his unfailing humor, we dedicate this book to the memory of Massachusetts Education Commissioner Mitchell D. Chester.

Contents

Foreword

"A Toast to Sofia and Hector's Future"

Mitchell D. Chester

> *"The nation that out-educates us today will out-compete us tomorrow The nation that out-educates us today will out-compete us tomorrow The nation that out-educates us today will out-compete us tomorrow The nation that out-educates us today will out-compete us tomorrow."*
>
> President Barack Obama
> January 7, 2010

We live in an interdependent and shrinking world—a world where the speed at which we are growing smaller and more interconnected is accelerating. In this global context, political boundaries—both state and national—are increasingly irrelevant to economic and social opportunity. Nations across the globe are taking President Obama's admonition to heart. The quality and aspiration of their education systems are central to each nation's well-being.

It was only a few decades ago that the US education system was viewed with envy. However, the evidence that America has lost its standing educationally is numerous. It includes the 2015 Program International Student Assessment (PISA) results in which the United States performs in the middle of the pack internationally in reading and science and near the bottom in mathematics.[1] In addition, according to the Organization of Economic Cooperation and Development (OECD), whereas the United States led the world in college attainment as recently as two or three decades ago, more than a dozen nations have surpassed us at this point.[2]

Of the many wake-up calls we might cite, one of the loudest is the performance of Shanghai, China. Not only did the province perform at the very top, without peer, in reading, mathematics, and science on both the 2009 and 2012 PISA administrations, but also the gap between their highest and lowest performing students was narrower than in many nations, including the United States. In light of PISA's premium on applying knowledge to novel situations, Shanghai's results defy the caricature of Chinese schools as bastions of rote, pedantic learning.

In short, many nations (and subnational units) are upping their educational game in pursuit of a bright future for their citizens. It can be argued that the United States is doing no worse than we were two or three decades ago, but while we have largely plateaued, many of the world's nations have doubled down, invested smartly, aimed high, and are now surpassing us.

This global perspective frames the import of college and career readiness to our nation's future. Increasingly, the careers that promise a livable wage are those for which solid academic and career preparation are necessary. The evidence for the linkage between employment, earnings, and academic credentials is well established.[3] Further, the toll on being unprepared for a career that provides a livable wage includes decreased physical and psychological health (Zimmerman, Woolf, & Haley, 2015), increased divorce rates,[4] and increased likelihood of being a criminal offender (Alliance for Excellent Education, 2013).

The value of this volume is situated in this global context. It is clear that many of the nation's high school graduates are prepared—often well-prepared—for college and/or career. Roughly two-thirds of graduates enroll in college, while more than 70% of those who do not enroll are employed.[5] Of those who attend college full-time, approximately 60% achieve a four-year degree within six years.[6] But full-time college enrollment is the exception rather than the rule (Complete College America, 2013).

At the same time, the evidence suggests that too many high school graduates are not ready to succeed in college and/or career. Using data from Massachusetts (arguably one of, if not the highest achieving state), more than one-third of high school graduates who enroll in the Commonwealth's public campuses are placed in at least one remedial, noncredit-bearing course. In our two-year institutions, in which low-income and first-generation college attendees disproportionately enroll, the remedial rate hovers between 60% and 70%. Nationally, fewer than one-in-four students who begin their postsecondary education with noncredit-bearing courses ever acquire a degree (Complete College America, 2012).

At a time when it is increasingly important to educate all, and not simply some, the United States is failing to prepare a large proportion of our students for college and careers. A growing segment of our school-age population includes student groups for whom our public education system has the worst track record: students of color, many students from non-English-speaking backgrounds, and students from low-income families—and who are the emerging majority of our school-age enrollment. We must vastly improve our success in preparing all students for college and career if we are to secure a promising future for our nation.

College and Career Readiness through the Experience of Two Students

A few years back, when visiting one of the Commonwealth's career/vocational/technical high schools, I met Sofia and Hector.[7] I visit schools often. Typically, I observe classes, meet with administrators and teachers, and hold focus groups with students. On this visit, of the dozen or so students I met with, Hector and Sofia made a particular impression on me. It is for their future that this volume on preparing students for college and careers pivots from academic to reality.

Sofia was a sophomore and Hector a junior when I met them in the spring of 2014. Both attended a low-performing, urban career/vocational/technical high school. Many of the school's enrollees came from low-income families, were of Latino heritage, or had been identified with a learning disability—with many of the students reflecting two, or all three, of these attributes. The school's academic track record was abysmal, with a graduation rate of about 25%. More than one in five students were expelled at least once during the school year. My observations of classes at the school revealed low level academic aspirations and often less than competent instruction.

I had identified the school as "underperforming" in 2010 as one of the initial cohort of schools designated for turnaround under legislation enacted that year. Underperforming status requires the school district to develop and implement a turnaround plan. By 2014, with little improvement in academic performance, including graduation rates, the district had engaged a turnaround management partner to secure improved academic and vocational opportunities.

At the time of our conversation, Hector and Sofia articulated aspirations for their futures that required a level of education beyond the minimum necessary for graduation. Hector had attended the school for all three grades and was looking forward to his senior year. He demonstrated a level of maturity and focus that I did not find common in his age group. His mother had just moved back to the city after living out-of-state for more than a year. She now was planning to start a college program. Hector was living with the friend who had taken him in when his mother left. He did not mention his father.

Hector's goal was to be accepted to college and earn a degree. He was enrolled in the Transportation Academy, where he focused on automotive technology. Hector planned to enroll in Advanced Placement (AP) courses that the school would be offering the next school year for the first time. He wanted to enhance his academic credentials in the eyes of college admissions officers.

At the time, I had little doubt that Hector was capable of succeeding with his goal. He was motivated and had demonstrated the capability to persist in school, despite the apparent absence of the familial and peer-group norms often associated with academic success. Nonetheless, I had little confidence that the school had prepared him academically for success. Knowing the school's educational record and having observed many academic as well as vocational classes at the school, I had no reason to expect that Hector was prepared to succeed in demanding academic course work, nor was I assured that the teachers who would teach the AP courses were sufficiently prepared.

Sofia's profile was decidedly different than that of Hector. While both reported disrupted home and family contexts, Sofia displayed little of Hector's assuredness and focus. As a sophomore, Sofia was now enrolled in the third high school of her career. Her transfers reflected both evolving family circumstances, as well as personal and academic challenges she encountered in the first two high schools.

Sofia also was enrolled in the school's Transportation Academy, where she focused on automotive collision repair. She came across as personable, but tentative in her responses. While Sofia willingly participated in our conversation, her responses to questions about her academic and career aspirations demonstrated limited resolve about college or career. She expressed a commitment to stabilizing her life, staying engaged, and leaving high school with a marketable trade. She chose auto collision because she did not know much about it. She hoped that the lack of prior knowledge would compel her to focus. Sofia exhibited little knowledge of the course options open to her or how academic decisions she made now would impact the range of possible careers she might pursue.

I came away from my conversation with Sofia deeply concerned about the prognosis for her future. Although I found her continued enrollment despite three high school placements in two years to be an encouraging sign, I also knew that mobility during high school is associated with reduced likelihood of persistence to graduation. The combination of the school's mediocre academic record and Sofia's faltering school trajectory left me less than optimistic that she would be successful in completing her high school career, let alone be well prepared for success after high school.

The context of an underperforming high school, with a mediocre program of instruction in basic academic skills (i.e., literacy and mathematics) and low graduation rates, portends poorly for both college and career preparedness. Nonetheless, the case of Sofia and Hector highlights the intersection of college and career readiness, as well as the role of academic and nonacademic skills and dispositions. If we are unable to prepare Sofia and Hector to succeed in opportunities after high school, then we not only shortchange two of our youth, but we hinder the future of our nation as well.

Defining and Measuring College and Career Readiness

What does it mean to be ready? The first part of this volume addresses the challenge of defining the knowledge, skills, and attributes associated with college and career readiness, including the discrete as well as overlapping elements of college versus career readiness. Readiness is a multidimensional construct, and no single measure will capture accurately the dimensions of readiness.

Getting the constructs right is more than an academic exercise. I suspect that Sofia and Hector's teachers and administrators had little more than conventional wisdom and intuition to back their strategies for designing programs that would support readiness for college and careers. Conventional wisdom promoted the institution of AP courses, although there was no evidence that the school had a plan for ensuring the requisite knowledge and experiences to support AP success. Intuition drove the purchase of software designed to generate potential college choices based on student survey responses.

Hector understood that success in AP courses would carry more weight in college admissions than non-AP courses. He was interested in demonstrating his college readiness. Sofia understood that a high school diploma and a credential for a marketable trade would offer her a path to self-sufficiency.

What was lacking at Hector and Sofia's school was a design based on a robust understanding of competencies and experiences that prepare a student well for success after high school. Academic courses were fully uncoupled from vocational courses. The students participating in internships linked to their vocational/technical majors numbered in the single digits. Success in programs was largely defined by behavioral and attitudinal metrics—attendance and discipline. While showing up and conducting oneself maturely are dispositions valued by employers, these are insufficient in and of themselves to establish readiness.

As the chapters in this part illustrate, the interlocking dimensions of academic achievement, disposition, aptitude, and experience weave together to determine preparation for college and careers. Focusing on only one or two dimensions increases the likelihood of misclassification. Take the case of the Eton College summer 1949 science report card for a then 15-year-old boy who was ranked last out of 250 boys in his year group in biology:

> It has been a disastrous half. His work has been far from satisfactory. His prepared stuff has been badly learnt, and several of his test pieces have been torn over; one of such pieces of prepared work scored 2 marks out of a possible 50. His other work has been equally bad, and several times he has been in trouble, because he will not listen, but will insist on doing his work in his own way. I believe he has ideas about becoming a Scientist; on his present showing this is quite ridiculous, if he can't learn simple Biological facts he would have no chance of doing the work of a Specialist, and it would be sheer waste of time, both on his part, and of those who have to teach him.[8]

This report card belonged to the young Brit, John Gurdon. After Eton, he pursued developmental biology and studied nuclear transplantation and cloning. In 1995, the Queen of England knighted John Gurdon, and in 2012, he was awarded the Nobel Prize for Physiology or Medicine "for the discovery that mature cells can be reprogrammed to become pluripotent." The reader will note that Sir John's professor did not contribute any of the chapters in this volume.

Validating College- and Career-Readiness Performance Levels and Uses

How do we know when someone is ready? This part of the book identifies some of the challenges and approaches to providing sound inferences about readiness. Different approaches to measuring readiness may yield discrepant inferences. Understanding the basis of a given measure's claims is essential to judging its usefulness for a given decision.

While the Massachusetts Comprehensive Assessment System (MCAS) often is identified as best in class when compared to other state assessments, the limitations of our high school exam have emerged since the test was implemented. The 10th-grade English language arts, mathematics, and science/technology/engineering MCAS has two statutory purposes: to measure achievement on the 10th-grade content standards and as criteria for earning a high school diploma. Beginning with the Class of 2002, earning at least a "Needs Improvement" score (the second lowest of four performance levels) on the English/language arts and mathematics tests are requirements for graduation, with a science/technology/engineering MCAS exam added as a further requirement effective with the Class of 2010.

Results in the early years of the high school MCAS were quite low, with as few as 24% and 33% scoring at the "Proficient" or "Advanced" levels in mathematics and English/language arts, respectively ("Needs Improvement" along with an Educational Proficiency Plan is the graduation requirement). The first administration of the science/technology/engineering assessment (2008) resulted in a "Proficient" or higher rate of 57%. Over time, achievement on each of the high school exams has improved steadily. In 2015, the "Proficient" and "Advanced" rates were 91% in English/language arts, 79% in mathematics, and 72% in science/engineering/technology.

To be fair, the MCAS high school tests were not designed to measure readiness for college or careers. The "Proficient" standard signals mastery of content through the 10th grade and is not a claim of readiness for college-level work or for the academic expectations of employers. As a result, there are a large number of students who are meeting the MCAS as well as their district curriculum requirements who subsequently are placed into noncredit bearing, remedial courses in college. From a policy perspective, the phenomena of increasing numbers of students performing well on the Commonwealth's high school assessments but being unprepared for academic success in higher education presents a conflicted set of signals to students, families, and educators. As well, more than two-thirds of Massachusetts's employers report that they have difficulty finding "people with the right skills for the positions they need to fill" (Massachusetts Business Alliance for Education, 2014).

This disjuncture between our legacy MCAS high school performance levels and college and career readiness is a key reason that Massachusetts participated in the Partnership for the Assessment of College and Careers (PARCC) and that we are building a next-generation MCAS. In addition to being a graduation requirement, goals for the new assessment are to provide reliable information about whether students are on track for success at the next grade level and ultimately for success after high school, as well as to signal to educators expectations that reflect an aspirational program of instruction.

As Massachusetts prepares our new assessment, we are attentive to measurement issues such as content and predictive validity. An assessment may predict readiness for college or careers while not providing particularly useful information about content mastery needed to be well prepared. A Mathematica study comparing the power of MCAS and PARCC to predict college outcomes is illustrative (Nichols-Barrer, Place, Dillon, & Gill, 2015). MCAS and PARCC both predict college success at about the same rate, with higher scores on each associated with higher grade point averages in college level courses. Although the PARCC college ready performance level predicts a higher level of college performance and lower levels of remediation in mathematics than the MCAS "Proficient" level, in English language arts the performance levels are similar.

The authors of the Mathematica report note, however, that predictive validity is just one of several considerations when selecting or designing assessments of college readiness. For example, the differences in content knowledge, problem-solving skills, and degree of writing production required by PARCC and MCAS may promote different kinds of instructional practices. It is an article of faith that successful education systems align curriculum, instruction, and assessment. For our assessments to complement the efforts of educators who are designing programs of instruction to prepare students for success after high school, it is important that assessments signal our aspirations for curriculum content and not simply predict performance.

Interestingly, even when focused on prediction, the strongest correlations between MCAS or PARCC scores and first-year college GPAs account for no more than 20% of the variance in GPA. The MCAS and PARCC results are similar to correlations observed when comparing SAT scores and first-year college grades (Nichols-Barrer et al., 2015). These analyses illustrate the limitations of relying on a single measure to predict college success. Success depends on many factors, of which academic preparation is but one. Having made this point, I anticipate that certifying academic readiness for college-level coursework undoubtedly is a more achievable goal than predicting success.

Much of the discussion about high school content and performance standards has aimed at identifying the level of preparation necessary to succeed in an entry-level, credit-bearing course. In the case of a curricular or assessment program designed to certify readiness to succeed in an entry-level course, it is critical that students understand the extent and limitations of the readiness claim. For example, the level of mathematics preparation necessary to succeed in an engineering program is likely more ambitious than the preparation needed to succeed in an entry-level, credit-bearing mathematics course as part of a liberal arts program. The student who wants to pursue an engineering program should know that the readiness certification is short of what he or she needs to succeed.

Improving College and Career Readiness

While accurately defining and measuring the knowledge, skills, and attributes that contribute to college and career readiness is an evolving endeavor, providing a program of study and experiences that ensure student preparation is today's challenge. The final part of this volume offers insight into the holy grail of education—how we improve all students' readiness for college and careers. This effort is underway in virtually every state and district in the nation and almost always involves a combination of better and earlier identification of students who are not on track to being prepared for success after high school, interventions designed to advance students who are not on track, improved overall academic achievement, and attention to intrapersonal qualities and dispositions that influence readiness.

Over the past decade, Massachusetts's four- and five-year graduation rates have risen steadily (from respective rates of 79.9% and 82.7% in 2005–2006 to 87.3% and 88.5% in 2014–2015) while dropout rates have declined (from an annual cohort rate of 3.8% in 2006–2007 to 1.9% in 2014–2015). The improvements in both rates are the result, at least in part, of increased attention on the part of educators to students at risk of failing to persist to graduation. The increased attention involved a deliberate statewide initiative.

Beginning with the 2010–2011 school year, Massachusetts undertook a graduation rate initiative involving the 133 high schools with dropout rates above the statewide average (which was then 2.9%). Over the ensuing years, the Department of Elementary and Secondary Education convened the schools to identify and implement prevention, intervention, and recovery approaches. In addition, Massachusetts established three new Gateway to College National Network early college sites.

Beginning with the 2012–2013 school year, Massachusetts began publishing a student-level early warning index.[9] Through analysis of historical data, the Department identified factors that predict student success, including assessment scores, attendance rates, course grades, and discipline records. The factors are combined to produce individual student index scores that are tied to each of several academic milestones: 3rd-grade reading proficiency; 6th-grade reading and mathematics proficiency; 9th-grade course credits; and high school graduation. The index provides a likelihood measure of meeting each academic milestone and has become an important complement to the graduation rate initiative. The early warning index is a metric that school districts increasingly are employing to identify students in need of special attention and intervention.

As a result of these initiatives, student groups that historically trailed their counterparts on measures of educational attainment have made some of the strongest progress. For example, students from low-income backgrounds achieved a 15.9 percentage-point graduation rate gain over the past decade (from 62.3% in 2005–2006 to 78.2% in 2014–2015). African-American and Hispanic/Latino students have achieved respective graduation rate gains of 13.1 and 15.3 points since the 2005–2006 school year (through the 2014–2015 school year). Over the same period, White students achieved a 5.0-point gain. As with the graduation rate, the dropout rate reduction for African-American and Hispanic/Latino students exceeded the rate of improvement statewide.

Despite these gains, the graduation rate for African-American and Hispanic/Latino students trails that of White students by 14.1 and 19.4 points, respectively—a staggering gap in an age where a high school diploma is a minimum and likely not sufficient education credential. Likewise, the dropout rate for African-American students is almost three times that of White students (3.0% versus 1.1%). Hispanic/Latino students had a dropout rate four times that of White students (4.4%) in 2014–2015. The racial/ethnic gaps in attainment are more stark when examining gender disaggregations. On virtually every measure, male educational attainment trails that of female attainment for each racial/ethnic group.

Although the size of the disparities is troubling, the gap narrowing is promising. The Commonwealth's success to date in improving student persistence to graduation is both an opportunity and a challenge. The opportunity is presented by the fact that we are succeeding in engaging more and more students, particularly students of color and students from low-income backgrounds, and helping them secure a high school diploma. The challenge is to ensure that graduating students are ready to meet the expectations of higher education, employers, and citizenship. If a student graduates, but is poorly prepared for these expectations, then we have limited that individual's life opportunities. To the extent that we fail to provide a course of study and experiences that prepare students who we historically have served least well and who represent an increasing proportion of our population, we are limiting our state and nation's future.

Beginning with the 2016–2017 school year, Massachusetts is producing a new early warning index for high school students, designed to identify the likelihood of success in postsecondary education. The index is tied to three college success milestones: (1) enrollment in postsecondary, (2) enrollment in credit-bearing courses, and (3) persistence to the second year of postsecondary enrollment. This new index complements the efforts that districts are undertaking to achieve readiness for postsecondary success and not simply high school graduation.

Conclusion

In the past decade, the attention of policymakers and practitioners has expanded from an initial focus on increasing high school graduation rates to include preparation for success after high school. This expanded focus is propelled by heightened awareness of the efforts of other nations to improve their competitive standing by elevating their educational aspiration. The frequent misalignment between high school programs of study and success after high school provides a local-level reality check for this global context. As we saw, in Massachusetts, many of the students who have done what we have asked of them—they have passed the high school exit exam and met their district curriculum requirements—subsequently learn they are not prepared for the expectations of higher education and employers.

In this foreword, I have provided real-world contexts and applications for essential college- and career-readiness constructs that this volume explores: defining and measuring readiness, validating readiness performance levels and their use, and improving college and career readiness. The insights and frameworks that are presented herein are valuable resources for policymakers and practitioners who are tasked with applying them to real-world circumstances. I have employed examples from Massachusetts as well as the experiences of two students to illustrate the challenges of securing preparation for success after high school.

Sofia's immediate aspirations were to stabilize her life, stay engaged, and leave high school with a marketable trade. To this end, she saw her school's automotive collision repair program as a value-added experience that included the possibility of earning industry certifications. This is a good bet on Sofia's part, because the vocational technical high school's automotive collision repair program is recognized as preparation for employment. Through internships during high school as well as placement services after high school, many students gain employment in their field right out of school.

At the time that I am writing this foreword, Sofia remains enrolled at the same career/vocational/technical high school and is in her senior year. She continues to pursue automotive collision repair. Sofia's academic track record is less than strong, but she remains on track to graduate. Hopefully, the vocational preparation she is experiencing will establish a viable vocational and career pathway for her.

Hector now is a high school graduate. He began working in a warehouse shipping department three days after graduation and is not currently pursuing college. His high school failed to implement the AP program that then-juniors at the school were led to believe would be offered in their senior year. Perhaps, Hector would be employed at the warehouse and not pursuing college even if his high school had delivered on the AP courses. Perhaps, even if he had experienced a strong high school academic program, his personal circumstances would have dictated immediate workforce entry. His failure to secure an automotive technology career path is a puzzle. It is likely that his high school failed to provide a work/study placement that would have been an opportunity for Hector to connect with an employer in his area of study.

While the reader may dismiss Sofia and Hector's plight as too distant from the central effort to define, measure, and secure college and career readiness, I would suggest that their future is our future. To illustrate, by 2035, the number of school-age citizens in Massachusetts is predicted to stay fairly flat, while the number of citizens age 65 and older will almost double. As a result, the proportion of the state's population that is of traditional working age (ages 19–65) will be a smaller percentage of the total population.[10] This shift in the age demographic will be accompanied by a shift in the racial and ethnic makeup of the school-age population, with increasing proportions of school-age youth comprising citizens of color and ethnic minorities. In other words, we will be educating greater numbers of Sofias and Hectors and will count on them to be prepared for postsecondary education and/or careers: for their own fulfillment, to ensure a robust economy for Massachusetts, as well as for the future of the nation.

While college and career readiness are multidimensional constructs, with some elements over which schools have limited influence, there is no doubt that the academic and experiential dimensions of K–12 education are strongly determinative of the opportunities that high school graduates are prepared to pursue. It is with this conviction as backdrop that this volume contributes important understandings and insights to the pursuit of college and career readiness.

Notes

1 https://www.oecd.org/pisa/data/
2 https://www.oecd.org/unitedstates/CN%20-%20United%20States.pdf
3 http://www.bls.gov/emp/ep_chart_001.htm
4 http://www.pewresearch.org/fact-tank/2015/12/04/education-and-marriage/
5 http://www.bls.gov/news.release/hsgec.nr0.htm
6 https://nces.ed.gov/fastfacts/display.asp?id=40
7 While the references are to two actual students, I have selected the names Hector and Sofia to protect the students' identity.
8 http://www.telegraph.co.uk/news/science/science-news/9594351/Sir-John-Gurdon-Nobel-Prize-winner-was-too-stupid-for-science-at-school.html
9 http://www.doe.mass.edu/ccr/ewi/
10 University of Massachusetts, Donahue Institute, Population Estimates Program, 2015

References

Alliance for Excellent Education. (2013). *Saving futures, saving dollars: The impact of education in crime reduction and earnings.* Washington, DC: Author.

Complete College America. (2012, April). *Remediation: Higher education's road to nowhere.* Retrieved from http://www.completecollege.org/docs/CCA-Remediation-final.pdf.

Complete College America. (2013, October). *How full-time are "full-time" students?* (Policy Brief). Retrieved from http://completecollege.org/pdfs/2013-10-14-how-full-time.pdf.

Massachusetts Business Alliance for Education. (2014, March). *The new opportunity to lead: A vision for education in Massachusetts in the next 20 years.* Boston, MA: Author. Retrieved from http://www.mbae.org/new-report-offers-a-vision-for-education-in-the-next-20-years/.

Nichols-Barrer, I., Place, K., Dillon, E., & Gill, B. (2015, October). *Predictive validity of MCAS and PARCC: Comparing 10th grade MCAS tests to PARCC Integrated Math II, Algebra II, and 10th grade English language arts tests.* Cambridge, MA: Mathematica Policy Research. Retrieved from http://www.mathematica-mpr.com/~/media/publications/pdfs/education/parcc_ma_assessment_final.pdf.

Zimmerman, E. B., Woolf, S. H., & Haley, A. (2015, September). *Understanding the relationship between education and health: A review of the evidence and an examination of community perspectives.* Content last reviewed September 2015. Rockville, MD: Agency for Healthcare Research and Quality. Retrieved from http://www.ahrq.gov/professionals/education/curriculum-tools/population-health/zimmerman.html.

Acknowledgments

This book is the result of several years of brainstorming, research, and writing, along with our contributors' tireless efforts to draft and revise chapters that we felt would advance the fields of measurement and educational practice. We are deeply indebted to the 23 authors who contributed to this volume. We appreciate our authors' willingness to develop and share their work, subject it to our review, respond to questions, and turn around edits on an ambitious production schedule. Obviously, this volume would not have taken shape without their thoughtful and timely contributions. We would also like to acknowledge support from our employers—ACT, Inc., Questar, SRI International, and Pearson. We are each grateful to our bright and enthusiastic colleagues who not only contributed research ideas (and, in some cases, chapters) but also assumed many responsibilities that allowed us to complete this book as we had envisioned it. Special thanks are owed to Wayne Camara (ACT), who approached us with this opportunity, and Marten Roorda (ACT), Jamie Post Candee (Questar), and Viki Young (SRI International), who supported our efforts throughout. We also wish to acknowledge Catherine Lacina and Kelly Larson, whose editing and formatting contributions were invaluable, and Daniel Schwartz and Matthew Friberg, our editorial team at Routledge, for their wisdom and encouragement.

Introduction

Katie Larsen McClarty, Matthew N. Gaertner,
and Krista D. Mattern

State of College and Career Readiness

Though higher education costs continue to rise, the economic and societal returns on a college education are clear. College graduates experience lower levels of unemployment and higher annual wages, resulting in over $1 million more in lifetime income than high school graduates (Abel & Deitz, 2014). Regions with higher proportions of college graduates benefit from lower crime rates, better health, and greater civic participation (Oreopoulos & Slavanes, 2009). Unfortunately, just 40% of adults ages 25–64 hold either a two-year or four-year college degree (Lumina Foundation, 2016).

Recent trends are not uniformly dismal. High school graduation rates are on the rise; most years we can take some comfort in the fact that more students are finishing high school on time this spring than last spring. The graduation rate has now reached 82%, an all-time high, and 10 percentage points higher than 20 years ago (NCES, 2016). But by just about any metric, the majority of these students are graduating underprepared for postsecondary opportunities. College readiness rates have not followed graduation rates upward. In fact, the percentage of students classified as college ready by the ACT and the SAT assessments has been relatively flat for the last five years, stuck around 25%–27% based on the ACT and 42%–44% as measured by the SAT (ACT, 2016; Adams, 2015). Each year, 60% of students who enroll in college are first referred to noncredit, developmental education courses (Bailey, 2009). This path is usually a dead end; less than 25% of students who start in developmental education successfully complete their degree within eight years (Attewell, Lavin, Domina, & Levey, 2006).

Colleges that emphasize retention, good standing, and completion are understandably concerned about the preparedness of students walking through their gates, and they aren't the only ones. Employers also cite a talent shortage, with 46% of US businesses reporting at least some difficulty finding adequate candidates (Manpower Group, 2016). One in five employers noted that applicants lack hard skills, or task-related qualifications. This skills gap can have a direct impact on the economy, reducing employers' ability to meet customer needs, provide effective customer service, improve efficiencies, innovate, and expand (Giffi et al., 2015).

Whether for college or career, boosting postsecondary readiness rates has become a centerpiece of education reform efforts in the United States. In 2009, President Obama set a goal that by 2020, America would have the highest proportion of college graduates in the world. The Lumina Foundation's goal is more specific: by 2025, 60% of Americans should hold postsecondary degrees, certificates, or other high-quality credentials.

To meet these ambitious goals, postsecondary preparation and completion initiatives have emerged, spanning life stages from prekindergarten through college. For example, programs such as Head Start are designed to provide low-income preschool students and their parents with education, health and nutrition, and social services. Long-term tracking of program participants shows they have an increased school attainment and are more likely to attend college, relative to similar peers (Ludwig & Phillips, 2008). In elementary school, smaller class sizes increase students' likelihood of enrolling in and completing college. The effects are most dramatic for minority students and those attending poorer schools (Dynarski, Hyman, & Schanzenbach, 2013).

In 2010, several states came together to create and adopt a more rigorous set of college- and career-readiness content standards—the Common Core State Standards (National Governors Association Center for Best Practices and Council of Chief State School Officers, 2010). Even states such as Texas and Virginia, which did not adopt the Common Core, issued their own set of CCR standards describing what students should know and be able to do at each grade level to be on track toward college and career readiness by the end of high school.

Following the adoption of new standards, many states and organizations redesigned their assessments and associated performance levels. The US Education Department funded two consortia of states to develop new CCR assessments—the Partnership for the Assessment of Readiness for College and Careers (PARCC) and the Smarter Balanced Assessment Consortium (SBAC). The National Assessment Governing Board (NAGB) also began a research program to develop a "postsecondary preparedness" performance level on the National Assessment of Educational Progress (NAEP). In 2013, NAGB approved reporting on 12th grade preparedness for college, and the first reporting showed 39% of 12th grade students prepared in mathematics and 38% prepared in reading.

Assessment programs have helped identify student deficiencies, but it has often fallen to colleges to remediate these deficiencies. Remediation has traditionally been delivered through a series of developmental, noncredit-bearing courses, but a growing body of research shows this approach is not very effective (Bailey, Jaggars, & Scott-Clayton, 2013). In response, many states have legislated new developmental education policy for colleges and universities. For example, in 2012, Connecticut passed Public Act 12–40, which eliminated traditional developmental education and required colleges to offer remedial support embedded within credit-bearing courses. Similarly, the Florida legislature passed Senate Bill 1720 in 2013, which exempted recent Florida high school graduates and active military members from assessment and placement into developmental courses. Students who are not exempt are presented with options for developmental education, but they are not required to enroll. Moreover, all developmental education courses offered in the state must be accelerated through specific instructional strategies (i.e., corequisite, modularization, compression, or contextualization).

Our Philosophy on College and Career Readiness

As editors of this book, we recognize that not everyone goes to college, and not everyone wants to go. However, the percentage of high school students who do not attend some form of postsecondary education by the age of 26 is extremely small—just 12% (Hull, 2014). Even among the 12% who do not enroll in college, two-thirds begin high school believing they will go to college, and over a quarter still have college aspirations at the age of 26. In addition, the share of US jobs available for those without postsecondary training is shrinking. By 2018, it is projected that only 37% of jobs will not require at least some postsecondary training (Carnevale, Smith, & Strohl, 2010). Therefore, in this book, we take a broad view of college—defining it as postsecondary training that leads to a degree, certificate, or other high-quality credential. This encompasses universities, colleges, community colleges, technical colleges, and other training institutions.

Furthermore, though not all students will go to college, we believe that students should be prepared to make that choice. In fact, most high school students do have college aspirations. For example, 96% of Chicago Public Schools students in 2005 hoped to earn a vocational, associate, or bachelor's degree. Notably, 83% of the students wanted to attain a bachelor's degree or higher (Roderick et al., 2008). Students are not the only ones interested in a college degree. Ninety-two percent of parents believe their child will attend college (Bushaw & Lopez, 2010). Why? Quite simply, more job opportunities, better income, and ultimately better life outcomes.

Therefore, we advocate for educational decisions that keep college doors open for students. This means designing course sequences in middle school that put students on track to complete upper-level science and mathematics courses in high school. Students who complete more rigorous high school mathematics courses are more likely to earn a bachelor's degree (Adelman, 2006), and taking a generally more rigorous curriculum is associated with higher grades in high school and college and better odds of college enrollment and persistence (Wyatt, Wiley, Camara, & Proestler, 2011).

A second way to expand opportunity is by providing job exploration opportunities to students early on. According to Gottfredson's (1981) developmental theory of occupational aspirations, it is during middle school—ages 9–13—when student differences in social class and ability become more apparent and, in turn, affect educational and career goals. For example, two-thirds of boys and girls are interested in science at a young age, but less than a quarter of physics, computer science, or engineering college graduates are women (De Welde, Laursen, & Thiry, 2007). Evaluating different career opportunities and their associated educational requirements is important, because middle-school students who are driven by college aspirations are more likely to meet minimum college qualifications by high school graduation, submit college applications, and ultimately attend college (Deci & Ryan, 1985; Hill & Wang, 2015).

State policies that require (and fund) all students to take a college admissions exam are another way to keep doors open. Universal testing admissions policies have gained traction over the last decade and are even easier to implement with the new Every Student Succeeds Act (ESSA) federal legislation. States that implement a mandatory admissions testing policy show an increase in four-year college enrollment, particularly among minority students and those from poorer schools. Moreover, the additional students who enroll in college also persist there—at the same rate as other students with similar high school credentials (Hyman, 2016).

In sum, we argue that keeping college doors open throughout middle and high school does not seem to harm career prospects for students who ultimately do not begin postsecondary training, and it substantially improves outcomes for students who do. For example, students who complete Algebra II in high school are more likely to enroll, persist, and complete college. However, completing Algebra II has little to no effect on students who enter directly into the workforce (Gaertner, Kim, DesJardins, & McClarty, 2013). Thus, though not all students may pursue college, most students will, most students and their parents have college aspirations, and education systems should prepare all students for this opportunity. Students may opt out of college, but schools should prepare them to have that choice.

Goals of This Book

With that philosophy as a background, the goal of this book was to convene a cross-disciplinary group of experts to synthesize the current state of college- and career-readiness research, best practices in measurement and diagnostics, and leading intervention practices designed to prepare students for life after high school. Though college and career readiness is a common discourse among educators, researchers, policymakers, and the general public, that discourse tends to lack consistency and clarity about what college and career readiness actually means. Much of this book, therefore, is devoted to measurement concepts including construct definitions, assessments, performance levels, score interpretations, and test uses.

Measurement, however, is but one piece of the larger college- and career-readiness theory of action. Assessments provide diagnoses of individual- or group-level readiness. Achieving bold college completion goals, however, requires moving beyond measurement and diagnosis to improvement. As such, we also wanted to share research about interventions designed to prepare students for college and careers. We therefore adopted an inclusive approach, bringing together researchers from a variety of domains to address important questions for college- and career-readiness policy, practice, and research.

Parts and Chapter Overview

The book is divided into three parts: (1) *Defining and Measuring College and Career Readiness*, (2) *Validating College- and Career-Readiness Performance Levels,* and (3) *Improving College and Career Readiness.* The first part of the book contains four chapters that describe the knowledge, skills, and attributes associated with college and career readiness as well as how those constructs are measured. This part address similarities and differences between college readiness and career readiness, as well as the roles of academic achievement (content knowledge), noncognitive skills, and aptitude in preparedness and later-life success.

In Chapter 1, David Conley focuses on the definitions of college and career readiness. He begins by differentiating between "college eligible" and "college ready," with the latter requiring a much broader set of knowledge, skills, and attributes. Conley then outlines various college readiness models, describing the similarities and differences between them, before comparing college readiness with career readiness. Finally, he discusses the implications of a multidimensional definition of readiness for the creation and use of assessments. Conley emphasizes readiness profiles over readiness scores, which would provide a significant shift in how readiness is currently reported.

In Chapter 2, William McCallum and James Pellegrino also argue for a shift—from defining and measuring college readiness as a set of discrete knowledge and skills to a set of enduring practices and ways of thinking. They derive a definition of college and career readiness from existing content standards, using the Common Core State Standards in mathematics as an example. Then, they discuss the challenges that such a definition poses for traditional assessment. One particularly interesting challenge is the idea of measuring the robustness or durability of knowledge. How has a student progressed in learning, and how have mathematical concepts been transferred and connected over time? This calls for more than static snapshot-in-time type assessments and for assessment developers with a deep understanding of content connections.

Chapter 3 expands the definition of college and career readiness even further by including noncognitive skills. Matthew Gaertner and Richard Roberts make three central claims: (1) including noncognitive measures alongside academic measures provides better prediction of future outcomes, (2) noncognitive measures provide more nuanced college-readiness diagnoses than cognitive measures alone, and (3) results of noncognitive assessments provide actionable feedback for students and educators. Gaertner and Roberts acknowledge some of the limitations of current noncognitive measures but provide specific recommendations for how measurement and use of these constructs could be improved.

The final chapter in this part, Chapter 4, addresses the role of general cognitive ability in college admissions and outcomes, career hiring and performance, and later-life achievement. Jonathan Wai, Frank Worrell, and Christopher Chabris argue that current college- and career-readiness discourse lacks recognition of the important role of cognitive ability, or *g*. They begin by asserting that many common academic achievement measures actually have *g* as an underlying factor. They then demonstrate the relationship between *g* and important college and career outcomes. Wai et al. acknowledge and address some counterarguments before making recommendations for how to include general cognitive ability in areas such as career counseling, admissions and hiring decisions, and intervention studies.

The second part of the book includes five chapters that focus on defining and using college- and career-readiness performance levels. The first two chapters describe some common approaches for setting standards on college- and career-readiness assessments. The second two chapters focus on the use and implications of college- and career-readiness performance levels for institutions of higher education and for diverse student populations. The final chapter in this part addresses the challenges and "mixed messages" that arise from the widespread adoption of many different college-readiness measures and performance levels.

In the first chapter in this part, Chapter 5, Katie Larsen McClarty, Susan Cooper Loomis, and Mary Pitoniak describe a standard-setting approach that combines empirical evidence with judgments from subject matter experts. They describe the steps of the approach—defining outcomes, gathering evidence, synthesizing results, conducting the standard setting event, and reporting and monitoring—using real examples. The chapter places particular emphasis on the decisions needed by practitioners and policymakers in order for the approach to be effective.

Building on the theme of evidence-based standard setting, in Chapter 6, Wayne Camara, Jeff Allen, and Joann Moore detail an empirical process for setting college- and career-readiness performance standards and for linking those standards down through lower grade levels. Using examples from ACT and ACT Aspire, the authors describe how college-readiness levels are set on admissions tests, as well as how additional performance levels and performance level descriptors can be set in order to use admissions tests at the state level for accountability or other purposes. The final part of the chapter outlines different empirical approaches that can be used to vertically articulate standards at lower grade levels, allowing for "on track to college readiness" performance level interpretations.

In Chapter 7, Elisabeth Barnett and Vikash Reddy explore the use of college-readiness assessments in college placement decisions. They describe the historical underpinnings of placement testing, along with the limitations and consequences of inaccurate placement. Barnett and Reddy present a framework for changing placement assessments, including alternative measures, multiple measures, and broader conceptualizations of placement. They describe specific examples of each and integrate changes in placement policies with other key higher education issues, such as developmental education reform and technology advances.

In Chapter 8, Rebecca Zwick tackles the issue of fairness in college- and career-readiness assessments. Although Zwick acknowledges the promise of college- and career-readiness assessments for providing useful information for students, parents, and educators, she highlights several areas for careful consideration. As echoed by other authors in the book, single point-in-time measures focused solely on academic achievement may have limited predictive power. However, measures designed to increase prediction such as race or income may unintentionally perpetuate disadvantage. Moreover, "not ready" designations may actually precipitate declines in achievement instead of improvements. Rather than spurring students and educators to provide more intensive interventions, "not ready" designations can become self-fulfilling prophecies, discouraging effort rather than inspiring it.

The last chapter in this part, Chapter 9, addresses the challenges and "mixed messages" that arise from the widespread adoption of many different college-readiness measures and performance levels (e.g., college admissions tests, national tests, state-level tests). Krista Mattern and Matthew Gaertner outline several dimensions on which college- and career-readiness assessments may differ, leading to different interpretations of resulting test scores. They place particular emphasis on the consequences of having multiple college- and career-readiness assessments that provide inconsistent results and whether the current assessment trends are any better than historical ones.

The final part of the book includes four chapters focused on both general and specific strategies to improve college and career readiness. Whereas the first two parts focused on more traditional measurement issues, the third part expands and discusses leading practices for boosting readiness. Each chapter in this part includes an overview of best practices in interventions in the general topic area as well as descriptions and research evidence for a specific intervention approach.

Chapter 10 describes the importance of intervening early in supporting college and career readiness. Chrissy Tillery and Brent Duckor detail best practices in early intervention and introduce the federally funded GEAR UP model specifically. They explain the goals and components of the GEAR UP program before illustrating the effectiveness of the GEAR UP program overall and for each of the specific components. Tillery and Duckor conclude by describing issues that make college- and career-readiness program evaluation research challenging, not only for GEAR UP but also for all early intervention programs.

Chapter 11 covers academic interventions, with a specific focus on best practices in developing mathematics pathways between high school and college. Francesca Fraga Leahy and Carolyn Landel illustrate why structured, intentional mathematics pathways are superior to a series of discrete mathematics courses designed in isolation. Taking specific examples from the Dana Center Mathways Project, Leahy and Landel describe how mathematics pathways help address the traditional mathematics challenges of misalignment, ineffective remedial education structures, and outdated curricular and pedagogical strategies.

Chapter 12 turns to nonacademic psychosocial interventions. Kathryn Kroeper and Mary Murphy address both individual and contextual factors that can create barriers to college and career readiness. They detail research-based intervention strategies, describing how to implement them and why they work. Interventions covered in this chapter include growth mindset, social belonging, and utility value. Kroeper and Murphy explain how social psychological interventions boost psychological strength, which, in turn, impacts academic achievement outcomes and college and career readiness.

In the final chapter of the improving college- and career-readiness part, Chapter 13, Margaret Heritage illustrates how changes in formative classroom assessment can enable students to take more control of their learning outcomes and better prepare for college and careers. She argues that the assessment relationship must change from a vertical one—where teachers assess students and students only receive scores—to a horizontal one, where students receive feedback from teachers, peers, and their own self-assessment and then use that information to actively plan their own learning. Only students who are able to take feedback from a variety of sources, synthesize the information, and act accordingly will truly be prepared for college and careers.

This book spans a wide range of topics, so we use the conclusion to draw out common themes from each part. Furthermore, just as each individual chapter concluded with a part on implications for policy, practice, and research, we use the closing chapter to highlight what we believe are lessons learned and some of the most fruitful areas for additional exploration. It is our hope that this book is useful to a broad audience of researchers, practitioners, policymakers, and anyone interested in measuring and improving educational outcomes.

References

Abel, J. R., & Deitz, R. (2014). Do the benefits of college still outweigh the costs? *Current Issues in Economics and Finance, 20*(3). Retrieved from https://www.newyorkfed.org/research/current_issues/ci20-3.html.

ACT. (2016). *The condition of college and career readiness 2016.* Retrieved from http://www.act.org/content/act/en/research/condition-of-college-and-career-readiness-2016.html.

Adams, C. J. (2015, September 4). *2015 SAT, ACT scores suggest many students aren't college-ready: Scores either dipped or stayed the same.* Retrieved from http://www.edweek.org/ew/articles/2015/09/09/2015-sat-act-scores-suggest-many-students.html.

Adelman, C. (2006). *The tool box revisited. Paths to degree completion from high school through college.* Washington, DC: U.S. Department of Education.

Attewell, P., Lavin, D., Domina, T., & Levey, T. (2006). New evidence on remediation. *Journal of Higher Education, 77*(5), 886–924.

Bailey, T. (2009). Challenge and opportunity: Rethinking the role and function of developmental education in community college. *New Directions for Community Colleges, 145,* 11–30.

Bailey, T., Jaggars, S. S., & Scott-Clayton, J. (2013). Characterizing the effectiveness of developmental education: A response to recent criticism. *Journal of Developmental Education, 36*(3), 18–25.

Bushaw, W. J., & Lopez, S. J. (2010). *A time for change: The 42nd annual Phi Delta Kappa/Gallup poll of the public's attitudes toward the public schools.* Retrieved from http://www.gallup.com/poll/142661/Phi-Delta-Kappa-Gallup-Poll-2010.aspx.

Carnevale, A. P., Smith, N., & Strohl, J. (2010, June). *Help wanted: Projections of jobs and education requirements through 2018.* Retrieved from https://cew.georgetown.edu/cew-reports/help-wanted/.

Deci, E. L., & Ryan, R. M. (1985). *Intrinsic motivation and self-determination in human behavior.* New York: Plenum Press.

De Welde, K., Laursen, S., & Thiry, H. (2007). *Women in science, technology, engineering, and math (STEM): Fact Sheet.* Retrieved from http://www.socwomen.org/fact-sheets/.

Dynarski, S. M., Hyman, J. M., & Schanzenbach, D. W. (2013). Experimental evidence on the effect of childhood investments on postsecondary attainment and degree completion. *Journal of Policy Analysis and Management, 32*(4), 692–717.

Gaertner, M. N., Kim, J., DesJardins, S. L., & McClarty, K. L. (2013). Preparing students for college and careers: The causal role of Algebra II. *Research in Higher Education, 55*(2), 143–165.

Giffi, C., Dollar, B., Drew, M., McNelly, J., Carrick, G., & Gangula, B. (2015). *The skills gap in U.S. manufacturing: 2015 and beyond.* Retrieved from http://www.themanufacturinginstitute.org/Research/Research.aspx.

Gottfredson, L. S. (1981). Circumscription and compromise: A developmental theory of occupational aspirations. *Journal of Counseling Psychology, 28,* 545–579.

Hill, N. E., & Wang, M-T., (2015). From middle school to college: Developing aspirations, promoting engagement, and indirect pathways from parenting to post high school enrollment. *Developmental Psychology, 51*(2), 224–235.

Hull, J. (2014, September). *The path least taken: A quest to learn more about high school graduates who don't go on to college.* Retrieved from http://www.centerforpubliceducation.org/pathleasttaken.

Hyman, J. (2016). ACT for all: The effect of mandatory college entrance exams on postsecondary attainment and choice. *Education, Finance, and Policy.* Advance online publication. doi: 10.1162/EDFP_a_00206.

Ludwig, J., & Phillips, D. A. (2008). Long-term effects of Head Start on low-income children. *Annals of the New York Academy of Sciences, 1136,* 257–268.

Lumina Foundation. (2016, April). *A stronger nation 2016.* Retrieved from https://www.luminafoundation.org/stronger_nation2016.

Oreopoulos, P., & Salvanes, K. G. (2009). How large are returns to schooling? Hint: Money isn't everything. *NBER Working Paper No. 15339.* Retrieved from http://www.nber.org/papers/w15339.

Manpower Group (2016). *2016 talent shortage survey.* Retrieved from http://www.manpowergroup.com/talent-shortage-2016.

National Center for Education Statistics [NCES]. (2016, May). *The condition of education 2016.* Retrieved from http://nces.ed.gov/programs/coe/.

National Governors Association Center for Best Practices & Council of Chief State School Officers. (2010). *Common core state standards.* Washington, DC: Authors.

Roderick, M., Nagaoka, J., Coca, V., Moeller, E., Roddie, K., Gilliam, J., & Patton, D. (2008, March). *From high school to the future: Potholes on the road to college.* Retrieved from http://consortium.uchicago.edu/downloads/1835ccsr_potholes_summary.pdf.

Wyatt, J. N., Wiley, A., Camara, W. J., & Proestler, N. (2011). *The development of an index of academic rigor for college readiness* (College Board Research Report 2011–11). Retrieved from https://research.collegeboard.org/sites/default/files/publications/2012/7/researchreport-2011-11-development-index-academic-rigor-college-success.pdf.

Part 1

Defining and Measuring College and Career Readiness

1 The New Complexity of Readiness for College and Careers

David T. Conley

This chapter explores the idea that students need to be ready, not just eligible, to enter postsecondary education. For students to become truly ready, they need to develop knowledge and skills in many more areas than just reading and mathematics. Simply attending college in some form is no longer sufficient. Once they enter a postsecondary program, students must be highly likely to succeed in their chosen degree or certificate program.

Numerous existing readiness standards paint a more complex picture of what it takes to succeed in postsecondary education and be ready for the workplace. They demonstrate that readiness consists of many more factors than reading and math skills, among them the ability to be an adaptive learner with knowledge and skills that transcend core academic content. Students who are competent in the full range of readiness factors improve their likelihood of postsecondary success and are better equipped to meet the demands of a dynamically changing economy and society.

The "Eligibility" Model

Historically and currently, students have had to be *eligible to be admitted* to college much more than *ready to succeed* in college. To be eligible, students complete courses with titles approved by colleges and achieve grades deemed sufficient by admissions offices, take standardized tests, and, in the case of selective colleges, provide a potpourri of additional information (Clinedinst, Koranteng, & Nicola, 2015).

Although elite colleges have long considered information from a much wider range of sources, most college-going students need only take the proper classes, earn decent grades, and perform reasonably well on an admissions test. A letter of recommendation and a transcript that indicates participation in extracurricular activities may also enhance chances of being admitted. However, admission to most postsecondary institutions is a somewhat mechanical process for most students. In fact, 53% of US postsecondary institutions take all applicants, and an additional 18% admit 75% or more of applicants (National Center for Education Statistics, 2014).

This method worked well when the basic purpose of admission requirements was to sort students into "college material" and "not college material." But, as a college education has become something that is needed for success in an ever-increasing number of careers, equity concerns become a higher priority. Making judgments based on course titles, particularly advanced courses, overlooks the fact that many students do not have access to all the necessary or desirable preparatory courses. Students are often allowed to create plans of study that will not meet eligibility requirements, or they receive little help or support when they struggle in a college-prep program. Students who get off track are then enrolled in less challenging courses, thereby ending any hope of becoming eligible for college.

Many of those who do achieve eligibility still demonstrate gaps and shortfalls. Estimates of the proportion of regularly admitted students placing into remedial, or developmental, English and math classes range from 20% to well over 50% (Attewell, Lavin, Domina, & Levey, 2006; Bailey, Jeong, & Cho, 2010; Sparks & Malkus, 2013). At the same time, large percentages of students accepted as fully eligible and not subject to remediation nevertheless do not complete the first year of college (Bettinger & Long, 2009). Sixty percent end up switching institutions (Adelman, 2006); about 80% change majors at least once (Ramos, 2013). First-year college grade point averages (GPAs) drop from .31 to .84 of a point below high school GPAs in core subjects (Allen & Radunzel, 2016).

Several developments over the past 30 years have made the eligibility model largely obsolete. Most important is the dramatic upskilling of the US economy (Carnevale, 1992). Low-skill jobs are being replaced by career pathways that require higher entry-level skills combined with the ability to add new skills and be adaptable throughout a career (Carnevale, Strohl, & Gulish, 2015). These new jobs expect workers to think more independently and deeply, and even to change the nature of the work they do (Pellegrino & Hilton, 2012).

Upskilling has been accompanied by the elimination of entire occupations and career pathways, which creates employment instability that results in workers not being able to remain with one employer for an entire career. Technological upheaval transforms workplaces and expectations for workers' skills overnight. One result is decreasing opportunity and mobility for lower skill workers (Carnevale, Jayasundera, & Cheah, 2012).

This trend will only increase as automation continues reshaping the workplace (Chui, Manyika, & Miremadi, 2016). It is estimated that jobs paying $20 per hour and less have an 83% chance of being automated, while jobs paying between $20 and $40 per hour face a 31% chance of being automated (Frey & Osborne, 2013). In sum, the new economy rewards individuals who are knowledgeable, skilled, educable, flexible, and adaptive. In almost every case, meeting these criteria will require education beyond high school.

From Eligibility to Readiness

Traditional eligibility models can incorporate a wide range of factors (Rigol, 2003). They are not as clear on what it takes to be ready to succeed in postsecondary education and the workplace. The following section introduces a number of readiness models. They have many important commonalities, which are discussed here.

First, they all are composed of elements that are *actionable*. In other words, essentially all students can develop the necessary skills or behaviors. This means that some variables that are important in predictive models but not actionable are not incorporated, primary among them parental income and parent education level. While these are known to be among the most important factors in predicting postsecondary success, they are also among the least malleable. A readiness approach emphasizes developing the skills, knowledge, attitudes, characteristics, and capabilities that can benefit all students. Most of these also help counteract the effects of more limited educational and economic opportunities.

Second, they require information from multiple sources, including performance in other subject areas, attitudes toward learning content, thinking skills and strategies, mastery of key learning techniques, mindset and motivation, and ability to make a successful transition from high school to a postsecondary environment. Additionally, all of this information needs to be examined with an eye toward longitudinal trends rather than point-in-time judgments such as cut scores.

And while many colleges already consider an array of information, few, if any, have devised a system that communicates to students before the fact what is necessary to be ready to succeed at their institution. And while many use an index composed of an admission test score and high school grade point average, many others rely on some version of a "black box" model for admissions: a lot of information goes in and a decision comes out, without much clarity on how the decision was made (Rangappa, 2013).

A third characteristic of the eligibility model, perhaps more of an unfortunate side effect, is that students may not learn much about themselves as they seek to meet eligibility requirements. Admissions to a subset of colleges has become increasingly competitive (Jackson, 2015), which can have the paradoxical effect of deterring students from exploring who they are and why they want to keep learning beyond high school. Over a third of students change colleges, and nearly half change more than once. About half of transfers occur during the first two years (Shapiro, Dundar, Wakhungu, Yuan, & Harrell, 2015). Students transfer for a variety of reasons, but poor fit is one important cause. Students who know more about themselves and why they go on to postsecondary education will make better choices, which benefits both students and the institutions they attend.

Fourth, the eligibility approach, with its myriad deadlines and varying requirements, excludes many students from less privileged backgrounds, because they, for example, scored poorly on an admissions test because they didn't fully appreciate its importance. The information from a more comprehensive readiness model could give more students from disadvantaged backgrounds an opportunity to demonstrate their drive, depth of knowledge in a subject area that may not be tested by admissions exams, and other personal characteristics that make them strong candidates to succeed and to bring something unique to campus. Many smaller liberal arts schools have focused specifically on students from underrepresented racial groups and low-income backgrounds and have developed admissions procedures that emphasize potential to succeed as much as performance in math and English (Smith-Barrow, 2015).

A postsecondary institution that implements a readiness approach would first need to adopt an explicit readiness model and then boost its capacity to collect and analyze information that captured student strengths in all areas of that framework. Doing so is not necessarily easy or cheap, but the potential payoff is in students who are more likely to succeed. This can result in reduced remediation rates, increased retention, and reduced time to completion.

Models of College and Career Readiness

Getting a handle on the complexity of college and career readiness requires a conceptual model that incorporates the full range of variables that contribute to readiness. Many models have been developed. They agree in a number of important ways about what constitutes readiness but also contain their own unique elements. The following sections provide an overview of six readiness frameworks immediately followed by a summary of similarities and differences across the frameworks, which in turn frames a consideration of essential differences and similarities between college and career readiness. This is followed by recommendations for how to measure college and career readiness and future research priorities.

Standards for Success and the Four Keys to College and Career Readiness

One of the first set of standards to address readiness for college is Standards for Success (Conley, 2003a). These standards were derived from an analysis of entry-level course content and instructor priorities at top US universities. They are distinctive for their inclusion of a narrative description in each subject area that paints a comprehensive picture of a well-prepared learner. The Four Keys to college- and career-readiness model is derived from Standards for Success, additional empirical analysis of the content of entry-level college courses at a wide range of institution types, and 38 high schools that did a better than expected job of getting a wide range of students ready to succeed in college (Conley, 2003b, 2010; Conley et al., 2009). The model has 42 components grouped into four "keys."

- *Key cognitive strategies.* The thinking skills students need to learn material at a deeper level and to make connections among subjects.
- *Key content knowledge.* The big ideas and organizing concepts of the academic disciplines that help organize all the detailed information and nomenclature that constitute the subject area, along with the attitudes students have toward learning content in each subject area.

- *Key learning skills and techniques.* The student ownership of learning that connects motivation, goal setting, self-regulation, metacognition, and persistence combined with specific techniques such as study skills, note taking, and technology capabilities.
- *Key transition knowledge and skills.* The aspiration to attend college, the ability to choose the right college and to apply and secure necessary resources, an understanding of the expectations and norms of postsecondary education, and the capacity to advocate for oneself in a complex institutional context.

Noncognitive Factors and Context

The University of Chicago Consortium on Chicago School Research offers its own model with many similarities to the Four Keys and one notable difference (Nagaoka et al., 2013). Its model concentrates exclusively on what their researchers call noncognitive skills. The key elements are *academic behaviors*, those associated with being a good student; *academic perseverance*, the ability to remain focused and engaged in the face of distractions, setbacks, and obstacles; *learning strategies* necessary to comprehend and retain academic content; and *academic mindsets* that motivate students to stay engaged and give their best effort, including the belief that ability is not fixed and can be influenced by effort. This model also includes *social skills* such as cooperation, assertiveness, responsibility, and empathy that are not found in many other readiness models, in part because of their close linkage to personality models, which suggest that at least some of these skills may not be as amenable to significant change as are other factors.

ACT's Beyond Academics Framework

ACT has created its own "holistic" framework outlining what it takes to be ready to succeed in college (Camara, O'Connor, Mattern, & Hanson, 2015). It is based on research conducted by ACT over the past 50 years and shares many features with the Four Keys. Its four components are:

- *Core academic skills*, the domain-specific knowledge and skills necessary to perform essential tasks in the core academic content areas of English language arts, mathematics, and science.
- *Cross-cutting capabilities*, the general knowledge and skills necessary to perform essential tasks across academic content areas. This includes technology and information literacy, collaborative problem solving, thinking and metacognition, and studying and learning.
- *Behavioral skills*, interpersonal, self-regulatory, and task-related behaviors important for adaptation to and successful performance in education and workplace settings.
- *Education and career navigation skills*, the personal characteristics, processes, and knowledge that influence individuals as they navigate their educational and career paths (e.g., make informed decisions and develop achievable plans).

The Hewlett Foundation Deeper Learning Model and the National Research Council Deeper Learning Framework

The Hewlett Foundation's deeper learning model reflects the skills students need to succeed in postsecondary education and the workplace, and a conceptual model for deeper learning is presented in the National Research Council (NRC) report *Education for Life and Work* (Pellegrino & Hilton, 2012). Deeper learning emphasizes understanding of the fundamental concepts and principles of a subject area and their relationship to one another, not just the acquisition of isolated bits of factual information. The three-domain model includes:

- *The cognitive domain*: cognitive processes and strategies, knowledge, and creativity. Examples of competencies in this domain are critical thinking, information literacy, reasoning and argumentation, and innovation.
- *The intrapersonal domain*: intellectual openness, work ethic and conscientiousness, and positive core self-evaluation. Competencies include flexibility, initiative, appreciation for diversity, and metacognition, which is the ability to reflect on one's own learning and make adjustments accordingly.
- *The interpersonal domain*: teamwork, collaboration, and leadership. Examples are communication, responsibility, and conflict resolution.

Work-Ready Standards

The National Association of State Directors of Career Technical Education Consortium (NASDCTEc)[1] (2013) standards instead focus on the world of work. The Common Career Technical Core (CCTC) standards in 16 career pathways are designed for states to adopt. Examples of career pathways include architecture and construction, natural resources systems, and performing arts. In addition to the pathway-specific standards, the CCTC contains 12 statements of career ready practices that apply to all pathways. Examples of career ready practices include communicating clearly, effectively, and with reason; considering the environmental, social, and economic impacts of decisions; and employing valid and reliable research strategies.

These career ready practices paint a picture that is much different than basic employment skills; many have clear applications in academic as well as career settings.

The Common Core State Standards

Finally, the Common Core State Standards (Council of Chief State School Officers & National Governors Association, 2010) explicitly target college and career readiness as their goal. The grade 6–12 English Language Arts standards in reading, writing, speaking and listening, and language outline the skills necessary for college and career readiness. The mathematics standards at the high school level are organized by course and are less explicit about what constitutes readiness for college and careers. However, the Standards for Mathematical Practices enumerate eight areas that cut across courses and align well with the mathematical thinking skills college instructors identify as important.

Other College- and Career-Readiness Standards

Others have developed college- and career-readiness standards as well, including Achieve (American Diploma Project, 2004), whose standards were developed with input from the business community, ACT (2011), and the College Board (2006). Many states have gone on to develop their own versions of college and career readiness that are variations on one or more of the models presented here and include additional elements deemed important by states, such as citizenship readiness (College & Career Readiness & Success Center, 2014).

Key Commonalities and Differences across Frameworks

Reviewing these examples leads to several observations. First, the content knowledge for college and career readiness has a high degree of overlap across frameworks that include content specification, particularly in English and mathematics. What varies is the degree of specificity. Some remain at a higher level of conceptualization, such as Standards for Success and the Hewlett deeper learning framework, while others are more fine-grained.

Several—for example, the Chicago Consortium on School Research and Standards for Success—describe how students should think and the kinds of understandings they should develop, while others, most notably the Common Core State Standards, combine specific knowledge and skills with larger concepts that frame content knowledge. Clearly, some, such as the Hewlett deeper learning areas, were designed more as vision statements than content frameworks, while others—for example, the College Board standards—are more detailed and specific by grade level. Most combine elements of both content knowledge and nonacademic skills and behaviors, acknowledging that college and career readiness requires content knowledge and effective learning skills.

The frameworks presented here demonstrate reasonably high agreement on what constitutes readiness in content knowledge as well as for habits of mind and learning skills. It is possible to identify some common themes that emphasize student self-management, learning strategies such as problem solving, and social skills. Transition knowledge is only addressed in the Four Keys, although lack of skill in applying to college, garnering financial aid, and adjusting to the culture of college is a major factor in the postsecondary transition.

Finally, the balance between college ready and career ready for most of the models is tilted toward college over career. This should not be surprising, given that it is easier to define the content knowledge needed to be ready for entry-level college courses than it is to specify what it takes to succeed in a wide range of career pathways. The balance, however, is beginning to shift in the direction of greater emphasis on career readiness.

College Ready, Career Ready: Same or Different?

The tension between *college ready* and *career ready* is a consistent and recurring theme when the models are stacked up against one another. The initial effort to create college-readiness standards almost immediately spawned the question: what about students who aren't going on to a bachelor's degree? The implications of "career ready" are rarely unpacked; the important distinction here is between being prepared for an occupation versus a career. Many use the term "career ready" to mean both interchangeably, which is a serious error. The difference is critically important.

The conceptual model of career readiness I have developed consists of three levels. The first level is generic work readiness, which consists of the basic behaviors required to get and hold a job. These include being able to complete an application, interview successfully, show up on time, follow directions, not abuse substances on (and sometimes off) the job, get along with co-workers, and meet job responsibilities and customer needs. Unfortunately, a high proportion of entry-level applicants fail to meet these basic standards. Over 40% of respondents to a national survey of employers rated the overall preparation of applicants with a high school diploma as "deficient" for entry-level positions. More specifically, 70% of employers find entry-level applicants' professionalism and work ethic deficient (Casner-Lotto & Barrington, 2006).

The next level of employment readiness is occupation-specific training. Each job has unique training associated with it, which may involve operating a cash register, following a delivery route, or understanding company goals. While job-specific requirements do vary considerably, all require the ability to follow directions, understand organizational mission, and master specific skills, which may be very detailed. Once again, many workforce entrants are unable to adapt; they do not last long because they cannot listen and follow directions well, cannot adopt a customer-service mentality, or cannot work well on a team (Casner-Lotto & Barrington, 2006).

Finally, the third level—the one that requires formal education beyond high school—is career ready. The career ready worker must master the two previous levels *and* content knowledge specific to the career pathway. Being career ready entails mastering the knowledge and skills relevant to one's career cluster. Career readiness also includes learning about the values, norms, and functions of that cluster. Most important, being career ready means being able to continue to acquire new knowledge and skills throughout one's career.

Being college ready also requires the skills in levels 1 and 2. At level 3, college and career readiness begin to diverge. Those directly entering a career cluster acquire more job-specific knowledge. Someone pursuing a bachelor's degree tends to be prepared more broadly and with a greater emphasis on developing learning skills and cognitive strategies. This prepares baccalaureate seekers differentially for careers, less well for a specific entry-level job but often better for lifelong learning and career advancement (Carnevale, Rose, & Cheah, 2011).

Educators and policymakers alike often equate vocational training with career readiness. The problem is that vocational training can neglect broader academic skill development.[2] Getting all students to the level where they have acquired content knowledge and thinking skills sufficient to pursue a career, not just get a job, requires challenging curriculum that develops cognitive strategies and learning skills. Such curriculum works best when students are applying key content knowledge in context to solve real-world problems. This is the point at which college and career readiness can truly converge.

Measuring and Reporting Readiness

The term that is often used to describe a more comprehensive approach to gathering information on readiness is "multiple measures." While this term might trip nicely off the tongue, putting such a system in place can be devilishly complex. The act of linking performance measures, so that the whole is greater than the sum of the parts, requires data systems capable of capturing a wide range of information, including test scores, grades, student self-reports, and other performance information, and then interpreting all of this in relation to a readiness model or framework of the type presented earlier in the chapter.

Achievement tests in reading and mathematics are not enough. New forms of information are necessary that illustrate students' learning skills and techniques, their motivation and goal orientation, help-seeking capabilities, and their general understanding of how to succeed in college. Some of this can be inferred from academic performance (e.g., time management from proportion of assignments turned in on time). Other insights come from triangulating student self-reported information against tests and other external measures (e.g., motivation and engagement as a potential explanation for test scores). Finally, many learning skills can be observed reliably by teachers (e.g., ability to memorize material or technology skill mastery).

The Readiness Profile

Results need to be organized as an integrated profile rather than a series of isolated, disconnected numbers and ratings. The profile needs to be accessible to and actionable by students. More action-oriented and comprehensive portraits of student college readiness can be used by postsecondary institutions to pinpoint the skills and knowledge students have yet to develop (Conley, 2014). This more comprehensive approach contrasts with placement tests that yield generic information limited to reading and math skills and provide no insight into motivation or learning skills.

The goal of the profile is to determine the match between student knowledge and skill and their aspirations, goals, and areas of interest. The profile approach helps students learn more about themselves, which enables them to make decisions about the match between their profile results, their aspirations, and the requirements of postsecondary study.

At the same time, richer data provide educational institutions greater insight into the match between student preparation and the resources available to support them. The profile approach also highlights the degree to which students know what they want to get out of college and how well they understand what they must do to achieve their goals. Knowing this can help create or improve programs and strategies to get students more focused about what they want to accomplish in college.

What about students who are not ready in one or more academic subjects, such as mathematics? Should they be denied entry to college or to their chosen major? Should they be routed into the developmental track? What about students at less selective institutions? Do these students need and can they use this information?

If high schools provided comprehensive readiness profiles to postsecondary education for all entering students, it would be possible to tailor remediation or support much more to student needs and capabilities. This is particularly true if students know their college goals. Rather than generic math and English courses, students could learn the specific content and skills they need to increase their chances of success. Rather than waiting until they have problems in key areas such as time management, they could be enrolled proactively in workshops that teach these skills immediately upon matriculation. Rather than drifting along for the first semester, they could connect with an academic advisor before enrolling, and the advisor could use the profile to help students make wise course choices.

New Instruments and Student Success Courses

Using more information to inform student success is newer to open enrollment institutions than it is to more selective colleges and universities. Still, new instruments that give students greater insight into their readiness—such as the PAR framework, Engage, SuccessNavigator, and the Conley Readiness Index—are beginning to be employed by general-enrollment institutions to help enhance student success. Moreover, many colleges have instituted student success courses or first-year experience programs. Essex County College in Newark, NJ offers a required course for all entering students emphasizing self-assessment, self-management, and the development of life skills, goal-directed behavior, and effective study habits. Lone Star Community College in Texas will require all students to take a student success course as a part of the Best Start program, an important component of its accreditation process.

The goal of a student success course is to maximize student performance and retention in the first year. These programs would be more powerful with additional information gathered during high school and upon admission, and they would be less necessary if more students entered with greater awareness of where they stood on the readiness continuum. However, they are an important supplement to the admissions and placement process, which can overlook of students' true needs, interests, and capabilities.

Making Better Decisions

Ultimately, an explicit model of college and career readiness should identify student strengths and match students with the right programs and resources. The most fundamental goal is to empower students to take more ownership over their learning. The current eligibility-based admission system disempowers students because it tells them so little. Neither does it encourage them to decide where their interests and passions lie.

None of this is intended to force students to choose an occupation, career, or college major prematurely. Students in the US are fortunate because they can change their minds frequently; no dream is to be discouraged and no career is to be put off limits. Instead, students should be encouraged to determine what is possible, what is engaging, and what deserves a significant amount of their energy.

This will require a change in the secondary schooling. Instead of marching students through a course sequence that was established largely in the 1890s and focuses on isolated academic subjects, a profile demands learning experiences where students apply knowledge to real problems in a field of study. Assignments need to be more interdisciplinary and to afford students more opportunities to consider how they like to learn and work. They need to span the gulf between school and the world outside of school. They need to connect students with mentors who can help them consider their options. They need to allow students to sample different career options and work styles. In short, they need to tap the natural desire young people have to find out how they fit in to the world.

Implications for Policy, Practice, and Research

Research Priorities

Research should begin with fuller validation of existing readiness models by using longitudinal data to ascertain which elements of which models explain readiness in which situations and settings and for which types of student. This research would help identify which patterns of prerequisite skills are associated with success in which majors or programs, benefitting both students and colleges.

As noted previously, readiness models overlap in important ways but also contain unique elements. A first step would be to create a true taxonomy of college and career readiness. Work on such a taxonomy is ongoing (Mission Measurement, 2017). Figuring out what constitutes the "best" model would require considering predictive power, content validity, comprehensiveness, and confirmation via expert judgment. In the end, a consensus model may end up being a synthesis of existing models.

It will also be important to ascertain if readiness produces a more or less equitable result than an eligibility system. Does making readiness factors more explicit simply benefit those who already glean the privileged knowledge needed to access college, or does focusing on readiness result in more students from underrepresented groups preparing for, going on to, and succeeding in postsecondary education? Similarly, are profiles used to empower learners and increase success or to create a new set of exclusionary barriers for all but the most highly qualified?

Interestingly, few, if any, studies of readiness have been conducted. Most studies have used course transcript titles as proxies for course content and quality and then compared grades in high school and entry-level college courses (Adelman, 1999). A research agenda organized around readiness would take into account the research on the content and skill requirements of entry-level postsecondary courses. Such an agenda could conceivably suggest changes at both the high school and college levels to improve alignment and boost student success.

Implications for Policy and Practice

The issues raised in this chapter suggest several implications for policy and practice. One step that needs to be taken is to resolve the relationship between college and career readiness. Doing so could help K–12 schools prepare all students for life success without sorting students into "college bound" and "noncollege bound." Clarifying the similarities and differences between college and career readiness will also let colleges and employers make better decisions about readiness.

Researchers, policymakers, and practitioners also need to clarify what career readiness means. Career readiness currently suffers from a definitional problem. Any of a plethora of programs and approaches, old and new, are now labeled "career technical education." Until the field is prepared to consider what it really takes to be ready to progress through a career pathway, it will be impossible to reconcile college and career readiness. The overlap between the two entails, at the least, foundational content knowledge, cognitive strategies, and learning skills. College and career readiness are not the same, but neither are they entirely separate. Agreeing upon the nature of the overlap will support the next area where action is recommended.

Schools need to allow students to explore interests while not being forced to choose a future. Policies that give students credit for a wider range of learning experiences is one way to move in this direction. Another is to integrate more application-oriented activities into traditional academic courses, such as research assignments that require investigating a career field or learning how an expert in a particular area thinks. It will be important to determine how many young people end up knowing what they want to become and how many need the space to change direction multiple times. Today's secondary schools are not great at nurturing individual interests and goals; this must change if school is to remain relevant.

Finally, transcripts need to be reconceived to accommodate more diverse information and communicate that information to end users. Right now, college applicants are asked to accumulate information about themselves. Instead, transcript information should be organized for students in e-profiles built around a college- and career-readiness model that contain both high-stakes and low-stakes information, and that provide an estimate of readiness relative to aspirations. Profiles could then be used to help match students with postsecondary opportunities at an appropriate challenge level and likelihood of success. Just as important, students could be connected to support services tailored more to their needs.

This chapter's vision assumes that policymakers and educators accept the proposition that all students need to continue beyond high school in some form and that students can determine the postsecondary program best matched to their needs and goals. They need more information about readiness and themselves to do so.

The amount of change required to prepare the vast majority of students for post-high school learning is substantial. While many schools have adopted the rhetoric of "all students college and career ready," few have yet taken many of the steps necessary to make this more than a catch phrase. College-going rates continue to increase while first-year college success remains relatively flat (National Center for Education Statistics, 2016). Enabling more students to succeed in postsecondary education will require schools to adopt an explicit college-readiness model, develop the wide range of skills beyond content knowledge necessary for college and career success, and generate more information on readiness. Few incentives exist currently for high schools or colleges to take these steps. It will be up to policymakers in partnership with educators and employers to create the incentives and supports that will motivate and sustain the system-level change necessary for all students to become college and career ready.

Notes

1 Now known as Advance CTE.
2 High quality career technical education (CTE) programs integrate academics, cognitive strategy development, and occupational training. However, many programs that are labeled CTE should more accurately be described as vocational-technical training, because they do not achieve the integration that characterizes high quality CTE programs.

References

ACT. (2011). *ACT college readiness standards.* Retrieved from http://www.act.org/standard/.

Adelman, C. (1999). *Answers in the tool box: Academic intensity, attendance patterns, and bachelor's degree attainment.* Washington, DC: U.S. Department of Education.

Adelman, C. (2006). *The toolbox revisited: Paths to degree completion from high school through college.* Washington, DC: U.S. Department of Education.

Allen, J., & Radunzel, J. (2016). *Comparing high school grade point average (GPA) to first-year college GPA.* Iowa City, IA: ACT.

American Diploma Project. (2004). *Ready or not: Creating a high school diploma that counts.* Washington, DC: Achieve.

Attewell, P. A., Lavin, D. E., Domina, T., & Levey, T. (2006). New evidence on college remediation. *Journal of Higher Education, 77*(5), 886–924.

Bailey, T., Jeong, D. W., & Cho, S.-W. (2010). Referral, enrollment, and completion in developmental education sequences in community colleges. *Economics of Education Review, 29*(2), 255–270.

Bettinger, E. P., & Long, B. T. (2009). Addressing the needs of underprepared students in higher education: Does college remediation work? *Journal of Human Resources, 44*(3), 736–771.

Camara, W., O'Connor, R., Mattern, K., & Hanson, M. A. (2015). *Beyond academics: A holistic framework for enhancing education and workplace success.* Iowa City, IA: ACT.

Carnevale, A. P. (1992). Skills for the new world order. *The American School Boards Journal, 179*(5), 28–30.

Carnevale, A. P., Jayasundera, T., & Cheah, B. (2012). *The college advantage: Weathering the economic storm.* Washington, DC: Georgetown Public Policy Institute, Center on Education and the Workforce.

Carnevale, A. P., Rose, S. J., & Cheah, B. (2011). *The college payoff: Education, occupations, lifetime earnings.* Washington, DC: Georgetown University Center on Education and the Workforce.

Carnevale, A. P., Strohl, J., & Gulish, A. (2015). *College is just the beginning: Employers' role in the $1.1 trillion postsecondary education and training system.* Washington, DC: Center on Education and the Workforce, McCourt School of Public Policy, Georgetown University.

Casner-Lotto, J., & Barrington, L. (2006). *Are they really ready to work? Employers' perspectives on the basic knowledge and applied skills of new entrants to the 21st century U.S. workforce.* Washington, DC: The Conference Board, Inc., The Partnership for 21st Century Skills, Corporate Voices for Working Families, The Society for Human Resource Management.

Chui, M., Manyika, J., & Miremadi, M. (2016). Where machines could replace humans—and where they can't (yet). *McKinsey Quarterly.* Retrieved from www.mckinsey.com/business-functions/digital-mckinsey/our-insights/where-machines-could-replace-humans-and-where-they-cant-yet.

Clinedinst, M., Koranteng, A.-M., & Nicola, T. (2015). *State of college admission.* Arlington, VA: National Association of College Admission Counselors.

College & Career Readiness & Success Center. (2014). *Overview: State definitions of college and career readiness.* Washington, DC: American Institutes for Research.

College Board. (2006). *Standards for college success.* New York: Author.

Conley, D. T. (2003a). *Standards for success: What it takes to succeed in entry-level university courses.* Paper presented at the American Association of Colleges and Universities, Seattle, WA.

Conley, D. T. (2003b). *Understanding university success.* Eugene: Center for Educational Policy Research, University of Oregon.

Conley, D. T. (2010). *College and career ready: Helping all students succeed beyond high school.* San Francisco, CA: Jossey-Bass.

Conley, D. T. (2014). New conceptions of college and career ready: A profile approach to admission. *The Journal of College Admissions, 223*, 12–23.

Conley, D. T., Bowers, C., Cadigan, K., Rivera, D., Gray, T., Groenewald, M., … van der valk, A. (2009). *Creating college readiness.* Eugene, OR: Educational Policy Improvement Center.

Council of Chief State School Officers & National Governors Association. (2010). *Common core state standards.* Washington, DC: Authors.

Frey, C. B., & Osborne, M. A. (2013). *The future of employment: How susceptible are jobs to computerisation?* Oxford University: Oxford Martin School.

Jackson, A. (2015, May 18). The drop in Ivy League acceptance rates in the past decade is shocking. *Business Insider.*

Mission Measurement. (2017). Retrieved from http://www.missionmeasurement.com/about/.

Nagaoka, J., Farrington, C. A., Roderick, M., Allensworth, E., Keyes, T. S., Johnson, D. W., & Beechum, N. O. (2013). Readiness for college: The role of noncognitive factors and context. *VUE, Fall,* 45–52.

National Association of State Directors of Career Technical Education Consortium. (2013). *The common career technical core.* Silver Springs, MD: Author.

National Center for Education Statistics. (2014). *Digest of education statistics, 2014.* Washington, DC: U.S. Department of Education.

National Center for Education Statistics. (2016). *Conditions of education 2016.* Washington, DC: U.S. Department of Education.

Pellegrino, J., & Hilton, M. (Eds.). (2012). *Education for life and work: Developing transferable knowledge and skills in the 21st century.* Washington, DC: National Academy Press.

Ramos, Y. (2013, March 15). *College students tend to change majors when they find the one they really love.* Retrieved from http://borderzine.com/2013/03/college-students-tend-to-change-majors-when-they-find-the-one-they-really-love/.

Rangappa, A. (2013, September 5). Unrigging the admissions system. *Slate.* Retrieved from http://www.slate.com/articles/double_x/doublex/2013/09/getting_into_an_elite_school_forget_the_consultants_don_t_write_about_naked.html.

Rigol, G. W. (2003). *Admissions decision making models: How U.S. institutions of higher education select undergraduate students.* New York: The College Board.

Shapiro, D., Dundar, A., Wakhungu, P. K., Yuan, X., & Harrell, A. (2015). *Transfer and mobility: A national view of student movement in postsecondary institutions, fall 2008 cohort (Signature Report No. 9).* Herndon, VA: National Student Clearinghouse Research Center.

Smith-Barrow, D. (2015, January 23). For liberal arts colleges, enrolling minority students a challenge. *U.S. News & World Report.*

Sparks, D., & Malkus, N. (2013). *First-year undergraduate remedial coursetaking: 1999–2000, 2003–04, 2007–08.* Washington, DC: Institute for Education Sciences, National Center on Educational Statistics.

2 Conceptualizing and Measuring Progress toward College and Career Readiness in Mathematics

William McCallum and James W. Pellegrino

What Is College and Career Readiness?

Complaints about the preparation of high school graduates probably date back to the invention of high schools, but a good starting point for the modern era might be the 1983 report *A Nation at Risk*, which complained that, among other problems, "more and more young people emerge from high school ready neither for college nor for work." The report issued recommendations in five areas: content; standards and expectations; time; teaching; and leadership and fiscal support. The recommendations under content described the Five New Basics in high school: English, mathematics, science, social studies, and computer science. Foreign languages, fine and performing arts, and vocational education were also mentioned, along with the need for K–8 education to prepare students for high school in "English language development and writing, computational and problem solving skills" and "foster an enthusiasm for learning and the development of the individual's gifts and talents." This set of recommendations might be taken as a broad definition of college and work readiness circa 1983, although it should be noted that the report does not claim that there exists a single construct called college and work readiness.

By the mid-2000s, a policy coalition was beginning to emerge around the idea that there is a single construct. The 2004 Achieve publication *Ready or Not* issued a call for states to "create a system of assessments and graduation requirements that—considered together—signify readiness for college and work." The heart of the publication was a set of benchmarks for Mathematics and English that described what high school graduates should know and be able to do when they graduate. This set of benchmarks formed the basis for the American Diploma Project, a precursor effort to the Common Core to help states align their standards. Somewhere between 2004 and 2006, Achieve changed "work" to "career" and started talking about the "college and career readiness agenda." This was an important shift. It is difficult to argue that the all jobs need the same preparation as college. But a career implies more than just a job; it implies the ability to keep growing and learning. Here is the definition of college and career readiness on Achieve's website:

> From an academic perspective, college and career readiness means that a high school graduate has the knowledge and skills in English and mathematics necessary to qualify for and succeed in entry-level, credit-bearing postsecondary coursework without the need for remediation—or put another way, a high school graduate has the English and math knowledge and skills needed to qualify for and succeed in the postsecondary job training and/or education necessary for their chosen career (i.e. community college, university, technical/vocational program, apprenticeship, or significant on-the-job training).

This definition puts both college course work and postsecondary job training on the same footing, and posits a body of knowledge and skills in mathematics and English necessary for both.

When governors and superintendents launched the Common Core State Standards initiative in June 2009 through their national associations, the National Governors Association (NGA), and the Council of Chief State School Officers (CCSS), college and career readiness was a key design specification (NGA, 2009).

There were two phases of development of the Common Core: a preparatory phase during the summer of 2009 that resulted in a document entitled "College and Career Ready Standards" in September 2009 and a subsequent back mapping of these standards into grade-level standards that resulted in the Common Core State Standards in June 2010. The latter was the document that states adopted as their own standards. For a more detailed account of the process, including a description of the evidence consulted, see Zimba (2014).

It is not our purpose in this paper to debate the validity of college and career readiness as a construct. Indeed, such a debate cannot proceed without a definition of the construct. Rather, our intent here is to use the standards as a starting point to (1) extract a definition of college and career readiness from the text of the standards and (2) discuss challenges that definition poses for assessment. We will focus this chapter on the mathematics standards, though several of the concepts would apply to the English Language Arts (ELA) or science standards as well.

We propose three aspects of college and career readiness that one may discern in the design of the mathematics standards.

Knowledge and skills. The content standards describe what students should know and be able to do by the time they leave school.

Mathematical practice. The standards for mathematical practice describe ways of engaging in mathematics designed to support students' retention and use of mathematics in their future courses and careers.

Durability. How durable is the mathematical knowledge that students carry with them into their future and careers? Although this question cannot be answered directly until time has passed, the standards define a progression of learning starting in kindergarten, designed to put students' knowledge, skills, and practice on firm foundation by the time they leave high school.

A full description of these aspects is in the standards themselves. We summarize that description here and indicate the challenges that each makes to assessment. In the next section, we discuss those challenges in more detail. It is worth noting that, whereas the first and third of these aspects could well apply to the Common Core State Standards for ELA, the second is quite specific to the nature of mathematics as a discipline. However, there are parallels in the NRC Framework for K–12 Science Education (NRC, 2012) and the derivative Next Generation Science Standards (Achieve, 2013) where one of the three primary dimensions of the NGSS is the science and engineering practices.

Knowledge and Skills

The high school standards call for course work in algebra, geometry, probability, and statistics with specific attention to using these areas in mathematical modeling. They set the standard for students to take postsecondary, credit-bearing coursework without remediation. Additional standards, indicated by a (+), describe the "additional mathematics that students should learn in order to take advanced courses such as calculus, advanced statistics, or discrete mathematics" (Common Core State Standards Initiative, 2010).

An important difference from most previous state standards is the balance of conceptual understanding, procedural fluency, and applications of mathematics. Although the standards do not give explicit definitions of these terms, one may infer their meaning from the text of the standards. For example, grade 2 has the following cluster of standards:

Understand Place Value

1 Understand that the three digits of a three-digit number represent amounts of hundreds, tens, and ones; e.g., 706 equals 7 hundreds, 0 tens, and 6 ones. Understand the following as special cases:

    a 100 can be thought of as a bundle of 10 tens—called a "hundred."

    b The numbers 100, 200, 300, 400, 500, 600, 700, 800, 900 refer to one, two, three, four, five, six, seven, eight, or nine hundreds (and 0 tens and 0 ones).

2 Count within 1,000; skip-count by fives, tens, and hundreds.
3 Read and write numbers to 1,000 using base-ten numerals, number names, and expanded form.
4 Compare two three-digit numbers based on meanings of the hundreds, tens, and ones digits, using >, =, and < symbols to record the results of comparisons.

Here, the first and fourth standards are about ideas, whereas the second and third are about procedures. Demonstrating conceptual understanding includes the ability to talk about those ideas meaningfully, for example, by explaining how to think of the digits in 706 or how to use the meaning of digits to compare three-digit numbers, and to connect them to procedures like skip-counting. One may infer a definition of conceptual understanding as the ability to explain, use, and make connections between mathematical ideas.

A typical fluency standard is the grade 2 standard 2.NBT.B.5:

> Fluently add and subtract within 100 using strategies based on place value, properties of operations, and/or the relationship between addition and subtraction.

Here, one is clearly talking about a procedure, not an idea, although again ideas are called upon to support the procedure (place value, properties of operations, and the relationship between addition and subtraction). One may infer a definition of procedural fluency as the ability to carry out procedures quickly and accurately.

Finally, on the same page one finds the standard

> 2.OA.A.1 Use addition and subtraction within 100 to solve one- and two-step word problems involving situations of adding to, taking from, putting together, taking apart, and comparing, with unknowns in all positions, e.g., by using drawings and equations with a symbol for the unknown number to represent the problem.

Applying mathematics means using mathematical ideas, representations, and procedures to solve problems from outside mathematics. In grade 2, those problems are word problems with thin contexts designed for the purpose of testing a particular set of skills; in high school, students are expected to solve less well-defined situations.

The intertwining in the standards of conceptual understanding, procedural fluency, and applications of mathematics poses a challenge to assessment because it requires linked measurement of these strands of proficiency. A similar assessment challenge exists for the NGSS where proficiency is defined in terms of performance expectations that integrate three dimensions: core disciplinary ideas, science and engineering practices, and crosscutting concepts (see Pellegrino, Wilson, Koenig, & Beatty, 2014).

Mathematical Practice

The Standards for Mathematical Practice describe how competent practitioners do mathematics. They list eight aspects of mathematical practice: solving problems, reasoning, explaining, modeling, attending to precision, choosing tools, seeing structure, and expressing regularity. Although it has become popular to call these aspects "the practices," it is more appropriate to think of them as ways of looking at a single complex thing—mathematical practice. The standards are a first attempt to describe all the angles on that thing, drawing on research of Cuoco, Goldenberg, and Mark (1996) on habits of mind and Harel (2008) on ways of thinking and ways of understanding, and also drawing on the professional knowledge of research mathematicians about the nature of their discipline. Future research could reveal gaps in the list or ways in which one or more items in the list can be combined or reformulated.

The mistake of thinking of the practice standards as a list of eight discrete practices is easy to make when trying to design an assessment, because there is a natural tendency to design assessments around discrete pieces of knowledge. Another mistake is to look for all eight practices everywhere and all the time.

Durability

The knowledge that students take from school should last and stand them in good stead for the duration of their college experience and future career. Obviously, that cannot be directly measured: the only way to measure durability of something is to leave it for a while and see how it holds up. However, it is reasonable to suppose that an indicator of future durability is past durability. A student who burns the midnight oil cramming for the high school exit exam might do just as well as a student who goes into the exam with the wind in her sails, but we would expect the latter to do better in the future. Durability is an end state of a progression of learning, and it is difficult to discern it in a snapshot without having measured the progress toward it and assessed the strength of its roots, as well as its ability to support transfer of use in the future. The K–8 standards allow for such measurement through a division into domains. Domains are similar to the traditional division of standards into strands (e.g., number, data, algebra, geometry), but they have important differences. First, they do not span the entire gamut of K–12, but rather have a grade-specific beginning and end. Second, when strands swell into broad rivers, such as happens with number in the elementary grades, they are subdivided; thus, number in the elementary grades is divided into operations in base ten, algebraic properties of operations, and fractions. Each domain is further subdivided into clusters of standards, where the cluster heading itself contributes meaning to the standards within it. This design allows for focus and coherence.

Focus means not trying to do everything at once. Research on US standards circa 2000–2010 describes them as being a mile wide and an inch deep, the result of too many pet topics crammed into too many grades (see, e.g., Schmidt, Cogan, Houang, & McKnight, 2011). Structuring the standards into domains of appropriate length, rather than strands that traverse the entire school career, allows teachers and students time in each grade level to concentrate on important topics, so that students can move on to new topics in the next grade level.

Coherence means making sure that the sequence of ideas follows the natural progression dictated by both the structure of the subject and by what is known about how children learn. It means making connections between related topics within a grade level, and making sure that ideas flow from one grade level to the next in a way that is visible to the teacher and the learner.

The focus and coherence of the standards were designed to help with the progression of learning. An implicit hypothesis in the design is that focusing on the important work of each grade helps you make decisions about what to leave out without compromising progress, and that making the teaching of mathematics into a coherent story that builds logically and makes sense from one grade to the next helps struggling students find a pathway to catch up with their comrades rather than wander lost in the woods. The challenge is to design assessments that can test this hypothesis by measuring movement along one or more continua in addition to particular states along those progressions.

Conceptually Linking Assessments to Learning

Before discussing issues of assessment design and interpretation as they pertain to each of the three major aspects of college and career readiness discussed above, we need to make explicit two conceptual frames that link the assessment of student competence to attainment of the standards. The first has to do with critical relationships among curriculum, instruction, assessment, and standards. The second has to do with the nature of assessment in general and the role of theories and data on student cognition in the design and use of assessment in education.

Curriculum, Instruction, Assessment, and Standards

Assessment does not and should not stand alone in the educational system. Rather, it is one of three central components—curriculum, instruction, and assessment—that are linked, although the nature of their linkages and reciprocal influence is often less explicit than it should be. *Curriculum* consists of the knowledge and skills in subject matter areas that teachers teach and students are supposed to learn. The curriculum generally consists of a scope or breadth of content in a given subject area and a sequence for learning. Content standards in a subject matter area typically outline the goals of learning, whereas curriculum sets forth the more specific means to be used to achieve those ends. *Instruction* refers to methods of teaching and the learning activities used to help students master the content and objectives specified by a curriculum. Instruction encompasses the activities of both teachers and students. It can be carried out by a variety of methods, sequences of activities, and topic orders. *Assessment* is the means used to measure the outcomes of education and the achievement of students with regard to important competencies. Assessment may include both formal methods, such as large-scale assessments, and less formal classroom-based procedures, such as quizzes, class projects, and teacher questioning.

A precept of educational practice is the need for alignment among curriculum, instruction, and assessment. Alignment means that the three functions are directed toward the same ends and reinforce each other rather than working at cross-purposes. Ideally, an assessment should measure what students are actually being taught, and what is actually being taught should parallel the curriculum one wants students to master. If any of the functions is not well synchronized, it will disrupt the balance and skew the educational process. Assessment results will be misleading, or instruction will be ineffective. Alignment is often difficult to achieve because a central conception is lacking about the nature of learning and knowing around which the three functions can be coordinated. Alignment among curriculum, instruction, and assessment is better achieved if all three are derived from a scientifically credible and shared knowledge base about cognition and learning in a subject matter domain. The model of learning would serve as a nucleus around which the three functions would revolve. Standards that are based on the best available theories and empirical knowledge about the progress of student learning can serve such a function. Thus, the link between standards and assessment is always mediated by their respective connections to curriculum and instruction. Such connections are more apparent when assessment is used in close proximity to classroom processes of teaching and learning. But those connections are decidedly less apparent, and sometimes even ignored, when assessments are much more distal to the classroom as is typically the case for large-scale assessments of achievement at given grade levels. In fact, the latter are often designed to be "curriculum neutral" with a purported direct connection or "alignment" between the standards and assessments. However, the latter assumption is untenable, and interpretations about the development and growth of student competence based on assessment results are always confounded with how standards have been interpreted and translated relative to classroom-based practices of curriculum, instruction, and assessment.

Assessment as a Process of Reasoning from Evidence

Educators assess students to learn about what they know and can do, but assessments do not offer a direct pipeline into students' minds. Assessing educational outcomes is not as straightforward as measuring height or weight; the attributes to be measured are mental representations and processes that are not outwardly visible. Thus, an assessment is a tool designed to observe students' behavior and produce data that can be used to draw reasonable inferences about what students know. Deciding what to assess and how to do so is not as simple as it might appear.

The process of collecting evidence to support inferences about what students know represents a chain of reasoning from evidence about student learning that characterizes all assessments, from classroom quizzes and standardized achievement tests to the conversation a student has with the teacher as they work through a proportional reasoning problem. In the 2001 report *Knowing What Students Know: The Science and Design of Educational Assessment* issued by the National Research Council, the process of reasoning from evidence was portrayed as a triad of three interconnected elements—the *assessment triangle* shown in Figure 2.1 (Pellegrino, Chudowsky, & Glaser, 2001). The vertices of the assessment triangle represent the three key elements underlying any assessment: a model of student *cognition* and learning in the domain of the assessment; a set of assumptions and principles about the kinds of *observations* that will provide evidence of students' competencies; and an *interpretation* process for making sense of the evidence. An assessment cannot be designed and implemented without consideration of each. The three are represented as vertices of a triangle because each is connected to and dependent on the other two. A major tenet of the *Knowing What Students Know* report is that for an assessment to be effective and valid, the three elements must be in synchrony. The assessment triangle provides a useful framework for analyzing the underpinnings of current assessments to determine how well they accomplish the goals we have in mind, as well as for designing future assessments and establishing validity.

The *cognition* corner of the triangle refers to theory, data, and a set of assumptions about how students represent knowledge and develop competence in a subject matter domain (e.g., fractions). In any particular assessment application, research and theory on learning in the

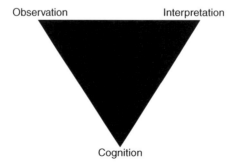

Figure 2.1 Assessment Triangle
Source: Reprinted from Pellegrino et al. (2001), with permission from National Academies Press.

domain are needed to identify the set of knowledge and skills that is important to measure for the context of use, whether that be characterizing the competencies students have acquired at some point in time to make a summative judgment or for making a formative judgment to guide subsequent instruction so as to maximize learning. A central premise is that the cognitive theory should represent the most scientifically credible understanding of typical ways in which learners represent knowledge and develop expertise in a domain.

Such research and theory would typically be drawn upon in developing the standards for a domain like mathematics, ELA, or science, as was the case for the Common Core for Math and ELA and in developing the NRC Framework for Science and NGSS. Quality standards are based on what is known from research and theory about knowledge and learning in a discipline and typically reflect a relatively high level of abstraction of that knowledge base. This is also why we can expect standards to change over time as research and theory on disciplinary learning and teaching inform our understanding of what is important to know and how that knowledge progresses with instruction.

Every assessment is also based on a set of assumptions and principles about the kinds of tasks or situations that will prompt students to say, do, or create something that demonstrates important knowledge and skills. The tasks to which students are asked to respond on an assessment are not arbitrary. They must be carefully designed to provide evidence that is linked to the cognitive model of learning and to support the kinds of inferences and decisions that will be made on the basis of the assessment results. The *observation* vertex of the assessment triangle represents a description or set of specifications for assessment tasks that will elicit illuminating responses from students. The assessment designer can use this capability to maximize the value of the data collected, as seen through the lens of the underlying assumptions about how students learn in the domain.

Every assessment is also based on certain assumptions and models for interpreting the evidence collected from observations. The *interpretation* vertex of the triangle encompasses all the methods and tools used to reason from fallible observations. It expresses how the observations derived from a set of assessment tasks constitute evidence about the knowledge and skills being assessed. In the context of large-scale assessment, the interpretation method is usually a statistical model, which is a characterization or summarization of patterns one would expect to see in the data, given varying levels of student competency. In the context of classroom assessment, the interpretation is often made less formally by the teacher and is usually based on an intuitive or qualitative model rather than on a formal statistical one.

A crucial point is that each of the three elements of the assessment triangle not only must make sense on its own, but also must connect to each of the other two elements in a meaningful way to lead to an effective assessment and sound inferences. Central to this entire process, however, are theories and data on how students learn and what students know as they develop competence for important aspects of the curriculum.

Challenges to Assessment of College and Career Readiness

The targets of inference for any given assessment should be largely determined by models of cognition and learning that describe how students represent knowledge and develop competence in the domain of interest (the *cognition* element of the assessment triangle) and the important elements of such competence. The cognitive model suggests the most important aspects of student achievement about which one would want to draw inferences and provides clues about the types of assessment tasks that will elicit evidence to support those inferences. In light of the aforementioned, we can now consider some of the many challenges to assessment design and interpretation brought up by each of the three aspects of college- and career-readiness definition.

Knowledge and Skills

Traditional approaches to assessment can lead to a view of subject matter as made up of discrete, measurable pieces of knowledge and skill. The standards fight with this view by emphasizing progressions of knowledge across grade levels, connections between different topics within a grade level, the uneven granularity of mathematical knowledge, and the intertwining of procedural fluency, conceptual understanding, and applications. All of these are difficult to assess if you are limited to an assessment design that insists on items of equal grain size, each tagged to one specific standard.

The standards are grouped into clusters, and the cluster headings themselves should be viewed as standards also, whose meaning distributes over the individual standards in the cluster. For example, the second grade cluster 2.NBT.A, entitled "Understand place value," contains the standard:

2.NBT.A.1. Count within 1000; skip-count by 5s, 10s, and 100s.

Taken together with its heading, the intent of this standard is to use skip-counting to support place value understanding. Skip-counting in general (by fives, threes, and so forth) is not a requirement of the standards; the activity is recruited in service of a higher goal. An assessment item for 2.NBT.A.1 should also aim at the higher-level target of 2.NBT.A, and there could be items that address 2.NBT.A that only operate at that higher level or that address multiple standards within the cluster.

Mathematical Practice

Because the Standards for Mathematical Practice are standards, a full assessment system must assess them, which is difficult to do under the practical constraints of most systems. The practices have a quantum aspect, in that they tend to disappear when you try to observe them directly. The assessment consortia, PARCC and Smarter Balanced, have designed items that attempt to measure the practices indirectly. For example, Figure 2.2 displays a released item from Smarter Balanced that can be answered in a number of ways. A student could simply calculate the value of every expression to see which one is correct. However, a student with the habit of looking for structure and with a conceptual understanding of the place value system will be able to do it more quickly. Thus, the time it takes to solve the problem can inform instruction and provide an incentive to teach mathematical practice and conceptual understanding.

Durability

Another difficulty in assessing college and career readiness, not specific to the standards, is that it cannot be measured at a single moment in time. It is possible to measure how much students know at any given moment, but it is difficult to measure how robust that knowledge is. Mathematical proficiency is strengthened by learning in progressions over time and by broadening at a particular moment in time, both with regard to subject matter connections and to the blending of procedural fluency, conceptual understanding, and applications. Some evidence that students have followed a progression leading to transferability of their mathematical knowledge is needed.

Consistent with these ideas, there has been considerable interest in the topic of "learning progressions" (see Duschl, Schweingruber, & Shouse, 2007; National Research Council, 2012; Wilson & Bertenthal, 2006). A variety of definitions of learning progressions (also called learning trajectories) now exist in the literature, with substantial differences in focus and intent

Which expression is equal to 5,007.992?

○ a
$$5 \times 1{,}000 + 7 \times 1 + 9 \times \left(\frac{1}{10}\right) + 9 \times \left(\frac{1}{100}\right) + 2 \times \left(\frac{1}{1{,}000}\right)$$

○ b
$$5 \times 1{,}000 + 7 \times 1 + 9 \times 10 + 9 \times 100 + 2 \times 1{,}000$$

○ c
$$5 \times 1{,}000{,}000 + 7 \times 1{,}000 + 9 \times \left(\frac{1}{1}\right) + 9 \times \left(\frac{1}{10}\right) + 2 \times \left(\frac{1}{100}\right)$$

○ d
$$5 \times 1{,}000{,}000 + 7 \times 1{,}000 + 9 \times 100 + 9 \times 10 + 2 \times 1$$

Figure 2.2 Example Smarter Balanced Grade 5 Assessment Task

(see, e.g., Alonzo & Gotwals, 2012; Corcoran, Mosher, & Rogat, 2009; Daro, Mosher, Corcoran, Barrett, & Consortium for Policy Research in Education, 2011; Duncan & Hmelo-Silver, 2009). Learning progressions are empirically grounded, testable hypotheses about how students' understanding of, and ability to use, core concepts and explanations and related disciplinary practices grow and become more sophisticated over time, with appropriate instruction. These hypotheses describe the pathways students are likely to follow as they master core concepts. The hypothesized learning trajectories are tested empirically to ensure their construct validity (does the hypothesized sequence describe a path most students actually experience given appropriate instruction?) and ultimately to assess their consequential validity (does instruction based on the learning progression produce better results for most students?). The reliance on empirical evidence differentiates learning trajectories from traditional topical scope and sequence specification.

Any hypothesized learning progression has implications for assessment, because effective assessments should be aligned with an empirically grounded cognitive model. A model of a learning progression should contain at least the following elements:

1   *Target performances or learning goals,* which are the end points of a learning progression and are defined by societal expectations, analysis of the discipline, and/or requirements for entry into the next level of education;
2   *Progress variables* that are the dimensions of understanding, application, and practice that are being developed and tracked over time. These may be core concepts in the discipline or practices central to mathematical work;
3   *Levels of achievement* that are intermediate steps in the developmental pathway(s) traced by a learning progression. These levels may reflect levels of integration or common stages that characterize the development of student thinking. There may be intermediate steps that are noncanonical but are stepping stones to canonical ideas;
4   *Learning performances* that are the kinds of tasks students at a particular level of achievement would be capable of performing. They provide specifications for the development of assessments by which students would demonstrate their knowledge and understanding; and,
5   *Assessments* that are the specific measures used to track student development along the hypothesized progression. Learning progressions include an approach to assessment, as assessments are integral to their development, validation, and use.

Research on cognition and learning has produced a rich set of descriptions of domain-specific learning and performance that have served to guide the development of the mathematics standards and that, in turn, can serve to guide assessment design aligned to those standards. That said, there is much left to do in mapping out learning progressions for multiple areas of the mathematics curriculum in ways that can effectively guide the design of instruction and assessment, including the design of systems of assessments that attempt to cover the progress of learning within and across grades.

Implications for Policy, Practice, and Research

Articulating standards for college and career readiness in mathematics serves as a starting place for a much larger conversation and debate about what students should know and be able to do when they exit high school. When that articulation is based on research, theory, and disciplinary arguments about knowing and learning mathematics, as is the case for the Common Core Standards in Mathematics, as well as much of the commentary that has followed their publication, then educators and researchers can also start to articulate and debate their implications for curriculum, instruction, and assessment.

While there are progressions of learning reflected in the standards, it is critical to recognize that they do not exist independently of instruction, and some are more easily identified and validated than others. There is a considerable amount of research that needs to be done to determine what aspects of hypothesized progressions in the standards might be invariant across instructional models and approaches versus those aspects that are dependent on instructional sequence, as well as the consequences of such variability on the outcomes for any proposed progression. In addition to assessment and measurement issues, a key aspect of this work is specifying the grain size or level of specificity at which to pursue such analyses.

So, while there is currently considerable interest in learning progressions, the field of practice and policy must be cautious in assuming that everything being espoused has a sound base and is "ready for prime time." There is a danger in leaping too readily to embrace the construct without questioning the evidentiary base behind any given progression that has been proposed. That said, there are potentially many benefits of recommending learning progressions as a way to think about the assessment of student learning. One benefit of carefully described learning progressions is that they can be used to guide the specification of learning performances—statements of what students would be expected to know and be able to do. The learning performances can, in turn, guide the development of tasks that allow one to observe and infer students' levels of competence for major constructs that are the target of instruction and assessment within and across grade levels.

The potential relevance of any learning progression will also vary with the purpose of the assessment and intended use of the information. This will be a function of the scope and specificity of the learning progression. The more detailed it is and the finer the grain size, the more useful it may be at levels close to classroom instruction. Learning progressions have potential roles to play in supporting and monitoring development and growth, and they may be especially relevant for aspects of diagnosis and instructional support. Finally, learning progressions can help us understand why working from a micro- to the macro-level understanding of student cognition and learning to generate assessments is more likely to lead to valid inferences about student achievement than the reverse. When we have detailed maps of the progress of student learning, at grain sizes that support instructional design and diagnostic assessment, we have a conceptual base that can be collapsed to make coarser judgments about aspects of growth and change appropriate to a broader timescale of learning. In doing so, we preserve the validity of the assessment, because we have a clear sense of the construct being measured and the level at which we can describe and understand student performance.

Research on the progression of learning and its assessment also must be done in the context of actual conditions of practice. Time constraints on schooling and the limits of instructional capacity and practice must be considered in the design of research aimed at studying progressions in mathematical competence. For example, much of our knowledge and assumptions about the progress of learning in mathematics is based on cross-sectional data, and there is a relative paucity of longitudinal data, especially data that span more than a single year of instruction. Collecting such data where there is an adequate description of the conditions of instruction may be well-nigh impossible, given the practicalities and restrictions imposed on researchers and teachers working in typical school settings. Thus, further work on the development of our understanding and assessment of mathematical competency may need to be done with carefully constructed cross-sectional student samples and assessment tools that permit reasonable inferences about the growth of competence toward college readiness. It is very unlikely that the types of data currently collected on existing large-scale assessments of grade level achievement will be sufficient to carry out such work. This caveat applies to the assessments developed by the multistate consortia known as PARCC (2014) (Partnership for Assessment of Readiness for College and Careers) and SBAC (2014) (Smarter Balanced Assessment Consortium). The grain size and specificity of what can be inferred from those assessments, within and across grades, is typically far too coarse to measure actual student growth in key areas of the standards.

In summary, much remains to be done to clarify assumptions about college and career readiness in mathematics. This includes developing methods of assessing various aspects of competence and then making judgments about the quality and adequacy of the observed performance relative to performance expectations. We also need programs of research concerned with validating assumptions about the interpretive meaning and value of different levels of achievement, including their predictive validity relative to justifiable criteria such as dimensions of performance in college and/or in the workplace. Designing, assembling, and executing such an agenda will require collaborations with the field of educational practice that includes agreements regarding the mutual benefits and commitments needed from multiple stakeholders, including those whose primary allegiances are within the research, practice, policy, and funding communities.

References

Achieve. (2013). *Next generation science standards*. Retrieved from http://www.nextgenscience.org/.

Alonzo, A. C., & Gotwals, A. W. (2012). *Learning progression in science: Current challenges and future directions*. Rotterdam, Netherlands: Sense Publishers.

Common Core State Standards Initiative (2010). *Common core state standards for mathematics*. Retrieved from http://www.corestandards.org/wp-content/uploads/Math_Standards.pdf.

Corcoran, T. B., Mosher, F. A., & Rogat, A. (2009). *Learning progressions in science: An evidence-based approach to reform*. New York: Columbia University, Teachers College, Consortium for Policy Research in Education, Center on Continuous Instructional Improvement.

Cuoco, A., Goldenberg, E. P., & Mark, J. (1996). Habits of mind: An organizing principle for a mathematics curriculum, *Journal of Mathematical Behavior, 15*(4), 375–402.

Daro, P., Mosher, F. A., Corcoran, T., Barrett, J., & Consortium for Policy Research in Education. (2011). *Learning trajectories in mathematics: A foundation for standards, curriculum, assessment, and instruction*. Philadelphia, PA: Consortium for Policy Research in Education.

Duncan, R. G., & Hmelo-Silver, C. (2009). Learning progressions: Aligning curriculum, instruction, and assessment. *Journal for Research in Science Teaching, 46*(6), 606–609.

Duschl, R. A., Schweingruber, H. A., & Shouse, A. W. (Eds.). (2007). *Taking science to school: Learning and teaching science in grade K-8*. Washington, DC: The National Academies Press.

Harel, G. (2008). What is mathematics? A pedagogical answer to a philosophical question. In R. B. Gold & R. Simons (Eds.), *Current issues in the philosophy of mathematics from the perspective of mathematicians*. Washington, DC: Mathematical Association of America.

National Governors Association (2009). Forty-nine states and territories join Common Core Standards Initiative. Retrieved from http://www.nga.org/cms/home/news-room/news-releases/page_2009/col2-content/main-content-list/forty-nine-states-and-territorie.html.

National Research Council (2012). *A framework for K-12 science education: Practices, crosscutting concepts, and core ideas.* Committee on a Conceptual Framework for New K-12 Science Education Standards, Board on Science Education. Washington, DC: National Academies Press.

PARCC (Partnership for Assessment of Readiness for College and Careers) (2014). The PARCC assessment: Item development. Information available at http://www.parcconline.org/assessment-development.

Pellegrino, J. W., Chudowsky, N., & Glaser, R. (Eds.). (2001). *Knowing what students know: The science and design of educational assessment.* Washington, DC: National Academies Press.

Pellegrino, J. W., Wilson, M., Koenig, J., & Beatty, A. (Eds.). (2014). *Developing assessments for the next generation science standards.* Washington, DC: National Academies Press.

Schmidt, W. H., Cogan, L. S., Houang, R. T., & McKnight, C. C. (2011). Content coverage differences across districts/states: A persisting challenge for U.S. policy. *American Journal of Education, 117*(3), 399–427.

SBAC (Smarter Balanced Assessment Consortium) (2014). The SBAC assessment: Item writing and review. Information available at http://www.smarterbalanced.org/smarter-balanced-assessments/item-writing-and-review/.

Wilson, M. R., & Bertenthal, M. W. (Eds.). (2006). *Systems for state science assessments.* Washington, DC: National Academies Press.

Zimba, J. (2014). The development and design of the Common Core State Standards for Mathematics, *New England Journal of Public Policy, 26*(1), Article 10. Retrieved from http://scholarworks.umb.edu/nejpp/vol26/iss1/10.

3 More than a Test Score

Defining and Measuring Personal Qualities

Matthew N. Gaertner and Richard D. Roberts

By most conventional metrics, college- and career-readiness rates in the United States have plateaued. To wit, in 2015, 28% of ACT test-taking high school graduates met all four exams' college-readiness benchmarks (English, reading, mathematics, and science) (ACT, 2015). In the two prior years (2014 and 2013), the figure was 26%. In 2012 and 2011, it was 25%. Not coincidentally, over the same time period, educators and policymakers have started pressing on two distinct yet complementary questions: (1) how can we accelerate these college-readiness trends? and (2) are we measuring all the right things? This book—particularly Part 3—devotes substantial attention to the first question. This chapter focuses on the second.

There is a place for test scores in modern educational evaluation and policy. We opened this chapter by citing a string of achievement metrics; and as measurement professionals, we have dedicated considerable energy to developing, refining, and analyzing results from standardized tests. But few teachers, students, and parents would disagree that assessment systems have historically placed inordinate emphasis on timeworn indicators of reading, writing, and arithmetic. This narrow focus on cognitive skills presents two problems. The first is limited test-criterion validity. In isolation, cognitive indicators often do not forecast future outcomes (e.g., college grades) with enough predictive power to provide convincing diagnoses about students' progress toward important goals. The second problem is limited actionable data. In short, cognitive traits like IQ may be difficult for students to change (Roberts, Stankov, Schulze, & Kyllonen, 2008). We do not mean to equate malleability with importance; influential constructs are influential, period. But constructs that are actionable may provide a better basis for targeted intervention and improvement.

Furthermore, overemphasizing cognitive traits shortchanges school systems' missions. Schooling is intended to build not just foundational academic skills but also self-regulation, teamwork, emotional maturity, and readiness for participation in democratic society (Stemler & DePascale, 2016). If the tools used to evaluate schools do not reflect democratic goals, it should not be surprising when schools stop pursuing those goals. Conversely, if educational systems are evaluated according to their diverse purposes, educators will be encouraged to cultivate their students' diverse skills—both cognitive and noncognitive. Therefore, in this chapter, we argue the relevance of noncognitive skills in defining and measuring college and career readiness, and we highlight specific examples amenable to measurement.

The chapter comprises an argument in three parts. First, we propose that assessment of noncognitive skills improves the prediction of future outcomes. Second, we argue incorporating noncognitive skills into assessment and evaluation frameworks provides more nuanced diagnoses. Third, we argue noncognitive skills represent comparatively actionable domains, relative to reading, mathematics, and writing. We conclude with implications for policy, practice, and research.

Before we begin, it is important to clarify our terminology. Names for noncognitive skills have proliferated nearly as fast as assessments to measure them. These skills are alternatively termed soft skills, character traits, foundational skills, 21st-century skills, transversal skills, and nonacademic traits (among many others). Ultimately, we believe the differences are as much semantic as they are material, providing varnish for a new generation of constructs (e.g., tenacity, grit) that are more similar to each other and to familiar personality traits than some researchers let on (Credé, Tynan, & Harms, 2016). We will use two terms interchangeably—psychosocial skills (i.e., the interaction of social factors and individual thought) and noncognitive skills.[1] With that bit of taxonomic housekeeping out of the way, we begin our first argument.

Better Prediction

When we use cognitive measures to predict future performance—in either the college or career domains—predictions are far from perfect. For example, predictive validity studies show the SAT and ACT explain between 26% and 28% of the variance in test-takers' freshman-year GPAs (Kobrin, Patterson, Shaw, Mattern, & Barbuti, 2008; Westrick, Le, Robbins, Radunzel, & Schmidt, 2015). Job performance predictions based on cognitive indicators alone are similarly precise: Schmidt and Hunter's (1998) meta-analysis covering 85 years of personnel selection research suggests that measures of mental ability explain 26% of the variance in job performance.

Considering noncognitive skills would improve these predictions. To explain how and why, a few examples are instructive. The cases that follow are by no means exhaustive; they are just a few studies with which we are particularly well acquainted. For further evidence, we suggest readers consult validity research covering the predictive utility of emotional intelligence (MacCann, Matthews, Zeidner, & Roberts, 2003; Roberts et al., 2006); the associations between motivation, interest-major congruence, and academic performance (Allen & Robbins, 2010); and the associations between the Five-Factor Model of personality and academic performance (Poropat, 2009). Notably, Poropat's extensive analysis demonstrates that noncognitive constructs like conscientiousness predict academic performance nearly as accurately as intelligence. In the examples that follow, we explore this phenomenon in more depth and provide references for further reading. We proceed roughly as learners do, from middle through high school, and on to both college and career readiness and success.[2]

School to College Readiness

One of the major concerns in college-readiness assessment—emphasized in this book and elsewhere in the literature—is that readiness information (1) comes too late in students' K–12 careers for meaningful corrective action and (2) focuses narrowly on cognitive domains, to the exclusion of affective and contextual factors. To address this concern, Gaertner and McClarty (2015, 2016) developed a college-readiness index for middle-school students. The index was based on data from the National Education Longitudinal Study of 1988 (NELS) and focused on six constructs: academic achievement (including cognitive tests), motivation, behavior, social engagement, family circumstances, and school characteristics. Derived from NELS variables via principal components analysis, these six middle-school factors explained 69% of the variance in GPA, SAT, and ACT scores at the end of high school. Moreover, motivation, behavior, and social engagement combined account for 48% of explainable variance in GPA, SAT, and ACT scores, while academic achievement accounted for 25%. These findings are not without precedent. For example, Casillas et al. (2012) show that behavioral factors explain more than a quarter of the variation in high school failure. Similarly, dropout prevention research stresses the importance of attendance and behavior in addition to course performance (Allensworth & Easton, 2005, 2007).

College Admissions and Success

In few arenas is predictive validity more fraught, consequential, and controversial than in college admissions. Selective colleges open doors to prized professions (Cantor & Englot, 2014); it should be no surprise that the college admissions process generates substantial anxiety among students (and their parents), who fear one poor performance on one cognitive test will dramatically alter their educational and career trajectories. Yet most colleges recognize that evaluating candidates on a single measure of a single dimension is not only unreliable but also anathema to their missions. Surveys of admissions officers repeatedly show standardized achievement tests do not override other admissions factors (e.g., Clinedinst, 2015). Instead, many selective universities practice "holistic review," a practice that, by definition, espouses the idea that college applicants are more than their test scores. The purpose of holistic review is to provide admissions officers with a nuanced understanding of candidates' skills relevant to institutional missions (Espinosa, Gaertner, & Orfield, 2015). Those skills include, but are not limited to, cognitive ability. For example, many universities seek out applicants who can generate original ideas, function in intercultural contexts, and respect individual differences (Willingham & Breland, 1982).

As such, arguments about the use of cognitive tests in college admissions are largely tautological: colleges should evaluate applicants on more than their cognitive ability, because colleges' selection criteria are explicitly much broader. But, for the sake of argument, let us pretend colleges were solely concerned with an applicant's predicted academic performance in college. Even then, noncognitive measures would add value. Research consistently shows that personality factors like conscientiousness (Camara, O'Connor, Mattern, & Hanson, 2015; Richardson, Abraham, & Bond, 2012), interests (Nye, Su, Rounds, & Drasgow, 2012), and striving (i.e., achievement relative to socioeconomic disadvantage; Carnevale & Strohl, 2010; Gaertner & Hart, 2015) improve predictions of college grades and graduation over admissions tests alone.

Job Selection and Success

In personnel selection, predictive validity evidence is probably the most important attribute of any assessment instrument. Above all else, employers want to know how well they can expect candidates to perform on the job. Through a series of meta-analyses, Schmidt and Hunter (1998) generated comprehensive findings about the predictive power of many commonly used personnel selection measures. While assessments of general mental ability predict job performance comparatively well, judicious personnel selection does not begin and end with an IQ test. Assessments of integrity and conscientiousness improve predictive validity by 27% and 18% (respectively), above and beyond tests of general mental ability. Structured employment interviews improve predictive validity by 24%. Predicting performance in job training programs is also made easier with noncognitive measures—particularly integrity (20%) and conscientiousness (16%).

Some Caveats

Before turning to this chapter's second argument, two points bear emphasis. First, it may seem intuitive that hiring and college admissions decisions—entry points for complex and multifaceted endeavors—should rely on more than aptitude or achievement tests. Still, these selection processes are only as valid as the measures upon which they are based and only as coherent as the theoretical frameworks that generate those measures. These caveats underscore the need for further theoretical clarity to support noncognitive measures—a point to which we will return in the final section of this chapter.

Second, in the passages before, we commented on the utility of diverse predictors to forecast a single (and usually rather conventional) outcome, such as college grades. It stands to reason that prediction models' left-hand sides (outcomes) should be expanded as well. Noncognitive personal qualities are worth measuring in and of themselves, not just as predictors of future academic performance. Educational systems should therefore consider measuring noncognitive skills as educational outcomes, not just inputs. This point is echoed with clarity and enthusiasm in Lipnevich, Preckel, and Roberts (2015). Specifically, schools at the primary, secondary, and tertiary levels consistently encode noncognitive skill development in their formal mission statements. Measuring students' cognitive development alone would make noncognitive skill development a distant secondary priority—especially when accountability ratings are at stake. Schools are tasked with cultivating productive and effective workers, and employers are not just looking for highly literate and numerate workers. The influential report *Are They Ready to Work?* identifies noncognitive skills such as work ethic, teamwork, oral communication, leadership, and creativity as particularly critical to workplace success, according to a large survey of employers (Casner-Lotto, Barrington, & Wright, 2006). In fact, these competencies were rated *more* important to overall job performance than reading comprehension and mathematics skills.

There are really two concepts that comprise predictive validity: (1) the validity, that is, the estimated association between the predictor and the outcome and (2) the criterion, that is, the appropriate outcome to target in the first place (MacCann, Duckworth, & Roberts, 2009). If face time at work is a key success indicator, industriousness (a subcomponent of conscientiousness) may be a key predictor. If coping with high-stakes competition is a core component of one's job, then perfectionism (another conscientiousness subcomponent) appears a construct-relevant predictor. These finer-grained predictors are useful not just for boosting predictive power but also for devising interventions that target discrete competencies rather than broad noncognitive traits.

More Nuanced Diagnoses

When assessments focus on narrowly defined cognitive domains, it follows that parents, teachers, and students receive narrow feedback. A low math test score one year may suggest lower math test scores in the future, and that relationship should not be undersold. But, in isolation, this feedback does not help educators pinpoint students' varied strengths and weaknesses. Measuring noncognitive skills, by contrast, helps us understand specific problems that require attention, may be sensitive to treatment, and—if ameliorated—can improve student outcomes.

To illustrate this point more concretely, let us return to the college-readiness indicator system for middle school students introduced earlier (Gaertner & McClarty, 2015). The middle-school indicator set includes measures of behavior (e.g., absences, disciplinary referrals) and motivation (e.g., locus of control, effort relative to ability). Gaertner and McClarty demonstrate how changes on these metrics may improve later-life outcomes for two NELS middle-school students who were not projected to meet SAT and ACT college-readiness benchmarks by the end of high school. By minimizing disciplinary referrals and cutting their absences in half (behavior) and spending more time on coursework outside normal class hours (motivation), these students would be reclassified as on track (i.e., projected to exceed the college-readiness benchmarks), absent any change in academic achievement.

It is important to emphasize that behavior and motivation are expansive constructs. Each must be unpacked (i.e., its component variables, like absences, must be examined) for students, parents, and teachers to make meaning of the diagnoses and take appropriate action. This is not a weakness of noncognitive skills, per se; it is a feature of all constructs. The same steps are appropriate for cognitive measures, where subject-area (e.g., mathematics) scores suffice as a screener, but subscores and item-level data help teachers pinpoint students' specific weaknesses.

Actionable Constructs

To support college and career readiness for all students, measurement alone is insufficient. Measuring a trait does not change it. Developing and applying interventions on the basis of those measures is the more sensible way to produce change.[3] It follows that more targeted and specific measures support more targeted and specific interventions. In this section, we discuss the promise of noncognitive measures for informing a fundamental question in educational practice: "What next?" Before we begin, however, we should clarify our views on malleable versus unmalleable constructs. Just because something cannot be changed does not mean it should not be measured. Some core features of cognitive performance (e.g., processing speed) or personality (e.g., extraversion) may be comparatively insensitive to intervention. Still, these factors have been shown in the literature cited throughout this chapter to influence later-life outcomes. Therefore, we see two reasons to keep measuring unchangeable phenomena and include these measures in predictive or causal models. The first reason is statistical, and the second is political.

Statistically speaking, discarding predictors that are strongly associated with an outcome introduces omitted variable bias (Greene, 2003). That is, the variance associated with omitted variables will be partially absorbed by the variables that remain in the model, leading to spurious inferences about a causal effect or the relative strength of a given predictor. Therefore, including influential predictors increases estimates' precision and decreases their bias, all else being equal.

Politically speaking, it may be disingenuous to ignore influential predictors. The classic illustrative example in educational contexts is socioeconomic status. Many variables that inform socioeconomic status indices (e.g., parents' education) are impervious to intervention. Still, not conditioning outcomes on socioeconomic status implicitly assumes that education can compensate for—and therefore should be accountable for alleviating—the harmful effects of socioeconomic disadvantage on academic outcomes. This logic flies in the face of classroom realities; it is politically and statistically untenable. Therefore, we caution analysts against equating "unchangeable" with "useless." We simply argue that constructs that are particularly sensitive to intervention are particularly useful in planning next steps, and many noncognitive attributes fit that criterion.

Many noncognitive skills are malleable; students can do something about them. In fact, psychosocial skills evolve not only during adolescence but also throughout adulthood. Walton and Billera (2009) provide a comprehensive review of the ways in which noncognitive measures change throughout the life span. Although personality traits are normatively stable over time (i.e., individuals' rank-orders do not change drastically over the course of their lives), and personality profiles (i.e., the configuration of factors like extraversion and emotional stability within individuals) remain relatively stable, this does not rule out other change. Mean-level traits change substantially over time. In particular, conscientiousness, emotional stability, and social dominance seem to increase across the life course (Roberts et al., 2017; Walton & Billera, 2016).

Change in some phases is more pronounced than others—in particular, young adulthood seems to be a period of rapid change—but noncognitive trait development is not restricted to early elementary-school years (Wrzus & Roberts, 2016). For example, conscientiousness is both changeable over time and highly predictive of academic success (Walton & Billera, 2016). Therefore, helping students accelerate their conscientiousness may, in turn, accelerate their academic progress. The literature suggests that a variety of interventions—medicinal (for extraversion and neuroticism; Tang et al., 2009), therapeutic (for emotional stability; De Fruyt, Van Leeuwen, Bagby, Rolland, & Rouillon, 2006), and experimental (for openness to experience; Jackson, Hill, Payne, Roberts, & Stine-Morrow, 2012; for conscientiousness; Burrus, Jackson, Holtzman, & Roberts, 2016)—can boost noncognitive skills.

If noncognitive skills change over time, which educational interventions are best positioned to improve those skills? In this section, we highlight a few promising practices, but we avoid great depth and detail. This book includes an entire section focused on interventions; readers principally interested in "what next?" questions will find Chapters 10–13 useful.

When surveying the landscape of interventions, we were struck by the proliferation of noncognitive constructs, each with its own name and associated treatments. We will not list all of them here. Readers interested in a more thorough review should consult a meta-analysis from Lazowski and Hulleman (2016), covering a variety of motivation-related interventions. Here, we will feature a few that are particularly relevant to schools and schooling. For example, expectancy-value interventions typically target students' feelings about the relevance of their coursework to their lives. When students (randomly assigned to the treatment) were asked to write about how their science lessons related to their lives, their GPAs improved significantly more than the GPAs of control-condition students (Hulleman & Harackiewicz, 2009). Attribution theory, on the other hand, focuses on interventions that seek to help students link their academic performance to effort rather than innate intelligence. Wilson and Linville (1982, 1985) showed such interventions hold promise. Subjects (again randomly assigned to a treatment group) watched a video explaining how students typically struggle with schoolwork during their freshman year, but eventually recover and progress. These students ultimately earned better grades and were less likely to drop out of high school, relative to their control-group counterparts.

Programs targeting attribution evoke one of the most well-known and widely researched noncognitive interventions—"growth mindset." We will not detail growth mindset here, because it is discussed at length in Chapter 12 of this volume. Rather, we will briefly emphasize a related concept—"growth mindset for practice" (Shechtman, Cheng, Stites, & Yarnall, 2016). Simply put, the idea that psychosocial skills are teachable is not universally integrated in teaching practice. "Growth mindset" is important for students, but it is also important for educators. Those who believe learners cannot change are likely to interpret behaviors through static labels and have low expectations that learners can master new competencies, while those who believe learners can change have higher expectations (Molden & Dweck, 2006; Neel & Lassetter, 2015).

Implications for Policy, Practice, and Research

In this chapter, we have argued for the measurement of noncognitive traits in educational settings, and we have provided three rationales—better prediction, more nuanced diagnoses, and actionable constructs. Next, we will list specific implications for schools, provide what we think are the most important next steps for researchers, and offer some options for putting noncognitive measures to use.

For Policy and Practice

To begin, we will invoke some conventional business wisdom that birthed test-driven accountability reforms at the turn of the 21st century: "You can't manage what you don't measure." Psychosocial skills assessments hold promise for not just diagnosis but also for educational evaluation. The argument for incorporating noncognitive measures in accountability systems is, on its face, rational. Schools' missions include cognitive and noncognitive skill building. Therefore, to the extent that it makes sense to hold schools accountable for student achievement, it must be equivalently sensible to hold them accountable for nurturing students' psychosocial skills. In fact, national and international assessments like NAEP, PISA, and PIACC have begun incorporating noncognitive measures, lending credibility to the idea that evaluative tests should cover more than reading, writing, science, and mathematics. Likewise, the Every Student Succeeds Act (2015) embraces at least the idea of *nonacademic* measures, requiring each state to include in its accountability system one measure (e.g., student engagement) that is not derived from a standardized math or reading assessment.

Still, high stakes demand caution, because the potential for measurement distortions and unintended consequences cannot be ignored. Different measurement tools are susceptible to different validity threats, and high-stakes settings may magnify those threats. So, in an effort to make these issues real and manageable for practitioners, we will list some common threats to inferences based on noncognitive measures, the circumstances in which they are most likely to surface, and some approaches researchers and educators have used to minimize them.

"Self-report" describes data that are collected via direct questions to students about their own psychological processes (e.g., "Chance and luck are important in my life"). Self-report questions are relatively easy to write and administer, but resulting data are vulnerable to two threats—reference bias and faking. Reference bias is the more conceptually complex problem; it happens when respondents' referent groups vary systematically. For example, imagine students with an internal locus of control (i.e., prone to attributing their life events to their own choices and behaviors; Rotter, 1966) being educated in an environment where internal locus of control is valued, taught, and emphasized (e.g., KIPP schools; KIPP, n.d.). When responding to the aforementioned "chance and luck" item, those students will respond relative to their proximal peer group—a group that will probably exhibit a high internal locus of control. As such, their internal locus of control estimates could be downwardly biased. Faking, by contrast, is easier to describe and grasp (Ziegler, MacCann, & Roberts, 2011). If students understand that there are stakes attached to their responses, they will respond in a way that maximizes their desired outcomes. For example, if they like their teacher, would like for their teacher to get a raise, and understand that demonstrating an internal locus of control will make that raise more likely, they will strongly disagree with the statement "Chance and luck are important in my life."

Of course, not all noncognitive measures are self-reported. Teachers' observations of student behavior, for example, may be slightly less vulnerable to self-report biases. That said, teacher observations may be more resource-intensive than student self-reports (a teacher will need to conduct and report on observations of all students), and observations are certainly not immune to bias. If teachers' observations were tied to their own evaluative ratings, the temptation to game the ratings would be too strong for observation-based inferences to be of much use. Another alternative is behavioral task performance. In this form of noncognitive measurement, students must complete a task, and their results or scores are not a matter of subjective interpretation. The most frequently cited example is the Marshmallow Test (Mischel, Ebbesen, & Raskoff, 1972). In this experiment examining delayed gratification, children were asked whether they would prefer an immediate reward (one marshmallow now) or a larger delayed reward (two marshmallows later). The children who delayed their gratification had better outcomes across a variety of domains, including SAT scores and body mass index. Of course, the Marshmallow Test is a contrived scenario, and its purpose is so well known today that it would be safe to assume the task is susceptible to faking.

More authentic and sometimes less obtrusive data collection tools are proliferating, and may be less vulnerable to the biases we have outlined here. For example, situational judgment tests present students with hypothetical scenarios and with various response options that are more (or less) appropriate given the situation. Validity evidence is beginning to accrue for this approach in educational settings, and the method can be pushed to provide formative noncognitive items (Lipnevich, MacCann, & Roberts, 2013). And in game-based settings, non-cognitive information (e.g., task persistence) could be collected via data mining. So-called "big data" measurement approaches may help reduce fakability concerns that plague the measurement of noncognitive factors when consequences are attached. Despite their promise, game-based and data-mining approaches to measuring noncognitive traits are relatively immature and untested. The field needs more reliability and validity evidence (convergent, divergent, and predictive) before these approaches can be put to evaluative use.

In some contexts, research on the use of noncognitive measures for evaluation is already underway. For example, West (2016) showed promising reliability and validity diagnostics for noncognitive measures slated for accountability use in California's largest school districts. We view these early findings with cautious optimism, and in line with the recommendations of Duckworth and Yeager (2015), we still adopt a "not yet" posture on noncognitive measures for accountability purposes. Overenthusiasm for attaching consequences to noncognitive measures could politicize and stunt an important line of research. Often cited and less often heeded, Campbell's Law deserves repeating: when quantitative measures are applied to track social processes, those measures may end up distorting the processes they were intended to monitor.

For Researchers

Most importantly for this book's audience, the research community still needs a unifying theoretical framework to support the development and application of noncognitive measures. We are in danger of creating psychosocial skills assessments so numerous that school systems will be overwhelmed by the variety of constructs and unable to organize them for purposeful application.

The best candidate has been around for quite some time and has already been referenced throughout this chapter—the Five Factor Model (FFM; Costa & McRae, 1992). Openness to experience, conscientiousness, extraversion, agreeableness, and neuroticism comprise the FFM, and we assert that most, if not all "new," psychosocial constructs fit within these five factors (Roberts, Martin, & Olaru, 2015). In psychology, the FFM has been the subject of empirical study for decades, and multiple large meta-analyses have demonstrated its utility for predicting future performance in the college and career domains (Poropat, 2009; Schmidt & Hunter, 1998). The FFM has been advocated by many (e.g., Poropat, 2009) as the preeminent taxonomy of psychosocial skills. Those who disagree have yet to agree on an alternative.

Still, consolidating noncognitive skills under the FFM will not completely suffice to advance research and practice in an organized way. We conclude this chapter with suggestions for further research focused on three questions. First, which of the five factors (and related subfactors) can we measure most reliably? Reliability is a critical feature of educational measures, especially those that are used for evaluative rather than exploratory purposes. Second, which of the five factors are most sensitive to intervention? Although unchangeable traits still deserve attention for statistical and practical reasons, those that are more responsive to interventions are more important for educational programs that intend to boost valued societal outcomes. Finally, which factors offer the biggest predictive bang for the buck, i.e., which most profoundly influence later-life success? Conscientiousness has been shown to be a strong predictor of academic and job performance outcomes; are there other predictive attributes that we can measure and that we can teach? Further researching the FFM's application to educational contexts will not just make us better measurers. It will broaden and strengthen our means to help students accelerate their academic progress and finish their K–12 careers ready for the next step.

Notes

1 As Easton (2013) points out, "Everybody hates this term [noncognitive] but everybody knows roughly what you mean when you use it."
2 College and career readiness is a potentially broad domain, which may extend back to early childhood. To circumscribe our discussion, we begin in middle school.
3 In principle, some assessment practices (e.g., formative assessment) are intended to "change" constructs, via integration in the learning process. We do not discuss formative assessment here; Heritage (2017) covers the topic in depth.

References

ACT (2015). *The condition of college and career readiness 2015.* Retrieved from http://www.act.org/content/act/en/research/condition-of-college-and-career-readiness-report-2015.html?page=0&chapter=3.

Allen, J., & Robbins, S. (2010). Effects of interest–major congruence, motivation, and academic performance on timely degree attainment. *Journal of Counseling Psychology, 57,* 23–35.

Allensworth, E., & Easton, J. (2005). *The on-track indicator as a predictor of high school graduation.* Chicago, IL: Consortium on Chicago School Research.

Allensworth, E., & Easton, J. (2007). *What matters for staying on-track and graduating in Chicago Public High Schools: A close look at course grades, failures and attendance in the freshman year.* Chicago, IL: Consortium on Chicago School Research.

Burrus, J., Jackson, T., Holtzman, S., & Roberts, R. (2016). Teaching high school students to manage time: The development of an intervention. *Improving Schools.* Advance online publication: DOI: 10.1177/1365480216650309.

Camara, W., O'Connor, R., Mattern, K., & Hanson, M. (2015). *Beyond academics: A holistic framework for enhancing education and workplace success (ACT Research Report Series 2015:4).* Iowa City, IA: ACT.

Cantor, N., & Englot, P. (2014). Defining the stakes: Why we cannot leave the nation's diverse talent pool behind and thrive. In R. Kahlenberg (Ed.), *The Future of Affirmative Action: New Paths to Higher Education Diversity after Fisher v. University of Texas.* Washington, DC: The Century Foundation, 27–34.

Carnevale, A., & Strohl, J. (2010). How increasing college access is increasing inequality, and what to do about it. In R. Kahlenberg (Ed.), *Rewarding strivers: Helping low-income students succeed in college.* Washington, DC: The Century Foundation, 71–190.

Casillas, A., Robbins, S., Allen, J., Kuo, Y., Hanson, M., & Schmeiser, C. (2012). Predicting early academic failure in high school from prior academic achievement, psychosocial characteristics, and behavior. *Journal of Educational Psychology, 104,* 407–420.

Casner-Lotto, J., Barrington, L., & Wright, M. (2006). *Are they really ready to work? (Report BED-06-Workforce).* Retrieved from www.conference-board.org/publications/publicationdetail.cfm?publicationid=1218.

Clinedinst, M. (2015). *State of college admission.* Arlington, VA: National Association for College Admission Counseling. Retrieved from http://www.nacacnet.org/research/PublicationsResources/Marketplace/research/Pages/StateofCollegeAdmission.aspx.

Costa, P., & McCrae, R. (1992). *Revised NEO Personality Inventory (NEO-PI-R) and NEO Five-Factor Inventory (NEO-FFI) professional manual.* Odessa, FL: Psychological Assessment Resources.

Credé, M., Tynan, M., & Harms, P. (2016). Much ado about grit: A meta-analytic synthesis of the grit literature. *Journal of Personality and Social Psychology.* Advance online publication: URL: http://psycnet.apa.org/?&fa=main.doiLanding&doi=10.1037/pspp0000102.

De Fruyt, F., Van Leeuwen, K., Bagby, R., Rolland, J., & Rouillon, R. (2006). Assessing and interpreting personality change and continuity in patients treated for major depression. *Psychological Assessment, 18,* 71–80.

Duckworth, A., & Yeager, D. (2015). Measurement matters: Assessing personal qualities other than cognitive ability for educational purposes. *Educational Researcher, 44*(4), 237–251.

Easton, J. (2013). *Using measurement as leverage between developmental research and educational practice.* Keynote delivered at the Center for Advanced Study of Teaching and Learning Meeting, Charlottesville, VA. Retrieved from https://ies.ed.gov/director/pdf/Easton062013.pdf.

Espinosa, L., Gaertner, M., & Orfield, G. (2015). *Race, class, and college access: Achieving diversity in a shifting legal landscape.* Washington, DC: American Council on Education.

Every Student Succeeds Act of 2015, Pub. L. No. 114–95 § 114 Stat. 1177 (2015–2016).

Gaertner, M., & Hart, M. (2015). From access to success: Affirmative action outcomes in a class-based system. *Colorado Law Review, 86*(2), 431–475.

Gaertner, M. N., & McClarty, K. L. (2015). Performance, perseverance, and the full picture of college readiness. *Educational Measurement: Issues and Practice, 34*(2), 20–33.

Gaertner, M. N., & McClarty, K. L. (2016). The case for a middle-school college-readiness index. *Educational Measurement: Issues and Practice, 35*(3), 35–37.

Greene, W. (2003). *Econometric analysis.* Upper Saddle River, NJ: Prentice Hall.

Heritage, M. (2017). Changing the assessment relationship to empower teachers and students. In K. L. McClarty, K. D. Mattern, & M. N. Gaertner (Eds.), *Preparing students for college and careers: Theory, measurement, and educational practice.* New York: Routledge.

Hulleman, C., & Harackiewicz, J. (2009). Promoting interest and performance in high school science classes. *Science, 326*, 1410–1412.

Jackson, J., Hill, P., Payne, B., Roberts, B., & Stine-Morrow, E. (2012). Can and old dog learn (and want to experience) new tricks? Cognitive training increases openness to experience in older adults. *Psychology and Aging, 27*, 286–292.

KIPP (n.d.). *Five Pillars.* Retrieved from http://www.kipp.org/our-approach/five-pillars.

Kobrin, J., Patterson, B., Shaw, E., Mattern, K., & Barbuti, S. (2008). *Validity of the SAT* for predicting first-year college grade point average (College Board Research Report No. 2008–5).* New York: The College Board.

Lazowski, R., & Hulleman, C. (2016). Motivation interventions in education: A meta-analytic review. *Review of Educational Research, 86*(2), 602–640.

Lipnevich A. A., MacCann C., & Roberts R. D. (2013). Assessing noncognitive constructs in education: A review of traditional and innovative approaches. In Saklofske D. H., Reynolds C. B., & Schwean V. L. (Eds.), *Oxford handbook of child psychological assessment.* Cambridge, MA: Oxford University Press, 750–772.

Lipnevich, A., Preckel, F., & Roberts, R. (2015). Psychosocial constructs: Knowns, unknowns, and future directions. In P. Kyllonen, R. Roberts, & L. Stankov (Eds.), *Extending intelligence: Enhancement and new constructs.* New York: Lawrence Erlbaum Associates, 375–394.

MacCann, C., Duckworth, A., & Roberts, R. (2009). Empirical identification of the major facets of con-scientiousness. *Learning and Individual Differences, 19*, 451–458.

MacCann, C., Matthews, G., Zeidner, M., & Roberts, R. (2003). Psychological assessment of emotional intelligence: A review of self-report and performance-based testing. *International Journal of Organizational Analysis, 11*(3), 247–274.

Mischel, W., Ebbesen, E., Raskoff, A. (1972). Cognitive and attentional mechanisms in delay of gratification. *Journal of Personality and Social Psychology, 21*(2): 204–218.

Molden, D., & Dweck, C. (2006). Finding "meaning" in psychology: A lay theories approach to self-regulation, social perception, and social development. *American Psychologist, 61*(3), 192–203.

Neel, R., & Lassetter, B. (2015). Growing fixed with age: Lay theories of malleability are target age-specific. *Personality and Social Psychology Bulletin, 41*(11), 1505–1522.

Nye, C., Su, R., Rounds, J., & Drasgow, F. (2012). Vocational interests and performance: A quantitative summary of over 60 years of research. *Perspectives on Psychological Science, 7*, 384–403.

Poropat, A. (2009). A meta-analysis of the five-factor model of personality and academic performance. *Psychological Bulletin, 135*(2), 322–338.

Richardson, M., Abraham, C., & Bond, R. (2012). Psychological correlates of university students' academic performance: A systematic review and meta-analysis. *Psychological Bulletin, 138*, 353–387.

Roberts, B., Luo, J., Briley, D., Chow, P., Su, R., & Hill, P. (2017). A systematic review of personality trait change through intervention. *Psychological Bulletin, 143*(2), 117–141.

Roberts, R., Martin, J., & Olaru, G. (2015). *A rosetta stone for noncognitive skills: Understanding, assessing, and enhancing noncognitive skills in primary and secondary education.* New York: Asia Society and ProExam.

Roberts, R., Schulze, R., O'Brien, K., MacCann, C., Reid, J., & Maul, A. (2006). Exploring the validity of the Mayer-Salovey-Caruso Emotional Intelligence Test (MSCEIT) with established emotions measures. *Emotion, 6*, 663–669.

Roberts, R., Stankov, L., Schulze, R., & Kyllonen, P. (2008). Extending intelligence: Conclusions and future directions. In P. Kyllonen, R. Roberts, & L. Stankov (Eds.), *Extending intelligence: Enhancement and new constructs.* New York: Lawrence Erlbaum Associates, 363–378.

Rotter, J. (1966). Generalized expectancies of internal versus external control of reinforcements. *Psychological Monographs, 80*(609), 1–28.

Schmidt, F., & Hunter, J. (1998). The validity and utility of selection methods in personnel psychology: Practical and theoretical implications of 85 years of research findings. *Psychological Bulletin, 124,* 262–274.

Shechtman, N., Cheng, B., Stites, R., & Yarnall, L. (2016). *Personal success skills for adults: Essential competencies for those striving to build sustainable careers in the 21st century workforce.* Chicago, IL: Joyce Foundation.

Stemler, S. E., & DePascale, M. (2016). Aligning Mission and Measurement. In A. A. Lipnevich, F. Preckel, & R. D. Roberts (Eds.), *Psychosocial skills and school systems in the 21st century. Theory, research, and practice.* New York: Springer, 57–92.

Tang, T., DeRubeis, R., Hollon, S., Amsterdam, J., Shelton, R., & Schalet, B. (2009). Personality change during depression treatment: A placebo-controlled trial. *Archives of General Psychiatry, 66,* 1322–1330.

Walton, K. E., & Billera, K. A. (2016). Personality development during the school-aged years: Implications for theory, research, and practice. In A. A. Lipnevich, F. Preckel, & R. D. Roberts (Eds.), *Psychosocial skills and school systems in the 21st century. Theory, research, and practice.* New York: Springer, 93–111.

West, M. (2016). *Should noncognitive skills be included in school accountability systems? Preliminary evidence from California's CORE districts.* Washington, DC: Brookings.

Westrick, P., Le, H., Robbins, S., Radunzel, J., & Schmidt, F. (2015). College performance and retention: A meta-analysis of the predictive validities of ACT[*] scores, high school grades, and SES. *Educational Assessment, 20*(1), 23–45.

Willingham, W., & Breland, H. (1982). *Personal qualities and college admissions.* New York: College Entrance Examination Board.

Wilson, T., & Linville, P. (1982). Improving the academic performance of college freshmen: Attribution therapy revisited. *Journal of Personality and Social Psychology, 42,* 367–376.

Wilson, T., & Linville, P. (1985). Improving the performance of college freshmen with attributional techniques. *Journal of Personality and Social Psychology, 49,* 287–293.

Wrzus, C., & Roberts, B. (2016). Processes of personality development in adulthood: The TESSERA framework. *Personality and Social Psychology Review.* Advance online publication: DOI: 10.1177/1088868316652279.

Ziegler, M., MacCann, C., & Roberts, R. (Eds.). (2011). *New perspectives on faking in personality assessment.* New York: Oxford University Press.

4 The Consistent Influence of General Cognitive Ability in College, Career, and Lifetime Achievement

Jonathan Wai, Frank C. Worrell, and Christopher F. Chabris

Advice given to students on college and career readiness includes interests, knowledge, and skills, but often leaves out cognitive abilities. Gottfredson (2003a) attributed this omission to counselors believing it is not appropriate to tell students that they are unlikely to be able to achieve a certain goal because of their ability level, but it may be equally inappropriate to withhold pertinent information from students if costly failures are likely to follow. Although multiple abilities are important, in this chapter, we focus on the largest source of common variance in achievement: general cognitive ability, or *g* (e.g., Chabris, 2007; Jensen, 1998).

General cognitive ability contributes to performance in educational settings (Kuncel, Hezlett, & Ones, 2004) and occupations (Hsu & Wai, 2015; Schmidt & Hunter, 1998, 2004) and also contributes to a variety of life outcomes (Gottfredson, 2003b; Jensen, 1998), including health (Wraw, Deary, Gale, & Der, 2015).

Because an individual's general cognitive level is important to account for in any education and career decision, it should be included in any college- and career-readiness discussion and accounted for by any intervention (and empirical tests of such interventions) designed to improve college and career readiness.

Measurement of General Cognitive Ability

How can general cognitive ability be measured? Spearman (1927) proposed that *g* enters into performance on any mental test, and therefore the precise content of mental tests is unimportant. Indeed, almost any difficult cognitive test that includes a diverse set of tasks or question types will measure *g* to some extent, regardless of the specific items or analytic technique (Chabris, 2007; Ree & Earles, 1991). Researchers have shown that measures traditionally thought of as aptitude or achievement tests, such as SAT or ACT, actually measure general cognitive ability to a large degree (Frey & Detterman, 2004; Koenig, Frey, & Detterman, 2008), and *g* is consistently measured in tests designed to measure a variety of abilities and achievements (Johnson, te Nijenhuis, & Bouchard, 2008; Schult & Sparfeldt, 2016). Cognitive *g* and academic achievement *g* are essentially the same (Kaufman, Reynolds, Kauman, & McGrew, 2012). Even when measures are specifically designed to assess fluid intelligence or novel tasks (e.g., using Sternberg's Triarchic Abilities Test; Sternberg, Grigorenko, Ferrari, & Clinkenbeard, 1999), empirical reanalyses have revealed *g* (Brody, 2003).

Given this volume's focus on college and career readiness, our emphasis is on common tests used for college admissions as an indicator of *g*. Various measures will be stronger or weaker measures of *g*; however, data across a variety of mental measures, ranging from IQ tests to achievement tests, show very similar patterns of prediction with later educational and occupational outcomes.

Utility of General Cognitive Ability Tests in College/Graduate School Selection

Research supporting the use of standardized tests in college admissions (e.g., Kobrin, Patterson, Shaw, Mattern, & Barbuti, 2008), graduate school admissions (e.g., Kuncel & Hezlett, 2007), and even for hiring (e.g., Schmidt & Hunter, 1998, 2004) is largely based on the predictive validity of such measures; these findings have been replicated across decades and are even predictive when considering only the top 1% of the ability distribution (e.g., Makel, Kell, Lubinski, Putallaz, & Benbow, 2016; Wai, Lubinski, & Benbow, 2005). Standardized tests have additional advantages over course grades, letters of recommendation, interviews, and other predictors or admissions criteria, because they are objective and lack bias from third-party judgments.

Undergraduate Performance

Studies of predictive validity on the SAT have a long history. Fishman and Pasanella (1960) and Morgan (1989) showed that a *combination* of high school grade point average (HSGPA) and SAT scores was a better predictor of first-year college GPA than SAT scores or HSGPA alone. In a study of the 2006 cohort of SAT takers (N = 196,364 from 110 colleges and universities across the United States), Kobrin et al. (2008) reported range-restriction corrected correlations with first-year GPA of .53 for the combined SAT scores, .54 for HSGPA, and .62 for combined SAT scores and HSGPA together.

Moreover, SAT test scores also predict college GPA beyond the first year. Using the 2006 validity cohort, researchers reported corrected correlations with second-year GPA of. 50 for the combined SAT scores, .51 for HSGPA, and .58 for combined SAT scores and HSGPA (Mattern & Patterson, 2011a), and corrected correlations with third-year GPA of .45 for the combined SAT scores, .46 for HSGPA, and .52 for combined SAT scores and HSGPA (Mattern & Patterson, 2011b). SAT and ACT scores also predict cumulative GPA at the end of the fourth year and predict whether students graduate from college (Schmitt et al., 2009).

Graduate Performance

The predictive validity of the Graduate Record Examination (GRE) scores for graduate school performance has been studied for decades (e.g., Stricker & Huber, 1967). Kuncel, Hezlett, and Ones (2001) conducted a meta-analysis of GRE and undergraduate GPA as predictors of graduate school performance, showing that GRE scores had similar or higher predictive validity coefficients than undergraduate GPA for a variety of academic outcomes, including:

- first-year graduate GPA (GRE general scores [$.34 \leq \rho \leq .38$], subject GRE [$\rho = .45$], and undergraduate GPA [$\rho = .33$]);
- cumulative graduate GPA (GRE general scores [$.32 \leq \rho \leq .36$], subject GRE [$\rho = .41$], and undergraduate GPA [$\rho = .30$]);
- comprehensive examination scores (GRE general scores [$.26 \leq \rho \leq .44$], subject GRE [$\rho = .51$], and undergraduate GPA [$\rho = .12$]);
- faculty ratings of performance (GRE general scores [$.35 \leq \rho \leq .47$], subject GRE [$\rho = .50$], and undergraduate GPA [$\rho = .35$]); and
- degree attainment (GRE general scores [$.11 \leq \rho \leq .20$], subject GRE [$\rho = .39$], and undergraduate GPA [$\rho = .12$]).

Both the GRE and Graduate Management Admission Test (GMAT) have been shown to predict performance in business schools. A meta-analysis showed that for business student performance, the GMAT, and especially the quantitative score, is a superior predictor to undergraduate GPA (Young, Klieger, Bochenek, Li, & Cline, 2014). Similarly, a systematic review including the GRE, GRE Subject Tests, GMAT, Law School Admission Test (LSAT), Medical College Admission Test (MCAT), Miller Analogies Test (MAT), and Pharmacy College Admission Test (PCAT) showed that all these tests were strong predictors of academic outcomes, including overall graduate GPA, qualifying exam scores, degree completion, research productivity, citation counts, faculty ratings, and licensing exam performance (Kuncel & Hezlett, 2007).

Predictions of Performance by Demographic Subgroups

To date, the predictive validity of traditional cognitive test scores (e.g., IQ tests, ability tests) on educational and occupational outcomes is quite similar across gender, ethnic-racial, and socioeconomic groups (Neisser et al., 1996; Nisbett et al., 2012). However, research on college admissions tests has yielded more varied findings. For example, Young (2001) found admissions tests slightly underpredict the college GPAs of Asian Americans and slightly overpredict the GPAs of African Americans and Hispanic Americans. Moreover, there was less predictive power for African-American and Hispanic students' GPA than for Asian Americans and European Americans.

Young (2001) also reported consistent gender differences in predictive power. Multiple correlations are typically higher for women than for men, although the difference between genders disappears in more selective institutions. Studies also indicate a slight underprediction of women's college grades. A recent systematic review by Higdem et al. (2016), controlling for socioeconomic status, replicated previous findings. In short, these findings indicate that although predictive validity coefficients differ somewhat, these differences do not result in substantial differential prediction of school performance.

Cognitive Ability in Hiring and Job Performance

Some companies use SAT scores as screeners for interviewing and hiring (Dewan, 2014), but do cognitive test scores actually predict job performance beyond degree completion? Yes. One set of evidence comes from validity studies of general mental ability on job performance (e.g., Schmidt & Hunter, 1998, 2004), and another set of evidence comes from studies of SAT and GRE scores on performance outcomes after schooling (e.g., Ferriman-Robertson, Smeets, Lubinski, & Benbow, 2010; Kuncel & Hezlett, 2010; Park, Lubinski, & Benbow, 2008).

A century of research has shown that general cognitive ability is highly predictive of both training outcomes and job performance. Schmidt and Hunter (1998) systematically meta-analyzed 85 years of research, finding that the best predictor of job performance was a combination of general mental ability scores with another measure, such as integrity tests or structured interviews. Schmidt and Hunter (2004) found that, first, cognitive scores predicted scores on performance measures both in job training and in job performance after training, and these validity coefficients increased with job complexity. Second, they showed the correlation between job performance and experience decreases over time from the first three years to after 12 years of experience; however, the correlation between cognitive test scores and job performance increases over the same time period. Third, they showed general mental ability predicts the acquisition of job knowledge and has a larger indirect effect on job performance via job knowledge and a smaller direct effect on job performance in both civilian and military jobs, respectively.

Other research illustrates that general cognitive ability is positively related to creativity, objective leader effectiveness, training success for both military and civilian groups, and performance in occupations ranging from low to high complexity (Kuncel et al., 2004; Ones, Viswesvaran, & Dilchert, 2005). Similar to findings relating SAT scores to college GPAs, in 174 studies on more than 36,000 workers, supervisors' ratings of employees' job performance were found to be linearly related to general cognitive ability (Coward & Sackett, 1990). Like Schmidt and Hunter, Coward and Sackett also observed that the association between general cognitive ability and job performance differs as a function of degree of job complexity. For example, general cognitive ability is more strongly linked with job performance of high complexity jobs (Kuncel & Hezlett, 2010; Kuncel et al., 2004; Ones et al., 2005).

Kuncel and Hezlett (2007) examined the predictive validity of a variety of graduate school admissions tests on subsequent performance on professional licensing examinations. They found that LSAT scores had a correlation of about .30 with Bar examination scores and that MCAT scores had a correlation coefficient of about .65 with medical licensing examination scores. Similarly, SAT scores predict outcomes well beyond college, including career choice and long-term occupational outcomes such as patents, publications, income levels, and even university tenure (Ferriman-Robertson et al., 2010; Wai et al., 2005).

General Cognitive Ability and Long-Term Educational and Occupational Outcomes

In this section, we review the evidence of the prediction of long-term educational and occupational outcomes for both the full range and the right tail of the distribution.

Educational Outcomes

SAT scores have been shown to be linearly related to longer-term college GPA across the entire range of scores (Cullen, Hardison, & Sackett, 2004) and related to multiple outcomes (Berry & Sackett, 2009), including performance in graduate school. A meta-analysis by Kuncel et al. (2004) demonstrated that general cognitive ability as measured by MAT scores was predictive of a variety of academic criteria for graduate students, including first-year GPA, overall GPA, comprehensive examination scores, time to degree, degree attainment, research productivity, and faculty ratings.

However, the strongest evidence for the long-term predictive validity of college admissions test scores on educational performance comes from studies of gifted and talented youth who have participated in a 7th-grade talent search (e.g., Lubinski, Benbow, & Kell, 2014; Makel et al., 2016; Wai et al., 2005). Students in the talent search complete the SAT before they are 13 years old, around 7th grade. Even within the top 1% of general cognitive ability, general ability scores, as measured by the SAT in the Study of Mathematically Precocious Youth (SMPY; Ferriman-Robertson et al., 2010) and by ability tests in Project Talent (Wai, 2014a), are shown to predict educational outcomes. SAT scores from age 13 were positively related to the earning of higher educational credentials, with clear differences within the top percent of scores (top quartile of the top 1% to bottom quartile of the top 1%) on earning, for example, doctorate degrees (Park et al., 2008; Wai, 2014a).

Occupational Outcomes

SAT scores within the top 1% of general cognitive ability are also related to long-term occupational outcomes. Within SMPY, higher ability was associated with a higher rate of publications, patents, income, and university tenure (Wai et al., 2005). Other research using Project Talent and SMPY data shows general cognitive ability in youth is related to the cognitive complexity of later occupations (Wai, 2014a).

Another way to examine the importance of general cognitive ability for long-term achievement is to reverse the selective filter and examine the people in elite occupations and see to what extent these people scored high—for example, in the top 1%—on general cognitive ability tests when younger. A number of studies looking at people in elite occupations—CEOs, billionaires, 30-millionaires, federal judges, House of Representatives members, Senators, Davos attendees, and people listed among the most powerful men and women—show that roughly 50% of the people in the extreme right tail of achievement in the United States are very likely to be in the top 1% of general cognitive ability (Wai, 2013, 2014b; Wai & Lincoln, 2016; Wai & Rindermann, 2015). This combination of prospective and retrospective longitudinal data shows that cognitive ability matters in the development of occupational expertise (cf. Kuncel & Hezlett, 2010; Schmidt & Hunter, 2004).

Additional evidence supports the idea that cognitive ability predicts occupational outcomes. For example, the average general cognitive ability level of undergraduate institutions was recently linked to the per capita rate of science and technology prize winners (Hsu & Wai, 2015). The undergraduate education of every Nobel prize winner, Fields medalist, Turing award winner, and member of the National Academy of Sciences, Institute of Medicine, and National Academy of Engineering was examined, and their undergraduate schools' average general cognitive ability based on SAT and ACT scores was correlated about .50 with their ranking in producing the most prize winners per number of graduates over time. These results show that general cognitive ability at an aggregate level is also predictive of long-term outcomes that reach well beyond education to elite performance in occupational and scientific spheres. Results like this are consistent with a continual accrual of benefits from higher cognitive ability over the lifespan, as one has more opportunities to exploit or demonstrate cognitive ability and as one receives beneficial opportunities from the results achieved from cognitive ability.

Even among the Gifted, More General Cognitive Ability Has a Payoff

The idea of an "ability threshold"—or that beyond a certain point, ability no longer continues to be related to long-term outcomes—has been expressed in various forms throughout history. It has been recently popularized by the writer Malcolm Gladwell (2008, p. 79), who wrote, "The relationship between success and IQ works only up to a point. Once someone has an IQ of somewhere around 120, having additional IQ points doesn't seem to translate into any measurable real-world advantage." Data from SMPY and Project Talent do not support that notion. For individuals in the top 1% of general ability, even beyond an IQ of about 137 (the cutoff point for the top 1%), more ability pays off in educational and occupational outcomes. Even within highly ability-range-restricted samples of Fortune 500 CEOs, 30-millionaires, and billionaires, higher ability is associated with higher income, net worth, connections, and network power (Wai, 2013, 2014b; Wai & Lincoln, 2016; Wai & Rindermann, 2015). These findings do not mean that ability is all that matters, only that ability continues to have a positive payoff.

Alternative Perspectives and Considerations

The evidence reviewed in this chapter focused on general cognitive ability, because in any system, it is important to account for the largest source of variance (Lubinski, 2004). Although not addressed here, evidence suggests that domain-specific abilities are also important in predicting educational outcomes (Lubinski & Benbow, 2006; Subotnik, Olszewski-Kubilius, & Worrell, 2011). We summarize in this section the main counterarguments and contrary evidence to the literature reviewed in this chapter, in order to better place our conclusions in the appropriate context.

A key counterargument to the literature we reviewed is the assertion that general intelligence is a changeable rather than fixed construct. One cited piece of support is the literature on the Flynn effect (Flynn, 1984), which shows that IQ scores have been rising for many decades in the general distribution and the right tail (Wai & Putallaz, 2011). A multitude of factors have been proposed to explain the Flynn effect (e.g., schooling, nutrition, technology). Although some have argued that the Flynn effect might suggest a rise in *g*, the scientific consensus to date is that we are unclear whether the gains are truly on *g* (e.g., Wicherts et al., 2004).

Another issue is the role early intervention might play in increasing *g*. Although studies have found early gains, typically these gains disappear as children get older. A recent meta-analysis of 7,584 participants across 39 randomized controlled trials showed that after an intervention (e.g., intensive early education, Head Start, effortful control training) raised intelligence, the effects faded away. Crucially, this outcome is due to the experimental groups losing ground rather than the control groups catching up (Protzko, 2016). Though Head Start follow-up studies do suggest that there may be long-term benefits on academic outcomes for some participants—including fewer grade retentions and special education placements, and higher high school graduation rates (Barnett & Hustedt, 2005)—such benefits may flow from intervention effects on influential factors other than general cognitive ability.

There is also mixed, inconclusive evidence about whether intelligence might be raised through brain training. An independent review of the best studies put forth by the brain training companies to support their claims concluded that most of the studies are uninterpretable, do not meet best practice standards, or did not actually produce transfer to tasks beyond the "brain games" themselves (Simons et al., 2016). Similarly, listening to classical music or watching "enrichment videos" for babies also has no significant effect on *g* or later-life outcomes (Chabris, 1999).

Though there is research showing *belief* in the ability to change intelligence might affect performance (Dweck, Chui, & Hong, 1995; Kroeper & Murphy, 2017), the idea that intelligence can actually be easily or lastingly increased by targeted interventions presently appears to be a myth (Haier, 2014). Perhaps possibilities for the future could include "interventions based on sophisticated neuroscience advances in DNA analysis, neuroimaging, psychopharmacology, and even direct brain stimulation" (Haier, 2014, p. 3).

Implications for Policy, Practice, and Research

In this chapter, we reviewed literature showing cognitive ability is a general predictor of performance. We also showed college admissions tests contribute unique variance to the prediction of educational outcomes, educational attainment, and job performance, including at the most elite levels, and that the predictive validity extends well into the late stages of careers. This final section outlines several important considerations for how *g* should be considered in discussions of college and career readiness.

Counseling for College and Career Readiness

First, we consider the role of *g* in college and career counseling. There is a growing recognition in the United States that in an information age, tertiary education is needed by a larger percentage of the population. Thus, there are a number of educational initiatives intended to prepare students from low-SES and underrepresented minority backgrounds to enroll in college (Fleischman & Heppen, 2009). However, although more students who have not traditionally gone to college are entering undergraduate institutions, college graduation rates for underrepresented students with strong high school performance have not similarly increased (Worrell & Weinstein, 2016).

One reason may be because students are not well-matched with their postsecondary institution. Dillon and Smith (2013) examined the phenomena of college mismatch in a nationally representative sample of college goers from the National Longitudinal Survey of Youth 1997 cohort and concluded that mismatch often occurs because of the colleges students apply to and ultimately enroll in, rather than because of the college acceptance criteria. Study results on the impact of mismatch on college outcomes are mixed (e.g., Gaertner & Hart, 2015), with some suggesting no effect of mismatch (Alon & Tienda, 2005; Heil, Reisel, & Attewell, 2014), others suggesting undermatching results in lower educational aspirations (Jagešić, 2015), others suggesting overmatching has a negative impact (Furstenberg, 2010), and others suggesting that mismatch is negative (Sander, 2004). Perhaps a key takeaway for school counselors is that students should not only aim for a school that is a good academic match, but should also aspire to the highest reasonable school possible.

College Admissions versus Hiring

More colleges have recently been choosing to go "test optional," meaning students do not need to submit admissions test scores (Hiss & Franks, 2014). Considering the fact that companies are using general cognitive ability measures (including SAT scores) in hiring decisions (Dewan, 2014; Kuncel, Ones, & Klieger, 2014) and that general cognitive ability has been shown to assist in educational selection decisions and predict college outcomes as well as job level and job performance (Schmidt & Hunter, 1998, 2004), it is puzzling to see colleges retreating from the use of admissions tests (Wai, 2014c).

It is likely that colleges have been placing less emphasis on admissions tests to balance admitting higher-ability students with the desire for socioeconomic and ethnic diversity (De Corte, Lievens, & Sackett, 2007; Sackett, 2005). Many employers are more dedicated to productivity and the bottom line than diversity. However, discounting g in college admissions through the removal of cognitive ability tests can result in admitting students who are not academically prepared for college level work and, perhaps more importantly, for a career after college. Therefore, discounting ability in college admissions will have tradeoffs both short and long term. Additionally, this tradeoff is likely to have a greater impact on the more complex jobs that require higher levels of g (e.g., Kuncel & Hezlett, 2010; Wai & Rindermann, 2015).

Accounting for Measures of g in Observational Studies and Interventions

Measures of g need to be systematically accounted for in observational studies, because if g is omitted, explanatory or causal power may be misattributed to factors that may partly be caused by g (e.g., educational attainment, early childhood achievement). Measures of g also should be systematically accounted for in randomized intervention experiments. If researchers either (a) measure g or include a preexisting measure of g in the analysis of a randomized experiment or (b) stratify the randomization according to g, they will account for some variance that might otherwise be misattributed to the effect of the intervention (e.g., being in the treatment or control group). This concern is even more important when doing post-hoc analyses and analyses of subgroups, because those analyses in experimental studies have smaller samples, lower power, and are more likely to result in false positive inferences. As researchers and practitioners strive to increase college and career readiness, we recommend they both control for general cognitive ability and seek to intervene in other areas.

References

Alon, S., & Tienda, M. (2005). Assessing the "mismatch" hypothesis: Differences in college graduate rates by institutional selectivity. *Sociology of Education, 78,* 294–315.

Barnett, W. S., & Hustedt, J. T. (2005). Head Start's lasting benefits. *Infants & Young Children, 18,* 16–24.

Berry, C. M., & Sackett, P. R. (2009). Individual differences in course choice result in underestimation of the validity of college admissions systems. *Psychological Science, 20,* 822–830.

Brody, N. (2003). Construct validation of the Sternberg Triarchic abilities test comment and reanalysis. *Intelligence, 31,* 319–329.

Chabris, C. F. (1999). Prelude or requiem for the "Mozart effect"? *Nature, 400,* 826–827.

Chabris, C. F. (2007). Cognitive and neurobiological mechanisms of the law of general intelligence. In M. J. Roberts (Ed.), *Integrating the mind: Domain general versus domain specific processes in higher cognition* (pp. 449–491). New York: Psychology Press.

Coward, W. M., & Sackett, P. R. (1990). Linearity of ability-performance relationships: A reconfirmation. *Journal of Applied Psychology, 75,* 297–300.

Cullen, M. J., Hardison, C. M., & Sackett, P. R. (2004). Using SAT-grade and ability-job performance relationships to test predictions derived from stereotype threat theory. *Journal of Applied Psychology, 89,* 220–230.

De Corte, W., Lievens, F., & Sackett, P. R. (2007). Combining predictors to achieve optimal trade-offs between selection quality and adverse impact. *Journal of Applied Psychology, 92,* 1380–1393.

Dewan, S. (2014, March 29). How businesses use your SATs. *The New York Times.* Retrieved from http://www.nytimes.com/2014/03/30/sunday-review/how-businesses-use-your-sats.html.

Dillon, W. W., & Smith, J. A. (2013). *The determinants of mismatch between schools and colleges* (Working Paper 19286). Cambridge, MA: National Bureau of Economic Research. Retrieved from http://www.nber.org/papers/w19286.pdf.

Dweck, C. S., Chiu, C., & Hong, Y. (1995). Implicit theories and their role in judgments and reactions: A world from two perspectives. *Psychological Inquiry, 6*(4), 267–285.

Ferriman-Robertson, K., Smeets, S., Lubinski, D., & Benbow, C. P. (2010). Beyond the threshold hypothesis: Even among the gifted and top math/science graduate students, cognitive abilities, vocational interests, and lifestyle preferences matter for career choice, performance, and persistence. *Current Directions in Psychological Science, 19,* 346–351.

Fishman, J. A., & Pasanella, A. K. (1960). College admission selection studies. *Review of Educational Research, 30,* 298–310.

Fleischman, S., & Heppen, J. (2009). Improving low-performing high schools: Searching for evidence of promise. *The Future of Children, 19*(1), 105–134.

Flynn, J. R. (1984). The mean IQ of Americans: Massive gains 1932 to 1978. *Psychological Bulletin, 95,* 29–51.

Frey, M. C., & Detterman, D. K. (2004). Scholastic assessment or *g*? The relationship between the SAT and general cognitive ability. *Psychological Science, 14,* 373–378.

Furstenberg, R. (2010). Academic outcomes and Texas's top ten percent law. *Annals of the American Academy of Political and Social Science, 627,* 167–183.

Gaertner, M. N., & Hart, M. (2015). From access to success: Affirmative action outcomes in a class-based system. *University of Colorado Law Review, 86,* 431–475.

Gladwell, M. (2008). *Outliers: The story of success.* New York: Little, Brown, & Co.

Gottfredson, L. S. (2003a). The challenge and promise of cognitive career assessment. *Journal of Career Assessment, 11,* 115–135.

Gottfredson, L. S. (2003b). g, jobs, and life. In H. Nyborg (Ed.), *The scientific study of general intelligence: Tribute to Arthur R. Jensen* (pp. 293–342). New York: Pergamon.

Haier, R. J. (2014). Increased intelligence is a myth (so far). *Frontiers in Systems Neuroscience, 8,* 1–3.

Heil, S., Reisel, L., & Attewell, P. (2014). College selectivity and degree completion. *American Educational Research Journal, 51,* 913–935.

Higdem, J. L., Kostal, J. W., Kuncel, N. R., Sackett, P. R., Shen, W., Beatty, A. S., & Kiger, T. B. (2016). The role of socioeconomic status in SAT-freshman grade relationships across gender and racial subgroups. *Educational Measurement: Issues and Practice, 35,* 21–28.

Hiss, W. C., & Franks, V. W. (2014). Defining promise: Optional standardized testing policies in American college and university admissions. Retrieved from https://www.iacac.org/wp-content/uploads/2014/05/H59-Defining-Promise.pdf.

Hsu, S., & Wai, J. (2015). These 25 schools are responsible for the greatest advances in science. *Quartz.* Retrieved from http://qz.com/498534/these-25-schools-are-responsible-for-the-greatest-advances-in-science/.

Jagešić, S. (2015). Student-peer ability match and declining educational aspirations in college. *Research in Higher Education, 56*, 673–692.

Jensen, A. R. (1998). *The g factor: The science of mental ability*. Westport, CT: Praeger.

Johnson, W., te Nijenhuis, J., & Bouchard, T. J., Jr. (2008). Still just 1 *g*: Consistent results from five test batteries. *Intelligence, 36*, 81–95.

Kaufman, S. B., Reynolds, M. R., Liu, X., Kaufman, A. S., & McGrew, K. S. (2012). Are cognitive *g* and academic achievement *g* one and the same *g*? An exploration on the Woodcock-Johnson and Kaufman tests. *Intelligence, 40*, 123–138.

Kobrin, J. L., Patterson, B. F., Shaw, E. J., Mattern, K. D., & Barbuti, S. M. (2008). *Validity of the SAT for predicting first-year college grade point average* (College Board Research Report No. 2008–5). New York: The College Board.

Koenig, K. A., Frey, M. C., & Detterman, D. K. (2008). ACT and general cognitive ability. *Intelligence, 36*, 153–160.

Kroeper, K. M., & Murphy, M. C. (2017). Supporting college and career readiness through social psychological interventions. In K. L. McClarty, K. D. Mattern, & M. N. Gaertner (Eds.), *Preparing students for college and careers: Theory, measurement, and educational practice*. New York: Routledge.

Kuncel, N. R., & Hezlett, S. A. (2007). Standardized tests predict graduate student's success. *Science, 315*, 1080–1081.

Kuncel, N. R., & Hezlett, S. A. (2010). Fact and fiction in cognitive ability testing for admissions and hiring. *Current Directions in Psychological Science, 19*, 339–345.

Kuncel, N. R., Hezlett, S. A., & Ones, D. S. (2001). A comprehensive meta-analysis of the predictive validity of the Graduate Record Examinations: Implications for graduate students selection and performance. *Psychological Bulletin, 127*, 162–181.

Kuncel, N. R., Hezlett, S. A., & Ones, D. S. (2004). Academic performance, career potential, creativity, and job performance: Can one construct predict them all? *Journal of Personality and Social Psychology, 86*, 148–161.

Kuncel, N. R., Ones, D. R., & Klieger, D. M. (2014, May). In hiring, algorithms beat instinct. *Harvard Business Review*. Retrieved from https://hbr.org/2014/05/in-hiring-algorithms-beat-instinct.

Lubinski, D. (2004). Introduction to the special section on cognitive abilities: 100 years after Spearman's (1904) 'General abilities', objectively determined and measured. *Journal of Personality and Social Psychology, 86*, 96–111.

Lubinski, D., & Benbow, C. P. (2006). Study of mathematically precocious youth after 35 years: Uncovering antecedents for the development of math-science expertise. *Perspectives on Psychological Science, 1*, 316–345.

Lubinski, D., Benbow, C. P., & Kell, H. J. (2014). Life paths and accomplishments of mathematically precocious males and females four decades later. *Perspectives on Psychological Science, 25*, 2217–2232.

Makel, M. C., Kell, H. J., Lubinski, D., Putallaz, M., & Benbow, C. P. (2016). When lightning strikes twice: Profoundly gifted, profoundly accomplished. *Psychological Science, 27*, 1004–1018.

Mattern, K. D., & Patterson, B. F. (2011a). Validity of the SAT for predicting second-year grades: 2006 SAT validity sample. *College Board Statistical Report No. 2011–1*. New York: The College Board.

Mattern, K. D., & Patterson, B. F. (2011b). Validity of the SAT for predicting third-year grades: 2006 SAT validity sample. *College Board Statistical Report No. 2011–3*. New York: The College Board.

Morgan, R. (1989). *Analysis of the predictive validity of the SAT and high school grades from 1976 to 1985* (College Board Research Report No. 89–7). New York, NY: The College Board.

Neisser, U., Boodoo, G., Bouchard, T. J., Jr., Boykin, A. W., Brody, N., Ceci, S. J., ….Urbina, S. (1996). Intelligence: Knowns and unknowns. *American Psychologist, 51*, 77–101.

Nisbett, R. E., Aronson, J., Blair, C., Dickens, W., Flynn, J., Halpern, D. F., & Turkheimer, E. (2012). Intelligence: New findings and theoretical developments. *American Psychologist, 67*, 130–159.

Ones, D. S., Viswesvaran, C., & Dilchert, S. (2005). Cognitive ability in personnel selection decisions. In A. Evers, N. Anderson, & O. Voskuijl (Eds.), *The Blackwell handbook of personnel selection* (pp. 143–173). Oxford: Blackwell Publishing.

Park, G., Lubinski, D., & Benbow, C. P. (2008). Ability differences among people who have commensurate degrees matter for scientific creativity. *Psychological Science, 19*, 957–961.

Protzko, J. (2016). The environment in raising early intelligence: A meta-analysis of the fadeout effect. *Intelligence, 53,* 202–210.

Ree, M. J., & Earles, J. A. (1991). The stability of *g* across different methods of estimation. *Intelligence, 15,* 271–278.

Sackett, P. R. (2005). The performance-diversity tradeoff in admissions testing: Higher education admission tools for the 21st century. In W. Camara & E. Kimmel (Eds.), *Choosing students: Higher education admission tools for the 21st century* (pp. 109–125). Mahwah, NJ: Lawrence Erlbaum.

Sander, R. H. (2004). A systemic analysis of affirmative action in American law schools. *Stanford Law Review, 57,* 367–483.

Schmidt, F. L., & Hunter, J. E. (1998). The validity and utility of selection methods in personnel psychology: Practical and theoretical implications of 85 years of research findings. *Psychological Bulletin, 124,* 262–274.

Schmidt, F. L., & Hunter, J. (2004). General mental ability in the world of work: Occupational attainment and job performance. *Journal of Personality and Social Psychology, 86*(1), 162–173.

Schmitt, N., Keeney, J., Oswald, F. L., Pleskac, T. J., Billington, A. Q., Sinha, R., & Zorzie, M. (2009). Prediction of 4-year college student performance using cognitive and noncognitive predictors and the impact on demographic status of admitted students. *Journal of Applied Psychology, 94,* 1479–1497.

Schult, J., & Sparfeldt, J. R. (2016). Do non-*g* factors of cognitive ability tests align with specific academic achievements? A combined bifactor modeling approach. *Intelligence, 59,* 96–102.

Simons, D. J., Boot, W. R., Charness, N., Gathercole, S. E., Chabris, C. F., Hambrick, D. Z., & Stine-Morrow, E. A. L. (2016). Do "brain-training" programs work? *Psychological Science in the Public Interest, 17,* 103–186.

Spearman, C. (1927). *The abilities of man: Their nature and measurement.* New York: Macmillan.

Sternberg, R. J., Grigorenko, E. L., Ferrari, M., & Clinkenbeard, P. (1999). A triarchic analysis of an aptitude-treatment interaction. *European Journal of Psychological Assessment, 15,* 3–13.

Stricker, G., & Huber, J. T. (1967). The Graduate Record Examination and undergraduate grades as predictors of success in graduate school. *The Journal of Educational Research, 60,* 466–468.

Subotnik, R. F., Olszewski-Kubilius, P., & Worrell, F. C. (2011). Rethinking giftedness and gifted education: A proposed direction forward based on psychological science. *Psychological Science in the Public Interest, 12,* 3–54.

Wai, J. (2013). Investigating America's elite: Cognitive ability, education, and sex differences. *Intelligence, 41,* 203–211.

Wai, J. (2014a). Experts are born, then made: Combining prospective and retrospective longitudinal data shows that cognitive ability matters. *Intelligence, 45,* 74–80.

Wai, J. (2014b). Investigating the world's rich and powerful: Education, cognitive ability, and sex differences. *Intelligence, 46,* 54–72.

Wai, J. (2014c, August 28). Should the SAT be optional? *Quartz.* Retrieved from http://qz.com/254248/why-making-the-sat-optional-is-a-mistake/.

Wai, J., & Lincoln, D. (2016). Investigating the right tail of wealth: Education, cognitive ability, giving, network power, gender, ethnicity, leadership, and other characteristics. *Intelligence, 54,* 1–32.

Wai, J., Lubinski, D., & Benbow, C. P. (2005). Creativity and occupational accomplishments among intellectually precocious youth: An age 13 to age 33 longitudinal study. *Journal of Educational Psychology, 97,* 484–492.

Wai, J., & Putallaz, M. (2011). The Flynn effect puzzle: A 30-year examination from the right tail of the ability distribution provides some missing pieces. *Intelligence, 39,* 443–455.

Wai, J., & Rindermann, H. R. (2015). The path and performance of a company leader: An historical examination of the education and cognitive ability of Fortune 500 CEOs. *Intelligence, 53,* 102–107.

Wicherts, J. M., Dolan, C. V., Hessen, D. J., Oosterveld, P., van Baal, G. C. M., Boomsma, D. I., & Span, M. M. (2004). Are intelligence tests measurement invariant over time? Investigating the nature of the Flynn effect. *Intelligence, 32,* 509–537.

Worrell, F. C., & Weinstein, R. S. (2016). Epilogue. In R. S. Weinstein & F. C. Worrell (Eds.), *Achieving college dreams: How a university-charter district partnership created an early college high school* (pp. 389–395). New York: Oxford University Press.

Wraw, C., Deary, I. J., Gale, C. R., & Der, G. (2015). Intelligence in youth and health at age 50. *Intelligence, 53*, 23–32.

Young, J. W. (with Kobrin, J. L.). (2001). *Differential validity, differential prediction, and college admissions testing: A comprehensive review and analysis* (College Board Research Report No. 2001–6). New York: The College Board.

Young, J. W., Klieger, D., Bochenek, J., Li, C., & Cline, F. (2014). *The validity of scores from the GRE revised General Test for forecasting performance in business schools: Phase one* (GRE Board Research Report No. 14–01; ETS Research Report No. RR-14–17). Princeton, NJ: Educational Testing Service.

Part 2

Validating College- and Career-Readiness Performance Levels

5 Building External Validity into the Process

Evidence-Based Readiness Standards

Katie Larsen McClarty, Susan Cooper Loomis, and Mary J. Pitoniak

Performance standards give meaning to numerically represented test results. For example, a score of 350 is difficult to interpret without performance standards and associated performance level descriptors (PLDs). Performance standards categorize test scores into performance categories (e.g., basic, proficient, advanced), and PLDs provide a more granular description of the knowledge, skills, and abilities typically demonstrated by students at that level. Content-based interpretations provided by PLDs gained popularity as a result of the No Child Left Behind Act (NCLB, 2002), as each state sought to define proficiency in detail at each grade level. However, because state definitions were created independently, students performing well above the proficient level in one state might be below that level in another (Bandeira de Mello, 2011; Braun & Qian, 2007; Phillips, 2010).

Variation in proficiency definitions was not the only concern that arose under NCLB; in addition, increasing trends in student proficiency on state exams were not accompanied by increases in college readiness or decreases in the need for remediation (Aud et al., 2013). As a result, a new generation of assessments was built to include not only PLDs and content claims but also predictive readiness claims. In addition to knowledge, skills, and abilities, these new performance levels described how students would likely perform in the future. For example, the Partnership for the Assessment of Readiness for College and Careers (PARCC) designates performance level 4 as "Met Expectations." For the high school English Language Arts (ELA)/ Literacy, Algebra II, and Integrated Mathematics III assessments, students achieving level 4 or higher also receive PARCC's college- and career-ready designation. The PARCC level 4 PLDs describe the

> academic knowledge, skills, and practices in English language arts/literacy and mathematics students must demonstrate to show they are able to enter directly into and succeed in entry-level, credit-bearing courses and relevant technical courses in those content areas at two- and four-year public institutions of higher education.
>
> (PARCC, 2015, p. 2)

Note the explicit expansion upon NCLB-era PLDs; this statement includes not only claims about content knowledge but also general claims about future success. Similar performance levels with content and future performance claims are used by many other assessment groups, including the Smarter Balanced Assessment Consortia (SBAC), the National Assessment of Educational Progress (NAEP), and several individual states (e.g., Virginia, Texas, Michigan).

The validity of claims about students' content knowledge and future performance is critically important. Kane has proposed such claims be "outlined as an argument that specifies the inferences and supporting assumptions needed to get from test responses to score-based interpretations and uses" (2013, p. 1). That argument should consist of both an interpretation/ use argument that states the claims and a validity argument that evaluates them (Kane, 2013;

see also Kane 1992, 2006). In the context of setting performance standards, evidence needed to evaluate the validity of interpretations has traditionally been drawn from three sources: procedural, internal, and external (Kane, 2001; see also Hambleton & Pitoniak, 2006). Much of the evidence, however, has focused on content and process, via the procedural and internal sources (McClarty, Way, Porter, Beimers, & Miles, 2013). Although external validity includes criterion-related evidence, test-criterion links have historically received limited attention. When readiness claims are provided in the PLDs, however, it is important to include predictive validity evidence, in addition to traditional content-based evidence, in the standard-setting process.

One of the benefits of creating assessments and performance levels with both content and predictive claims is that they can bring more clarity and relevance to the assessments. While the content claims describe "what," the predictive claims describe "so what." Adding a predictive component can introduce urgency by helping students, parents, and educators understand a student's likelihood of future success given current performance. If a student achieves at a low performance level, the student has not only a limited grasp of grade-level knowledge and skills but also a low likelihood of being successful in postsecondary endeavors. The logic is straightforward: predictive readiness interpretations can provide a call to action, prompting intervention to remediate students' weaknesses and help get them on a path toward success.

The purpose of this chapter is to introduce a process for setting performance standards with both content and predictive readiness claims, using a combination of empirical evidence and expert judgment. We distinguish this approach from traditional standard-setting approaches, provide examples from programs that have implemented it, and discuss lessons learned. The topics are divided into five sections: (1) defining the content and predictive claims, (2) gathering existing evidence and conducting new studies, (3) evaluating and synthesizing evidence from multiple sources, (4) holding standard-setting meetings with panelists, and (5) reporting results and conducting ongoing monitoring. We conclude the chapter with implications for policy, practice, and research.

Defining College- and Career-Readiness Claims

The process of defining readiness claims involves two components: the intended interpretations and the outcomes.

Defining Claims

The first step in developing a college and career readiness (CCR) assessment is to clearly articulate the intended interpretations or claims that will be made using assessment results. However, as Conley (2017) argues, defining CCR is not a straightforward task, particularly when it comes to deciding whether college readiness is similar to or substantially different from career readiness and whether a single performance standard can represent both.

Some organizations choose to define CCR as the same, often suggesting that college (or some form of postsecondary training) is a necessary precursor to a career with upward mobility that could support a family. This view draws on some persuasive evidence. First, college takes many forms—from a technical certificate to a four-year degree. There are few career options, however, for those with only a high school diploma. In 1973, 72% of the jobs were held by those with a high school diploma or less; by 2020, that number is expected to fall to 36% (Carnevale, Smith, & Strohl, 2013). Therefore, to be prepared for a career, most students will need to complete some postsecondary education or training

Second, the skills required for jobs are similar to the skills required for college. The US Department of Labor sponsors the Occupational Information Network (O*NET),[1] which includes information about the reading, mathematics, science, speaking, writing, active listening, and critical thinking skills required for nearly 1,000 occupations. All these skill components are found in the Common Core State Standards, the Next Generation Science Standards, and many other state standards targeting CCR.

Finally, some research suggests alignment between not only the skill domains for college and careers but also between the requisite skill *levels*. ACT (2006) reported that the levels of reading and mathematics knowledge needed on their WorkKeys assessment to be prepared for a job were similar to the levels of reading and mathematics required on the ACT assessment to be prepared for entry-level college English and mathematics courses. More recently, Wei, Cromwell, and McClarty (2016) evaluated the quantitative text complexity of reading materials used in 150 different careers and found all levels of careers had texts at least as complex as the recommended CCR level in the Common Core State Standards. Research like this could support a policy decision to treat college and career readiness as the same and to set a single performance level indicative of both.

Not all agree, however, that college readiness and career readiness are the same. In fact, the Association for Career and Technical Education (ACTE) argues that typical career-readiness definitions have been limited to the academic domain. Although there are some core academic skills that are needed for both college and career readiness, career readiness also involves employability skills and technical, job-specific skills (ACTE, 2010). Further, the core academic skills (which are the primary focus of most content standards and CCR assessments) are differentially related to college and career outcomes. For example, taking Algebra II is associated with many positive college outcomes such as acceptance, course grades, and graduation, but there is little to no association between taking Algebra II and job attainment, advancement, or salary (Gaertner, Kim, DesJardins, & McClarty, 2013).

The National Assessment Governing Board (NAGB or Governing Board) made no a priori assumptions about the equivalence of college and career preparedness. Instead, they decided to let research findings determine whether college and career preparedness were the same or different. Findings from the Governing Board's NAEP Preparedness Research revealed that knowledge and skills included in the grade 12 mathematics assessment were largely considered "irrelevant" criteria for success in job training programs (Loomis, 2012; NAGB, n.d.).

Specifying Outcomes

Once the general outcome has been selected, be it college readiness, career readiness, or both, that general outcome must be made concrete. This concrete outcome may be included explicitly as part of the PLDs or may be used instead to provide focus for research studies and evidence gathering. Many organizations have accomplished this by specifying an outcome threshold (e.g., specific course grade, grade point average, persistence to second year of college, college graduation) along with a confidence level in that outcome. For example, ACT's college-readiness benchmarks represent a 50% likelihood of earning a B or better (which translates roughly to a 75% likelihood of earning a C or better) in entry-level college courses in the same content area (ACT, 2013). SAT's college-readiness benchmark, on the other hand, is associated with a 67% likelihood of earning a B+ cumulative grade point average in the first year of college (Wyatt, Kobrin, Wiley, Camara, & Proestler, 2011).

An important issue in setting a CCR performance level and defining the confidence level is the tradeoff between false positives and false negatives. Policymakers and standard setters will need to consider which type of error is more costly. Is it worse to use a lower confidence level and give someone a CCR designation when he or she is truly not ready, or to use a higher confidence level and hold that designation back from a student who truly earned it? Alternately, is the goal to simply maximize the classification accuracy?

Gathering Evidence for College- and Career-Readiness Claims

Once the intended claims and related outcomes are specified, the next step is to develop research, data collection, and analysis plans, which includes specifying the types of evidence that should inform the standard-setting process. When developing a new assessment, the specific data that would best support the predictive readiness claims described in the PLDs are often not available. For example, longitudinal studies tracking students from high school to college take years to conduct. Therefore, organizations may look to other sources of evidence to support predictive readiness claims until longitudinal data are collected. This section describes how to select evidence to gather and present as part of standard setting.

Types of Evidence

Different types of studies yield different types of data, and gaining data access can prove challenging because of confidentiality issues or legislative and contractual restrictions. Determining the types of evidence to be collected requires a careful examination of potential data sources. Several factors should be considered (McClarty et al., 2013):

- Can the desired data be obtained; e.g., if students' SAT scores are to be linked to their state assessment scores, are SAT scores available for all students?
- Is there a strong connection between the data and the intended outcome; e.g., would PISA data provide support for grade six mathematics outcomes?
- Are there legal issues related to personally identifiable information needed to match data records; e.g., are states comfortable providing student names or other information necessary to match data records?
- Are there enough project management resources available to handle coordination across the participants in the process; e.g., are staff available to manage data flow and communications across entities, such as state or federal departments of education, test publishers, higher education institutions, and educators?

Once workable data sources are identified, the types of studies to which those data lend themselves must be identified. Different types of studies provide evidence related to convergent, predictive, and content-based validity.

In a convergent validity study, scores on a CCR assessment are compared to scores on another assessment targeting a similar outcome (APA, AERA, & NCME, 2014). For example, Haertel, Beimers, and Miles (2012) describe comparing scores on an end-of-course algebra assessment administered as part of the American Diploma Project (ADP) to those on six state mathematics assessments. As part of the NAEP preparedness research agenda, scores on grade 12 NAEP assessments were compared to those obtained by the same students on the SAT, ACT, Accuplacer, and WorkKeys assessments (Loomis, 2012; NAGB, n.d.). These types of designs are employed for concordance or linking studies and provide a way to evaluate how performance standards compare across assessments.

Because a key component of CCR assessments is making predictive claims, conducting criterion-related, predictive validity studies is a logical step. Predictive validity studies examine the relationship between scores on the target assessment—in this case, the CCR assessment—and scores from a criterion measure obtained at a later time (APA, AERA, & NCME, 2014). In the ADP study (Haertel et al., 2012), performance on the algebra assessment, administered to college students at the beginning of a semester, was compared with course grades obtained by those students at the end of the semester. Longitudinal studies, which involve following the same student from grade to grade and on to college- or career-related outcomes, are challenging to conduct, but provide valuable evidence on the relationship between performance on the CCR assessment and multiple future criteria.

The third type of study is content-based, involving subject-matter experts making judgments about the level of performance a student should demonstrate on the CCR assessment to be prepared for future success. For the ADP project, faculty from higher education institutions reviewed test items and made judgments about the level of knowledge and skills students would need to complete a course successfully (Haertel et al., 2012).

Data sources will also vary: some studies will use existing data (e.g., state assessments) and some will require original data collection (e.g., administering an algebra assessment to college students). Using existing data may lower costs; however, validity research should not be completely bound by convenience. For example, longitudinal studies on the full population of interest are often the most costly and time consuming but provide the most valid information about the specified outcome. The usefulness and appropriateness of the data should be the key considerations. Test publishers and policymakers should carefully consider the advantages and disadvantages of each approach in terms of time, resources, costs, and validity of resulting interpretations.

Access to Evidence

We must underscore the importance of access to the data, and the time and resources required to get it. Confidentiality of school records, including test scores, is mandated by law (e.g., US Department of Education, n.d.). Similarly, private testing organizations have strict rules and procedures for allowing access to data. Obtaining information from a source that would yield relevant criterion-related data may prove challenging and take months. When linking studies are conducted between two assessments, issues of confidentiality and anonymity of student data must be resolved. For example, when linking NAEP to SAT as part of the NAEP preparedness research, a system of "pseudo-identifiers" was used to avoid this conflict. This procedure allowed NAEP data to be linked to SAT scores as a source of predictive postsecondary success data and to Florida's longitudinal student records as a source of confirmatory data.

Evaluating and Synthesizing Results

Once the evidence has been gathered, it must be evaluated and synthesized for use in standard setting. We recommend three steps: (1) evaluate the quality of evidence from individual studies, (2) synthesize evidence across studies, and (3) determine which studies to use for the next steps in the standard-setting process.

Evaluating Evidence

Though multiple study results can inform standard setting, not all data points should be given equal influence. Assessment developers and policymakers should establish criteria for evaluating study results. One important criterion is the comparability of outcome definitions. For example, if the performance level implies likely success in an entry-level college course, using data about the percentage of students referred to developmental courses is an incomplete comparison. Remediation rates represent the percentage of students not eligible to enroll in an entry-level college course, but they provide no information about success rates in entry-level courses.

Second, it is important to evaluate the comparability of the populations studied. For example, college-readiness rates published by ACT and the College Board primarily reflect the population of students who elect to take the ACT or SAT assessment, which is often a higher-performing group than the entire population. ACT or SAT scores in states that administer these assessments to all students may be more useful. Important population characteristics include sample size, student age, demographic characteristics, accommodations available, and recency of data.

Content alignment should be another consideration. How well does the CCR assessment align with either the content of introductory college-level courses or the content of a similar assessment? For example, NAEP preparedness research showed few of the knowledge and skills from its grade 12 mathematics assessment were required in the curriculum of 85 introductory mathematics courses in 122 institutions with job training programs in the five selected NAEP occupational areas (WestEd & EPIC, 2013).[2] In addition, an alignment study between the WorkKeys assessment and NAEP showed limited content overlap (Dickinson et al., 2014). This lack of content alignment supports NAGB's decision not to set a job-training-preparedness performance level for NAEP. Additionally, several studies compared PARCC with international assessments such as PISA, TIMSS, and PIRLS. Results showed only partial alignment between the PARCC assessments and the content assessed on the international exams (McClarty et al., 2015). Therefore, any student performance comparisons between those assessments should be interpreted cautiously and given less weight in the standard-setting process.

Finally, the statistical relationship between the CCR assessment and the outcome measure (or other similar assessment) should be evaluated. A strong correlation between the assessment scores and outcome measure provides evidence to support predictive claims. Conversely, a weak statistical relationship between the two provides a challenge for making any predictive performance-level claims.

Synthesizing and Presenting Evidence

After evaluating results of individual studies, evidence can be summarized to identify common themes and areas of overlap in the results. In this phase, higher-quality studies should be emphasized. Rather than a single location for a performance standard, this type of evidence synthesis will provide regions of the performance scale that could or could not be supported by existing data. This allows for empirical study evidence to be brought into the standard-setting process in combination with judgments by subject-matter experts or other stakeholders to support procedural, internal, and external validity.

Once the studies have been evaluated and synthesized, assessment program administrators must decide how to present the information to panelists, policymakers, or other stakeholders. For example, should all studies be presented or only those determined to be high quality or most relevant? Poor-quality studies will add noise, but it may be important to represent the entire process of evidence collection and evaluation.

Should each study be presented or only a summary? Showing individual studies may allow panelists to draw their own conclusions about areas of emphasis and overlap. This approach may be more useful for policymakers or data-savvy experts who want to dig into the results. For panelists not as familiar with data and these types of studies, however, showing all studies could result in cognitive overload. It may be more prudent to provide a panel of content experts with a summary of the study results, so they can focus on their area of expertise—content judgments. If individual study data are shown to panelists, it is important to have some way to communicate study quality. This can be done by discussing the quality criteria with the panelists and how each study fared. Moreover, all studies should be evaluated to determine whether they meet minimum quality criteria to be included at all.

Once the determination has been made about what data to share, the next question is how to share it. Results could be presented on an impact data scale—that is, the percentage of students that would be classified into a CCR category if the performance-level threshold were placed at a specific point along the score scale. This approach may resonate with policymakers who will be reporting pass rates. For content experts working in standard-setting meetings with actual items and test forms, however, results presented in terms of the test-reporting scale or number of points may be more relevant and easier to use.

Holding Standard-Setting Meetings with Panelists

The criteria for selecting panelists and conducting standard-setting procedures in an evidence-based process for CCR are generally no different than those recommended for any standard-setting process. Special considerations will be highlighted here.

Selecting Panelists

Standard-setting panelists must represent the interests of the relevant stakeholders (Hambleton & Pitoniak, 2006; Raymond & Reid, 2001). If standards are to be set for CCR jointly, then the stakeholders may be different than if standards are to be set for CCR as two separate levels of knowledge and skills requirements.

In general, panels should include both educators and employers. All panelists must have content training and experience, as well as direct experience with the students at the grade level for which standards are to be set. The noneducators would need to be familiar with children in the relevant grade level or work in organizations that serve students in those grade levels, for example. Content knowledge is essential to the judgment tasks. Practitioners and even postsecondary faculty in job training programs may lack the in-depth level of training and academic expertise in subject matter required for setting standards for assessments of high school mathematics and reading/language arts (Loomis, 2012).

A sufficient number of panelists must be identified and recruited to provide sufficient power for the statistical analyses. That number is typically estimated to be between 10 and 15 panelists (Raymond & Reid, 2001). A sufficient number of panelists is needed to assure that all relevant roles and attributes can be represented on the panel. Further, it is desirable to have replicate panels, if resources permit, to provide inter-panel reliability evidence.

Presenting and Using Evidence

Empirical study results can be shared with panelists at multiple points during the standard-setting meeting. Evidence, or a summary of the evidence, could be provided during the introductory session. Thus, the evidence would introduce both the testing program and any expectations based on study results before the panelists begin their judgments. Alternately, study results could be used during the judgment rounds as feedback data to help panelists evaluate the reasonableness of their recommended cut scores. If their recommendations are far from what would be suggested by the data, panelists may adjust their recommendations to be more in line with external information. Finally, external evidence could be presented just prior to or after the final round of judgments. The bulk of the meeting would focus on the content judgments, but panelists would have an opportunity to see how their judgments lined up with external evidence and to discuss potential rationales for any discrepancies. The earlier the data are introduced into the standard-setting process, the more influence they are likely to have on panelists' judgments.

Reporting Results and Conducting Ongoing Monitoring

Clear and accurate results reporting should be emphasized as much as conducting appropriate studies. In addition, monitoring is needed to evaluate whether evidence changes over time, which would in turn impact the validity of the original CCR claims.

Reporting Results

Given the effort required to conduct an evidence-based standard setting project, it is imperative that reporting clearly communicates the purposes and goals of the project and provides convincing evidence about the reasonableness of the results and accompanying recommendations.

What to report is fairly straightforward; the easy answer is "Everything!" Transparency is vital to the successful implementation of any standard setting work, and complete reporting on the procedures producing the results and supporting their adoption is essential to transparency. Clear statements of purpose and design are needed early in the process. CCR standards are either new or recent for most states and districts, and it is especially important that the audience understands the precise definition of CCR being used, along with that definition's caveats and criteria.

For effective reporting, the audience must also be identified and specified. Though program administrators should report everything, not everyone is interested in everything about the project. It is important to determine which stakeholders constitute the audience for specific aspects of the standard-setting project. It essential that the "need to know" audiences be identified early, made aware of their status as such, and provided a schedule of activities for when they will receive briefings and interim reports. Some stakeholders will want to know that they are privy to reporting earlier than others, and this must be taken into account when staging information distribution. Although the decision-making group must have access to all the data and findings, reports should provide a succinct summary, highlighting important details and findings. Providing too much data at one time or the wrong data to a specific stakeholder group can have the same effect as providing no data at all.

In order to keep key stakeholders informed and to promote transparency, it is important to consider which results to communicate, at what time. "Early and often" seems a sensible heuristic. Still, reporting CCR results requires more careful planning. There will be widespread interest in how many students are ready for college and career or are on track to be ready, and it is necessary to let stakeholders know what to expect well before the results are reported. The importance of preparation has been highlighted with the introduction of new assessments and CCR performance standards. States that provided predictive information and prepared the public for changes in performance generally experienced more positive acceptance of the results than states that did not provide this sort of information. For example, Croft, Guffy, and Vitale (2014) contrasted experiences in Kentucky with New York when both states adopted new assessments and CCR standards. The performance decrease in New York was met with alarm, while the larger decrease in Kentucky was not. The difference in public perception and acceptance was attributed to the fact that information about what to expect was distributed much earlier in Kentucky.

Finally, the CCR standard-setting project will require several months—probably more than a year—in order to determine both the content and performance standards. Though reports on the results must be relatively brief and focused, each new stage will provide new information that demands context. It is helpful to note how the reported information relates to the overall project purpose and where it fits in the stages of the project. If reporting is successful, the purposes and goals of the project should be clear to the audiences well before the final results are ready for reporting.

The Monitoring Process

Monitoring evidence is critical for maintaining the integrity of CCR standards. Monitoring addresses issues of reliability and validity—internal and external. Because setting CCR standards is a relatively new development in assessment, monitoring is even more important. Does the evidence change over time? Does the relationship between the test score and the criterion change over time? Is new evidence available to support or refute original findings? Would different evidence have produced different results? Monitoring should include ongoing data collection from the same sources originally used in the standard-setting process, identification of new sources of the same or similar types of evidence, and identification of new sources of different evidence. Monitoring may include cross-sectional data, longitudinal data, or preferably a combination of both.

Monitoring is a complex endeavor, so different aspects of the monitoring process may be assigned to different groups according to their expertise. Ultimately, however, policymakers are responsible for monitoring. They must determine who will perform the actual monitoring function, and they must oversee and evaluate the process. A schedule of updates should be established and publicized, so that stakeholders are aware that the evidence and results are being monitored. This way, monitoring reports are anticipated rather than alarming.

Implications for Policy, Practice, and Research

Building assessments with CCR performance levels that include both content and predictive claims can add value to score interpretations, and setting CCR performance standards is relatively straightforward when both the content claims and predictive claims associated with a performance level are aligned. Predictive claims may be supported by the external evidence, and content claims may be supported by the judgments of subject-matter experts.

What happens, however, when the empirical evidence and the expert judgments do not align? Policymakers may need to decide whether to place more emphasis on the content claims or the predictive claims. In addition, if the external evidence is too far out of alignment with the PLDs, policymakers may need to adjust either the predictive statements or the PLDs associated with the CCR performance level—or both—before holding a standard-setting meeting with panelists.

Because of the need for strong alignment between the content evidence and the external data, the process for selecting which studies to conduct and developing criteria for evaluating study quality is of primary concern for policy, practice, and research. The gold standard in predictive research studies is longitudinal analysis. Longitudinal studies, however, are often challenged by student mobility. Ideally, students would be tracked long enough to evaluate their success in college, career, or both. This would require tracking students for at least five years, which is both difficult and costly. In the absence of strong longitudinal research, policymakers should work collaboratively with researchers to develop criteria for evaluating and vetting study results. Although the studies provide empirical results, there are still many judgmental elements in the process, including who develops the evaluation criteria, how they are developed, and how they are applied to the study results. The established criteria may affect the overall synthesis of results and thereby the substantive conclusions.

More research is also needed to understand the impact of sharing external study data with standard-setting panelists, as well as which approaches panelists understand most accurately. The external data should not be given so much emphasis as to eclipse the procedural and internal validity evidence for standard setting. All sources should work together to support the resulting standards recommendations.

Ultimately, the goal is to collect and document evidence that supports the intended interpretations of the CCR assessment scores. Those interpretations often include both content and predictive claims, and evidence must be provided to support each. This chapter described some of the considerations for adding external evidence to support predictive claims, while maintaining the content-based interpretations associated with a CCR performance level.

Notes

1 https://www.onetonline.org/.
2 The five occupational areas selected for the NAEP preparedness research included automotive master technician; computer support specialist; heating, ventilation, and air conditioning (HVAC); licensed practical and licensed vocational nurse (LPN); and pharmacy technician.

References

ACT. (2006). *Ready for college and ready for work: Same or different?* Retrieved from http://www.act.org.

ACT. (2013). *What are the ACT college readiness benchmarks?* (Policy Brief). Iowa City, IA: ACT, Inc. Retrieved from http://www.act.org/research/policymakers/pdf/benchmarks.pdf.

American Educational Research Association, American Psychological Association, and National Council on Measurement in Education. (2014). *Standards for educational and psychological testing.* Washington, DC: American Educational Research Association.

Association for Career and Technical Education (ACTE). (2010, April). *What is career ready?* Retrieved from https://www.acteonline.org/WorkArea/DownloadAsset.aspx?id=2114.

Aud, S., Wilkinson-Flicker, S., Kristapovich, P., Rathbun, A., Wang, X., & Zhang, J. (2013). *The condition of education 2013* (NCES 2013–037). Washington, DC: U.S. Department of Education, National Center for Education Statistics. Retrieved from http://nces.ed.gov/pubsearch.

Bandeira de Mello, V. (2011, August). *Mapping state proficiency standards onto the NAEP scale: Variation and change in state standards for reading and mathematics, 2005–2009.* Retrieved from http://nces.ed.gov/nationsreportcard/pdf/studies/2011458.pdf.

Braun, H., & Qian, J. (2007). An enhanced method for mapping state standards onto the NAEP scale. In N. J. Dorans, M. Pommerich, & P. W. Holland (Eds.), *Linking and aligning scores and scales* (pp. 313–338). New York: Springer.

Carnevale, A. P., Smith, N., & Strohl, J. (2013, June). *Recovery: Projections of jobs and education requirements through 2020.* Georgetown Center for Education and the Workforce. Retrieved from https://cew.georgetown.edu/report/recovery-job-growth-and-education-requirements-through-2020/.

Conley, D. T. (2017). The new complexity of readiness for college and careers. In K. L. McClarty, K. D. Mattern, & M. N. Gaertner (Eds.), *Preparing students for college and careers: Theory, measurement, and educational practice.* New York: Routledge.

Croft, M., Guffy, G., & Vitale, D. (2014). *Communicating college and career readiness through proficiency standards.* Retrieved from http://files.eric.ed.gov/fulltext/ED560229.pdf.

Dickinson, E. R., Smith, E., Deatz, R., Thacker, A. A., Sinclair, A. L., & Johnston-Fisher, J. (2014). *The content alignment between NAEP and the WorkKeys assessments* (HumRRO Researh Report No. 054). Retrieved from https://www.nagb.org/content/nagb/assets/documents/what-we-do/preparedness-research/content-alignment/naep_workkeys_final.pdf.

Gaertner, M. N., Kim, J., DesJardins, S. L., & McClarty, K. L. (2013). Preparing students for college and careers: The causal role of Algebra II. *Research in Higher Education, 55*(2), 143–165.

Haertel, E. H., Beimers, J. N., & Miles, J. A. (2012). The briefing book method. In G. J. Cizek (Ed.), *Setting performance standards: Foundations, methods, and innovations* (2nd ed., pp. 283–299). New York: Routledge.

Hambleton, R. K., & Pitoniak, M. J. (2006). Setting performance standards. In R. L. Brennan (Ed.), *Educational measurement* (4th ed., pp. 433–470). Westport, CT: American Council on Education/Praeger.

Kane, M. T. (1992). An argument-based approach to validity. *Psychological Bulletin, 112,* 527–535.

Kane, M. T. (2001). So much remains the same: Conception and status of validation in setting standards. In G. J. Cizek (Ed.), *Setting performance standards: Concepts, methods, and perspectives* (pp. 53–88). Mahwah, NJ: Erlbaum.

Kane, M. T. (2006). Validation. In R. L. Linn (Ed.), *Educational measurement* (4th ed., pp. 17–64). New York: American Council on Education/Macmillan.

Kane, M. T. (2013). Validating the interpretations and uses of test scores. *Journal of Educational Measurement, 50,* 1–73.

Loomis, S. C. (2012, April). *A study of "irrelevant" items: Impact on bookmark placement and implications for college and career readiness.* Paper presented at the annual meeting of the National Council on Measurement in Education, Vancouver, British Columbia, Canada.

McClarty, K. L., Kobrin, J., Moyer, E., Griffin, S., Huth, K., Carey, S., & Medberry, S. (2015, April). *PARCC benchmarking study.* Presented in the symposium Use of Evidence-Based Standard Setting in PARCC Assessments at the 2015 National Council on Measurement in Education, Chicago, IL.

McClarty, K. L., Way, W. D., Porter, A. C., Beimers, J. N., & Miles, J. A. (2013). Evidence-based standard setting: Establishing a validity framework for cut scores. *Educational Researcher, 42,* 78–88.

National Assessment Governing Board. (n.d.) *Technical Report: NAEP 12th grade preparedness research: Judgmental standard setting.* Retrieved from https://www.nagb.org/what-we-do/preparedness-research/types-of-research/jss.html.

No Child Left Behind Act of 2001, P.L. 107–110, 20 U.S.C. § 6319 (2002). Retrieved from https://www.gpo.gov/fdsys/pkg/PLAW-107publ110/html/PLAW-107publ110.htm.

PARCC. (2015, September). *PARCC college-and career-ready determination policy and policy-level PLDs.* Retrieved from http://parcconline.org/assessments/test-design/college-career-ready.

Phillips, G. W. (2010). *International benchmarking: State education performance standards.* Washington, DC: American Institutes for Research.

Raymond, M. R., & Reid, J. B. (2001). Who made thee a judge? Selecting and training participants for standard setting. In G. J. Cizek (Ed.), *Setting performance standards: Concepts, methods, and perspectives* (pp. 119–157). Mahwah, NJ: Erlbaum.

U.S. Department of Education. (n.d.). *Protecting the privacy of student education records.* Retrieved from https://nces.ed.gov/pubs97/web/97859.asp.

Wei, H., Cromwell, A. M., & McClarty, K. L. (2016). Career readiness: An analysis of text complexity for occupational reading materials. *Journal of Education Research, 109,* 266–274.

WestEd, & EPIC. (2013, March). *National Assessment of Educational Progress grade 12 preparedness research project job training programs curriculum study.* Retrieved from http://www.epiconline.org/jtpcs/.

Wyatt, J., Kobrin, J., Wiley, A., Camara, W., & Proestler, N. (2011). *SAT benchmarks: Development of a college readiness benchmark and its relationship to secondary and postsecondary school performance* (College Board Research Report 2011–5). New York: The College Board.

6 Empirically Based College- and Career-Readiness Cut Scores and Performance Standards

Wayne J. Camara, Jeff M. Allen, and Joann L. Moore

This chapter provides a summary of empirical methods used to establish college- and career-readiness benchmarks, such as those on the ACT and SAT, as well as empirically based standard setting approaches that have been used by states and consortia in setting cut scores on assessments used for accountability purposes. Setting multiple cut scores on assessments in secondary education for differentiating various levels of proficiency (e.g., basic, proficient, and advanced) and setting linked cut scores for assessments at earlier grades are also discussed.

Using College- and Career-Readiness Assessments for Accountability

Effective with the 2017–2018 school year, the Every Student Succeeds Act (ESSA) gives states greater autonomy and flexibility over standards, assessments, and accountability systems. A provision within the law allows states to use national admissions tests such as the ACT and SAT, as well as consortia assessments—PARCC and Smarter Balanced—in lieu of traditional standards-based tests.[1] Districts may also petition states to allow such tests as an alternative measure. However, other provisions may require modifications in how admissions tests are used for accountability purposes, including alignment to academic content standards addressing the depth and breadth of such standards and language suggesting that accommodations for English Learners (ELs) and students with disabilities must result in college-reportable scores to ensure comparable benefits for all students.

Over 20 states required statewide testing with the ACT or SAT in 2016–2017, and 7 states received permission to use national admissions tests for federal accountability (Gerwertz, 2016). Several states used the ACT or SAT for high school accountability under No Child Left Behind, but augmentation was frequently required to ensure test content adequately aligned to state content standards. In addition, states have used results from admissions tests to inform state accountability, or simply to meet other educational goals, such as increasing college awareness or early identification of students with potential to succeed in postsecondary environments.

There are many outstanding issues for states wishing to use national admissions tests for federal accountability,[2] beyond alignment. For example, Martineau, Gong, and Zurkowski (2016) identified a number of challenges for states considering the use of nationally recognized high school assessments:

- Flexibility—National admissions tests tend to have less administrative flexibility and shorter testing windows compared to state tests, in order to maintain high levels of security.
- Floor effects—Admissions tests may have a smaller range of scores and lower precision of scores at the bottom of the score scale.
- Growth—If scores in earlier grades are needed, they will be on a different scale.[3]

- Growth for educator effectiveness—Course-level content is often inadequate to permit such uses, but this issue extends to other state assessments of domain rather than end-of-course content.
- Cognitive complexity—Both the ACT and SAT are largely restricted to multiple-choice items and an optional essay; absence of additional performance tasks and technology-enhanced items may constrain assessment of some skills.
- Accommodations and comparable benefits—Admissions tests have established standard accommodations for students with disabilities and, more recently, ELs. When additional accommodations are requested by a state, scores are not used for college admissions.
- Cut score coherence between admissions tests and other state tests may be lacking—Admissions tests have established a single college-readiness benchmark, which may not be consistent with a state's definition of readiness, and ESSA requires at least two cut scores.

National admissions tests appear to offer some advantages over typical state and consortia tests as well, such as:

- High levels of credibility with postsecondary institutions, recognized and universal acceptance for college admissions in US four-year colleges.[4]
- Over half of all four-year public institutions report using ACT or SAT scores for placement in entry-level math courses and over one-third use reading scores for placement, exceeding the use of national placement tests and locally developed assessments (Fields & Parsad, 2012).
- Higher student motivation because the admissions tests are perceived as important to students, parents, and educators.
- Significantly less testing time.
- Lower opt-out rates, primarily because of the aforementioned features.
- Higher levels of security, including less item exposure.[5]
- Consistency in the testing blueprint, score scale, and longitudinal trend data.
- Strong predictive validity evidence across subgroups and different institution types.

Finally, states and assessment programs continue to use college and career readiness as a unified term, suggesting that the same content standards and performance standards (e.g., cut scores, descriptors) are identical and valid for claims relating to college and career readiness. However, such claims have been made largely in the absence of evidence, and reviews of what little evidence has been reported on career readiness suggests significant differences across job families and college readiness (Camara, 2013; Conley, 2014). We admit that the term "college and career readiness" is convenient for policy purposes, as it aggregates all postsecondary outcomes to a single metric. However, it is insufficient in capturing the variation in knowledge, skills, and abilities required for success across different types of colleges, training programs, and entry-level occupations.

Setting College- and Career-Readiness Benchmarks on Admissions Tests

ACT established college-readiness benchmarks using an empirical approach in 2005 (Allen & Sconing, 2005; Allen, 2013); College Board used a similar approach for setting a college-readiness benchmark for the SAT in 2007 (Kobrin, 2007; Wyatt, Kobrin, Wiley, Camara, & Proestler, 2011). Judgment is part of any standard setting, but with empirical approaches, that judgment centers on appropriate outcomes (e.g., course grade), criteria of success (e.g., earning a grade of a B or higher), and probability of success (e.g., 50%, 60%, 70%), as opposed to item content and whether a "proficient student" would likely get an item correct.

ACT's benchmarks are the scores associated with a 50% chance (the probability) of obtaining a B or higher (the criterion) in a corresponding first-year, credit-bearing, college-level course (the outcome) in each subject area. The SAT benchmark is based on the SAT score associated with a 65% (probability) of obtaining a 2.67 or higher (criterion) first-year college GPA (outcome).[6]

Advantages of adopting ACT or SAT benchmarks as a state's "college ready" performance level include availability of state-specific impact data, established relationships between test scores and postsecondary outcomes, and cost savings (traditional content-based standard setting is not required). Another advantage is that it allows for direct comparisons with other states that have adopted the ACT or SAT benchmarks, direct comparisons to the national group of ACT or SAT examinees, or indirect comparisons from ACT-to-SAT- or SAT-to-ACT-tested populations using concordance tables. The ACT and SAT benchmarks define two performance levels (ready or not), but states typically require three cut scores to distinguish four levels (e.g., below basic, basic, proficient, and advanced) for accountability. Neither assessment program has developed national benchmarks for an upper (advanced) or lower (basic) level, but this could easily be done using the same or similar methods (Camara, 2013). The absence of national cut scores alone should not impede use of admissions tests for accountability, given that ESSA indicates such determinations are preferably made at the state and local levels.

ACT and College Board base their benchmarks on first-year college grades. There are other important outcomes of college success, such as cumulative grades, persistence, and graduation; however, these outcomes are more removed from high school performance and are directly influenced by postsecondary experiences (e.g., quality of college courses, college environment). Similar methods can be employed to establish career-readiness benchmarks, but the lack of access to empirical data on grades or performance from workforce training programs, certificate completion, job placement, or job performance is the largest obstacle to analysis of these outcomes (Camara & Quenemoen, 2012).

Setting State-Specific Benchmarks on the ACT and SAT

While college-readiness benchmarks have been set by ACT and College Board, states may prefer to set their own college-readiness benchmarks for various reasons. State-specific benchmarks may be intended for federal or state accountability, and legislation may require that they are set locally. Other uses of state benchmarks may include exemption from end-of-course exams or placement into college programs, which might not align with the achievement levels associated with national benchmarks.

Various methods could be used to set cut scores on college admissions tests for state use. Norm-referenced standard setting focuses on the percentage of examinees who meet or exceed a cut score (Cizek & Bunch, 2007), but it is not ideal for setting college- and career-readiness benchmarks, because it is not tied to the level of knowledge and skills required for students to be successful. Criterion or standard-based approaches (e.g., Angoff, Bookmark) have been predominant for several decades in educational settings. They do provide information about the level of knowledge and skills expected of students who meet the cut score, but they are not tied to actual success outcomes. Empirical or mixed approaches incorporating outcome data are becoming more common today because of this mutual benefit.

As discussed before, purely empirical approaches were used by admissions testing programs in establishing benchmarks. In addition, ACT assisted two states in establishing their own cut scores using empirical data. Panelists reviewed current performance standards, performance level descriptors (PLDs), and percentages of students meeting each performance level. Their task was to determine the appropriate probabilities of success in first-year college courses rather than probabilities related to individual test questions. Unlike a content-based standard setting, where panelists provide ratings of many items to arrive at a recommended cut score, each panelist in an empirical standard setting only provides a recommended cut score, focusing on the probability of college success and corresponding score they believe a minimally qualified student would obtain. A key component of the discussion centered on the definition of a minimally qualified student.

Table 6.1 shows an example rating sheet that can be used by panelists to provide their proposed cut scores. Multiple criteria and their associated probabilities of success, as well as state and national impact data, are included in the rating sheet. Panelists provide their rating by highlighting the row on the rating sheet where they would place the cut. Panelists are instructed to think about how they would define a *minimally proficient* (or basic or advanced) student in terms of their probability of success and place the cut score at this score. After the first round of ratings, additional impact and comparative data can be provided. Panelists are expected to adjust their ratings in subsequent rounds in light of additional evidence, so inter-rater reliability is not meaningful in this context. Within-group consensus is a more meaningful measure of reliability for empirical standard setting.

Impact Data

Impact data should show the impact of the cut scores on the population of interest, including the percent of students who are expected to meet or exceed each score. State and national comparisons should be accompanied by an explanation of any differences between populations and testing policies (e.g., in some states, all 11th graders take the ACT or SAT, whereas in other states, mostly college-bound students, who tend to be higher achieving, are likely to take the ACT or SAT). Similarly, comparisons of data from previous years should include cautions about changes in the populations tested as a result of the state's adoption of the test.

Impact data may also be broken down by subgroup, such as race/ethnicity, family income, and EL status. Other impact data could include the percentage of students meeting the cut score by level of coursework taken and high school grades. The impact of adjusting the cut score up or down may also be provided. Impact can be compared to the performance of students in that state on other assessments such as NAEP or previous state tests. Initial studies have linked benchmarks and cut scores on the ACT, ACT Aspire, and ACT Plan to both NAEP proficiency levels (Mattern & Lacina, 2015; Phillips, 2016) and results on PISA (ACT, 2011; Lu, 2015) to provide additional context for national and international comparisons.

Table 6.1 Example Rating Sheet for Empirical Standard Setting

| ACT Score | Probability of Success | | | Percentage At/Above | | |
| | A | B or Higher | C or Higher | State | | National |
				2013	2014	2013
15	0.04	0.19	0.47	93	94	94
16	0.05	0.22	0.51	83	83	85
17	0.07	0.26	0.55	67	68	73
18	0.08	0.30	0.59	55	55	64
19	0.10	0.34	0.62	49	49	58
20	0.13	0.39	0.66	43	43	52
21	0.16	0.44	0.69	37	37	48
22	0.20	0.49	0.73	31	34	44
23	0.24	0.54	0.76	29	28	39
24	0.29	0.59	0.78	23	24	33
25	0.34	0.64	0.81	17	17	27

Setting Multiple Cut Scores

Much of the discussion around setting multiple cut scores has focused on using the ACT or SAT for ESSA accountability. However, there may be reasons to set multiple "college and career ready" cut scores. For example, one could distinguish between different levels of preparedness, such as readiness for community college, workforce training, or a more selective four-year institution. Readiness could also be defined in terms of a student's planned program of study; for example, ACT's Math and Science Benchmarks are based on readiness in college algebra and biology, respectively, whereas ACT's more rigorous STEM Benchmark is based on success in higher level math and science college courses (Mattern, Radunzel, & Westrick, 2015).

One approach to setting lower (i.e., basic) and higher (i.e., advanced) cut scores is to base them on the probabilities of success in first-year credit-bearing college courses, consistent with the approach taken to establish the ACT and SAT benchmarks. The resulting achievement levels can then be easily described in terms of college success. The key task in this approach is the determination of the probabilities of success corresponding to each level of performance, requiring a consensus about the probabilities of success, the criterion, and the outcome that should be associated with each cut score. For example, should a student performing at the advanced level be required to have a higher probability of success (e.g., a 75% chance), a higher criterion (e.g., earning a B+ or higher), and/or success in a more advanced course (e.g., Calculus instead of Algebra)?

Another approach is to set lower (i.e., basic) and higher (i.e., advanced) cut scores based on standard error of measurement (SEM). On the ACT, the SEM is approximately two points for each subject area test; therefore, the basic cut score could be set at four points below the proficient cut score, and the advanced cut score could be set at four points above the proficient cut score to provide approximate 95% confidence that a student scoring at the basic (advanced) cut score is truly below (above) proficient. The advantage of this approach and two SEMs is that the basic and advanced cut scores are significantly different from the proficient cut scores from a measurement perspective. A disadvantage is that the resulting probabilities of success may not match expectations for student performance in first-year college courses.

Linkages to lower grade-level cut scores can also be used to inform basic and advanced cut scores. For example, ACT Aspire covers grades 3–10 and reports four achievement levels with the "Ready" cut score, indicating that students are on target to meet the ACT benchmark in grade 11. To set basic and advanced cut scores on the ACT (in this example), a regression approach can be used to predict the ACT scores associated with the basic ("Close") and advanced ("Exceeding") cut scores on the ACT Aspire grade 10 assessment. The advantage of this approach is that it ensures coherence of the cut scores across grade levels and utilizes the "Ready" benchmark to set lower and higher cut scores.

These methods can also be used in combination. For example, ACT assisted one state in combining SEM and regression approaches. The SEM and regression approaches produced cut scores that differed by at most two score points (approximately 0.4 standard deviations) across subject areas and performance levels. In most cases, the results from the SEM approach were also consistent with course success probabilities of 0.30 (basic) and 0.70 (advanced). However, because the SEM approach by itself does not take into account the probabilities of success, adjustments were made to make the probabilities of success for each cut score more consistent across subject areas. If SEMs are used as the basis for adding cut scores beyond a single college-readiness cut score, a minimum difference should be ensured between that cut and other cuts (e.g., at least two SEMs), meaning adjustments based on regression results or other data would only be used to increase the advanced cut and decrease the basic cut.

PLDs

Performance levels classify students based on their test performance (Haertel, 1999); cut scores are simply the numeric points on a scale used to separate students into each performance level category. PLDs describe what a student is expected to know and be able to do at a given performance level. There are at least three requirements when creating empirical PLDs: (a) determine the criterion (e.g., course grade), (b) determine the performance level on the criterion (e.g., grade of B or higher), and (c) decide on probabilities (e.g., 50%, 65%). For example, an *empirical PLD* could read as follows:

> Students meeting the Proficient standard in English have a 52% chance of earning a B or higher in a first-year credit-bearing college course in English and a 79% chance of earning a C or higher in the course.

Even when empirical standard setting is used, *content-based PLDs* may be desired to provide educators, students, and parents with descriptions of what students can typically do at different performance levels. Scale anchoring has often been employed to develop such content-based PLDs after cut scores have been established or as the initial basis for setting new cut scores on established assessments (Sinharay, Haberman, & Lee, 2011). This approach was employed to create ACT's College Readiness Standards (ACT, 2014). Content specialists reviewed score distributions of ACT items from several test forms, as well as data from ACT's College Course Placement Service (i.e., cut scores used for placement into college courses). Items that had been answered correctly by 80% or more of test takers scoring in each range were used to inform the standards, because students scoring in that range are likely able to demonstrate those knowledge and skills.

ACT recently assisted a state in setting its own content-based PLDs after an empirical standard setting. ACT content experts selected exemplar items from released test forms and exemplar writing samples from actual student responses to the ACT Writing test (i.e., essays). Exemplar items were selected for content coverage and varying difficulty and were categorized as *Basic*, *Proficient*, or *Advanced*, based on the score at which 67% of students got the item correct. Writing samples were selected across a range of score points. Item maps were created, providing information about the performance level and content standard being measured by each item. A workshop was conducted with content experts from across the state who reviewed items and writing samples from each performance level, arranged in order of increasing difficulty. For each item, panelists were asked to answer "What knowledge and skills does this item measure?" and "Why is this item more difficult than the items that preceded it?" After reviewing the exemplars, content experts provided preliminary PLD statements describing the knowledge and skills demonstrated by students taking the ACT, and panelists reviewed and revised the PLDs for clarity of wording, progression of knowledge and skills across performance levels, and completeness of coverage of the state standards. Similar approaches can be taken to establish PLDs in earlier grades.

Setting Cut Scores for Grades 3–10

Modern K–12 assessment systems should be coherent across grade levels, giving students and others consistent messages about readiness. To support coherence and interpretations of "on target for readiness," methods for setting cut scores for grades 3–10 include:

A   linking scores at each grade level to existing grade 11 cut scores,
B   linking scores at each grade level to a college or career outcome of interest,
C   traditional content-based standard setting at multiple grade levels, followed by articulation (vertically moderated standard setting), or
D   some combination of the first three approaches.

The focus of this section is on approach A. Approach A could also be used to smooth grade-specific cut scores obtained from content-based standard setting.

Even within one approach, different linking methods can be used. The choice of linking method determines what interpretations should be supported by the cut scores. For example, meeting an early grade cut score could imply that students are predicted to score at the grade 11 cut score, or it could mean that students are performing at the same point in the score distribution relative to students who meet the grade 11 cut score.

For new assessment systems, linking methods are constrained by data availability. Some methods require longitudinal data, but new assessment systems need early grade cut scores long before full longitudinal data (e.g., grades 3–11) are available. This section focuses on approaches for estimating "on target for readiness" cut scores for grades 3–10 without the benefit of longitudinal data. We will use the example of estimating ACT Aspire Readiness Benchmarks for grades 3–10 that are linked to the ACT Benchmarks (grade 11 cut scores), described earlier in this chapter. ACT Aspire is a relatively new assessment program that was launched in spring 2014; longitudinal data spanning grades 3–11 will not be available until 2022.

We will focus on three linking methods for setting early grade cut scores based on linkage to the grade 11 cut score. These three methods (shown in Table 6.2) belong to larger families of methods, of which there are many variants. For example, we will discuss simple linear regression as one example of projection, but there are many other methods within the regression family that could be used (e.g., Wright, 2016, examined seven different regression methods for estimating cut scores). The methods could be used for an assessment program that spans grades 3–11 (e.g., ACT Aspire and the ACT test) or with an assessment system that mixes programs (e.g., PARCC grades 3–8, PreACT grade 10, and the ACT grade 11). None of the methods require vertical scales.

Contrasting Three Linking Methods for Early Grade Cut Scores

After the first year of an assessment system, only cross-sectional data are available, and statistical moderation (Mislevy, 1992) can be used to set early grade cut scores based on distributional equivalence to the grade 11 cut score. Using statistical moderation, early grade cut scores are those having the same z-score (distance from the grade-level mean, in standard deviation units) as the grade 11 cut score. Alternatively, the cut scores could be set based on percentile rank equivalence. When test scores are normally distributed, z-score and percentile rank equivalence should yield very similar results.

Table 6.2 Three Methods for Determining Early Grade Cut Scores Linked to Grade 11 Cut Score

Linkage Method	Required Data	Formula for Grade k Cut Score
Statistical moderation	Cross-sectional (1 year)	$\mu_k + \left(C_{11} - \mu_k\right)\left(\dfrac{\sigma_k}{\sigma_{11}}\right)$
Projection (regression)	Full longitudinal (9 years)	$\mu_k + \left(C_{11} - \mu_k\right)\left(\dfrac{\sigma_k}{\sigma_{11}}\right)\left(\dfrac{1}{r_{k,11}}\right)$
Piecewise regression	Piecewise longitudinal (2 years)	$\mu_k + \left(C_{11} - \mu_k\right)\left(\prod\limits_{j=k}^{10}\left(\dfrac{\sigma_j}{\sigma_{j+1}}\right)^{m(j)}\right)\left(\dfrac{1}{\prod\limits_{j=k}^{10} r_{j,j+1}}\right)$ where $m(j) = -1$ when j is odd and $m(j) = 1$ when j is even.

Note: μ_k is the grade k mean, σ_k is the grade k standard deviation, C_{11} is the grade 11 cut score (ACT Benchmark), and $r_{k,j}$ is the correlation of grade k test scores and grade j test scores.

As more longitudinal data become available, additional methods become feasible. Projection methods (Mislevy, 1992) generally require longitudinal data. For example, a regression model for grade 11 scores on grade 3 scores is only available after the ninth year of an assessment program. However, we will demonstrate an approach for estimating the parameters needed for the projection method using only cross-sectional data and assumed correlations.

Another approach is piecewise regression, where the grade 10 cut score is determined based on a regression of grade 11 scores on grade 10 scores, and then the grade 9 cut score is determined based on a regression of grade 10 scores on grade 9 scores, and so on. The piecewise longitudinal approach is especially attractive because it's feasible after the second year of the assessment program; however, the magnitude of the correlation ultimately impacts the grade-to-grade linkages, and measurement error is compounded at linkages for lower grades.

The different methods lead to different interpretations of what it means to meet early grade cut scores. Statistical moderation results in similar impact (percent meeting cut scores) across grade levels and is often used for vertically moderated standard setting (Lissitz & Huynh, 2003). Using statistical moderation, a student who scores at the grade 3 cut score performed about the same, relative to grade-level peers, as a minimally ready 11th grade student.

Arguably, projection methods lead to the interpretation most consistent with the idea of being *on target for readiness*: students who meet the 3rd-grade cut score have a 50% chance of being ready in grade 11 (or, alternatively, students who meet the 3rd-grade cut score are expected to score at the grade 11 Ready cut score). Under the piecewise regression method, a student who meets the grade 3 cut score has a 50% chance of meeting the grade 4 cut score.

Assuming multivariate normal distributions for the test scores, formulas for the early grade cut scores can be derived for each of the three methods (Table 6.2). It's useful to inspect the formulas to understand when, and to what extent, the three methods lead to different solutions. Note that the formulas for the cut scores have the same general form, and all three formulas depend on the grade-level mean and deviation of grade 11 cut score from grade 11 mean. The cut scores are also dependent on test score standard deviations, and the statistical moderation and projection cut scores depend on vertical correlations.

When the grade 11 cut score is equal to the grade 11 mean ($C = \mu_{11}$), the three linking methods are equivalent. All of the early grade cut scores will deviate from the grade-level mean in the same direction: as the grade 11 cut score deviates more from the grade 11 mean, the early grade cut score deviates more from the grade-level mean in the same direction. The statistical moderation solutions are asymptotes for the projection-based cut scores: as the correlation approaches 1, the two sets of cut scores converge. Each solution assumes a common population of students across grade levels. Using cross-sectional data, this assumption is violated because different students are represented in each grade level. Student dropout and migration exacerbates this problem.

Applying Early Grade Methods to ACT Aspire Data

The cut score formulas using the three methods were applied to data from ACT Aspire. The mean and standard deviation parameters for each grade level were estimated from a norming study for ACT Aspire (ACT, 2016). The norming study weighted the test scores from each grade level to a common population and used piecewise longitudinal data to anchor score distributions across grades 8–10. These steps are important because the cut score formulas in Table 6.2 assume a common population across grade levels.

The cut score formulas using the regression approaches require knowing cross-grade correlations. The correlations for adjacent grade levels were estimated from existing ACT Aspire data, but the correlations required for the projection model (e.g., correlation of grade 3 and 11 scores) are unknown, because ACT Aspire is relatively new. The sensitivity of the projection solution to correlation was examined by assuming a broad range of plausible correlations.

Figure 6.1 summarizes the results for mathematics. For each grade level (3–10), cut scores using the three linkage methods were calculated. The cut scores are plotted on the vertical axis against grade level on the horizontal axis. ACT Aspire scores are vertically scaled, so increasing cut scores across grade levels are expected. The grade 11 cut score (ACT Mathematics Benchmark of 22) is above the grade 11 mean (19.3) and so the early grade cut scores are also above their respective means. The statistical moderation method suggests a grade 3 cut score of 416, while the projection method suggests grade 3 cut scores ranging from 416 to 418, depending on the correlation. In this case, it might be reasonable to set the projection-based grade 3 cut score as the midpoint of the range (417). The projection-based cut scores are sensitive to the correlation, because the grade 11 cut score is considerably above the grade 11 mean (by 0.54 standard deviations).

As noted before, differences in cut scores across the linking methods were amplified by the deviation of the 11th-grade cut score from the 11th-grade mean. A piecewise regression approach may seem like an attractive option after the second year of an assessment program because sufficient data are available, but we found that it can provide unreasonable results. For example, the grade 3 cut score using the piecewise regression formula was seven standard deviations above the grade 3 mean. From the formula for the piecewise regression solution (Table 6.2), the product term (involving correlations) represents compounded error and can cause early grade cut scores to deviate drastically from their mean. The compounded error term becomes more pronounced with (1) lower vertical correlations and (2) more intervening grade levels. With high correlations and few intervening grade levels, the piecewise regression approach may work well. As shown in Figure 6.1, the grade 9 and 10 cut scores using piecewise regression agree well with the other approaches.

A middle-ground approach to set the initial cut scores for ACT Aspire used projection for grades 8–10 and statistical moderation for grades 3–7. The cut scores for grades 3–7 are the same distance from the grade-level mean (in standard deviation units) as the grade 8 cut score. An argument supporting this approach is that the prediction of performance in grade 11 for students in grades 3–7 is less precise, and so cut scores based on statistical moderation are sufficient indicators for being on target, while maintaining consistent impact across the early grades. Cut scores should be updated over time because of changes in student growth among the assessed population, or possible drift in score scales.

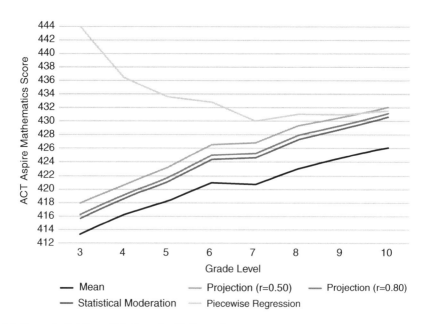

Figure 6.1 Example Cut Score Solutions for Mathematics

Implications for Policy, Practice, and Research

The use of empirical standard setting has increased in recent years. These methods can be contrasted with traditional approaches, which are not typically tied to outcome data and often result in significant differences in impact when comparisons are made across states and with national outcomes (e.g., NAEP proficiency versus state proficiency). An increasing focus on college and career readiness has driven the need to incorporate empirical data in standard setting. Rather than focusing on item content, empirically-based standard setting methods directly link performance on an assessment with postsecondary success. Of course, empirical methods can be combined with content-based methods in a variety of ways to mitigate the incoherence across states and with national data (as discussed in McClarty, Loomis, & Pitoniak, 2017).

In conducting an empirical standard setting, having access to relevant outcome data is essential. Both ACT and College Board rely on partnerships with colleges and universities to provide outcome data for models predicting success in college. Other outcome data would strengthen the link between performance in high school and success in college, such as remedial coursework completion rates and grades, and college degree completion. Career outcomes are needed to strengthen claims around career readiness.

Setting cut scores using empirical-based methods can result in a large drop in the percentage of students deemed proficient, which can lead to misunderstanding among the public and media. Croft, Guffy, and Vitale (2014) reviewed public responses to adopting more rigorous standards in four states, concluding that it is important to help the public understand that a drop in proficiency results from more rigorous standards, not necessarily a decline in performance. It is important to communicate such expectations in advance of score reporting and emphasize the rationale for increasing the rigor of standards. Tying the performance standards to college success or remediation rates can help explain the rationale and is one advantage of empirical approaches to standard setting.

With over 20 states using college admissions tests statewide and many states considering ways to use these tests for accountability, there is a risk that different cut scores will still be deployed to indicate college readiness or proficiency. States generally prefer their own performance standards, but this could undermine public confidence in results when readiness or proficiency rates change dramatically as standards or assessments are revised or cross-state comparisons are made. Because many students attend postsecondary institutions or attain employment outside their home state, state-specific performance standards have limited benefit and may hinder national goals related to increased readiness for college and work. If college and career readiness are truly the goals of K–12 education, then having a clear definition of college and career readiness that generalizes across states and institutions, with valid and reliable assessments used across K–12 and higher educational systems, should be a major consideration of any standard setting approach.

Notes

1 The specific language in ESSA provisions state "'nationally recognized high school academic assessment means an assessment of high school students' knowledge and skills that is administered in multiple States and is recognized by institutions of higher education in those or other States for the purpose of entrance or placement into courses in postsecondary education or training programs" (Rule, 4/19/16).

2 Final regulations for ESSA provisions related to the use of alternative national assessments recognized by higher education had not been issued at time of publication.

3 ACT and PreACT extend from grades 10–12; however, states also using ACT Aspire in grades 3–10 can use a common scale; SAT and PSAT extend from grades 8–12.

4 Approximately one-third of four-year colleges are test-optional with some group of students, but the vast majority of students applying to these colleges submit test scores. Only one four-year college will not review submitted admissions test scores.

5 State and consortia tests generally have extended windows of 3–6 weeks using one or several forms. Forms and/or items are reused across school days, as opposed to admissions tests, which generally have a single test date per form and reuse is much less frequent and proximal in terms of timing.

6 A review of these and other methods used to establish college-readiness benchmarks is available in Camara (2013) and Camara and Quenemoen (2012).

References

ACT, Inc. (2011). *Affirming the goal: Is college and career readiness an internationally competitive standard?* ACT Policy Report. Iowa City, IA: Author.

ACT, Inc. (2014). *The ACT technical manual*. Iowa City, IA: Author.

ACT, Inc. (2016). *ACT Aspire technical manual*. Iowa City, IA: Author.

Allen, J. (2013). *Updating the ACT college readiness benchmarks* (ACT Research Report No. 2013–6). Iowa City, IA: ACT, Inc.

Allen, J., & Sconing, J. (2005). *Using ACT assessment scores to set benchmarks for College Readiness* (ACT Research Report No. 2005–3). Iowa City, IA: ACT, Inc.

Camara, W. (2013). Defining and measuring college and career readiness: A validation framework. *Educational Measurement: Issues and Practice, 32*(4), 16–27.

Camara, W. J., & Quenemoen, R. (2012). *Defining and measuring college and career readiness and informing the development of performance level descriptors (PLDs).* Commissioned white paper for PARCC. Washington, DC: PARCC.

Cizek, G. J., & Bunch, M. B. (2007). *Standard setting: A guide to establishing and evaluating performance standards on tests.* Thousand Oaks, CA: Sage.

Conley, D. (2014). *Getting ready for college, careers, and the Common Core: What every educator needs to know.* San Francisco, CA: Jossey-Bass.

Croft, M., Guffy, G., & Vitale, D. (2014). *Communicating college and career readiness through proficiency standards.* Issue Brief, June 2014. Iowa City, IA: ACT, Inc.

Fields, R., & Parsad, B. (2012). *Tests and cut scores used for student placement in postsecondary education: Fall 2011.* Washington, DC: National Assessment Governing Board.

Gerwertz, C. (2016, January 6). Will states swap standards-based tests for SAT, ACT? *Education Week, 35*(15), 16–17.

Haertel, E. H. (1999). Validity arguments for high-stakes testing: In search of the evidence. *Educational Measurement: Issues and Practice, 25*(4), 5–9.

Kobrin, J. L. (2007). *Determining SAT benchmarks for college readiness.* College Board Research Notes RN-30.

Lissitz, R. W., & Huynh, H. (2003). Vertical equating for state assessments: Issues and solutions in determination of adequate yearly progress and school accountability. *Practical Assessment, Research, and Evaluation, 8*(10). Retrieved from http://PAREonline.net/getvn.asp?v=8&n= 10.

Lu, Y. (2015). *ACT Aspire scores associated with PISA scores: A preliminary analysis.* Iowa City, IA: ACT.

Martineau, J., Gong, B., & Zurkowski, J. (2016, June). *Preparing for ESSA's "nationally recognized high school assessment" provision.* Paper presented at the National Conference on Student Assessment in Philadelphia, PA.

Mattern, K., & Lacina, C. (2015). *Different assessments, different results: A cautionary note when interpreting state test results.* Iowa City, IA: ACT.

Mattern, K., Radunzel, J., & Westrick, P. (2015). *Development of STEM readiness benchmarks to assist educational and career decision making.* ACT Research Report 3. Iowa City, IA: ACT.

McClarty, K. L., Loomis, S. C., & Pitoniak, M. J. (2017). Building external validity into the process: Evidence-based readiness standards. In K. L. McClarty, K. D. Mattern, & M. N. Gaertner (Eds.), *Preparing students for college and careers: Theory, measurement, and educational practice.* New York: Routledge.

Mislevy, R. J. (1992). *Linking educational assessments: Concepts, issues, methods, and prospects.* Princeton, NJ: Educational Testing Service.

Phillips, G. W. (2016). *National benchmarks for state achievement standards.* Retrieved from http://www.air.org/sites/default/files/downloads/report/National-Benchmarks-State-Achievement-Standards-February-2016_rev.pdf.

Sinharay, S., Haberman, S. J., & Lee, Y.-H. (2011). When does scale anchoring work? A Case Study. *Journal of Educational Measurement, 48*, 61–80.

Wright, D. B. (2016). Regression methods for estimating cut scores. *International Journal of Research & Method in Education.* Advance online publication: doi: 10.1080/1743727X.2016.1167866

Wyatt, J., Kobrin, J., Wiley, A., Camara, W. J., & Proestler, N. (2011). *SAT Benchmarks: Development of a college readiness benchmark and its relationship to secondary and postsecondary school performance* (College Board Research Report 2011–5). New York: College Board.

7 College Placement Strategies

Evolving Considerations and Practices[1]

Elisabeth Barnett and Vikash Reddy

Introduction

Many postsecondary institutions—and community colleges in particular—require that students demonstrate specified levels of literacy and numeracy before taking college-level courses. Typically, students have been assessed using two widely available tests—ACCUPLACER and Compass. However, placement testing practices are beginning to change for three reasons. First, the Compass test will no longer be offered as of the end of 2016. Second, questions have been raised about the validity of commonly used placement tests. Third, there are emerging discussions about the need to consider other aspects of students' readiness to succeed in college, especially so-called noncognitive skills.

In this chapter, we discuss the history of college placement testing, with a focus on nonselective colleges. We describe the limitations of placement tests, the consequences of placement errors, and the movement toward changing systems of placement. We also provide a typology of the measures that can be used for placement, how they can be combined, and how colleges might use assessment results in more varied ways.

History of Assessment for Entering College Students

Higher education institutions need mechanisms to assess the college readiness of incoming students. Selective institutions use admissions requirements to screen students, accepting or rejecting them on the basis of their test scores and applications (Cohen, Brawer, & Kisker, 2014). Open-access institutions—which include community colleges and some four-year institutions—accept all or most students, but then must determine whether they are ready for college coursework. As such, placement testing is a near-universal part of the enrollment experience for incoming community college students (Bailey, Jaggars, & Jenkins, 2015). Students who are not deemed ready based on their placement test scores typically take remedial or developmental coursework before beginning college-level studies. Roughly 60% of incoming freshmen nationally require developmental instruction in English and/or math; the vast majority of these students are concentrated at nonselective two-year or less selective four-year colleges (National Center for Public Policy and Higher Education & Southern Regional Education Board, 2010).

For much of the 20th century, rigid policies with mandates for placement were accompanied by course prerequisite policies, academic probation and progression policies, and other requirements associated with entrance and graduation (Cohen et al., 2014). By the 1970s, however, the popularity of such policies was declining, as some argued that college students, as adults, should have the right to make their own decisions, even if this resulted in failing courses (Cohen et al., 2014; Hughes & Scott-Clayton, 2011). The laissez-fare approach to placement was short-lived, however, as legislators' and educators' support for testing and placement mandates grew amid concerns over high failure rates and dropout rates in the 1980s (Fonte, 1997; Rounds & Anderson, 1985). Two-year colleges reported having policies governing placement testing at twice the rate of their four-year counterparts (Abraham, 1987), and a national survey of community colleges found that over 90% used some sort of test to place incoming first-time students by the late 1980s (Woods, 1985).

At the same time, long-standing issues with standardized tests came to the fore in the 1980s. Early standardized tests, in particular IQ tests (Jencks, 1998), were criticized on the grounds that they reflected test-takers' racial and economic backgrounds, rather than their academic capacities, and that they ignored cultural knowledge and other student strengths (Byrd & Macdonald, 2005). The concerns primarily revolved around the potential for placement policies to disadvantage whole groups of students (see, for example, the Mexican American Legal Defense and Education Fund's 1991 lawsuit challenging legislation that mandated placement testing in California [Cohen et al., 2014; Hughes & Scott-Clayton, 2011]). Nonetheless, by the 1990s, mandatory testing and mandatory placement were included in an influential list of community college best practices (Boylan, 2002).

Of community colleges surveyed by the National Assessment Governing Board (NAGB) in 2010, 100% reported using a standardized test for math placement purposes, and 94% reported doing so for reading placement (Fields & Parsad, 2012). Among four-year institutions, 85% employed placement tests for math and 51% reported doing so for English. The 2010 NAGB survey also asked institutions about their use of the most common placement tools—SAT, ACT, ACCUPLACER, and Compass. While most used these tests, 14% of public two-year institutions and 38% of public four-year institutions reported using another assessment. In another 50-state survey of assessment practices, the National Center for Higher Education Management Systems found that only 15 states had a common set of placement tests (Zis, Boeke, & Ewell, 2010).

For any given placement test, there is substantial variation in the cut scores institutions use to designate students as college ready (Fields & Parsad, 2012; Hodara, Jaggars, & Karp, 2012). Only 12 states have statewide cut scores. One state has a cut-score policy that governs just its community colleges, and four states indicated they were developing a statewide policy. Even among these states, however, some allow institutions to set a cut score above that specified in the state policy (Zis et al., 2010).

Limitations of Current Practices

An accurate placement mechanism will direct students who are college ready into college-level coursework, while referring students who are academically underprepared to developmental coursework. Placing students correctly is crucial, as the consequences of incorrect placement—particularly underplacement—are severe. Of community college students who enroll in developmental coursework, just 28% earn a degree within eight years, compared with 43% of those who did not take any developmental coursework (Attewell, Lavin, Domina, & Levey, 2006). While these differences in outcomes could be attributed to differences in academic capabilities, a number of studies have employed a regression-discontinuity approach to compare similar students with placement test scores just above and below the cutoff and found that developmental enrollment has null or negative effects on short- and long-term outcomes (Bailey et al., 2015). A null impact on completion would indicate that students who score just below the cutoff and are referred to developmental education earn credentials at roughly the same rates as similar students who enter directly into college-level coursework. Thus, the introduction of pre-degree coursework does not improve college completion rates, but rather extends the time required to earn a credential and increases the cost to students and taxpayers (Crisp & Delgado, 2014; Scott-Clayton & Rodriguez, 2015).

Moreover, scores on entry assessments are not highly correlated with success in initial college-level courses. When used as the sole measure for course placement, these tests incorrectly place many incoming students (Bailey et al., 2015; Belfield & Crosta, 2012; Scott-Clayton, Crosta, & Belfield, 2012). For example, using data from a community college system in a large urban setting, Scott-Clayton (2012) demonstrated that high school grade point average (GPA) explained a greater share of variation in outcomes for gatekeeper English and math courses than placement test scores. A combination of placement test scores and high school achievement measures yielded the greatest explanation of variance. Using the richest set of predictors, the author then estimated the share of students who were placed in developmental coursework, even though they would likely have received a B or better in an entry-level college course, as well as the share of students who were placed into college-level coursework despite a high likelihood of failure. These shares were combined to produce a "severe error rate" (Scott-Clayton, 2012, p. 25), which ranged from 24% in math to 33% in English. Similar findings have emerged in research conducted in a number of different settings (Belfield & Crosta, 2012; Scott-Clayton & Rodriguez, 2015).

Another limitation of using single measures for placement is the inability of such measures to distinguish different student needs for remediation. Students differ in their comfort with mathematical concepts, their exposure to math in high school, their ability to interpret test questions given their English language proficiency, and the time since their last math course (Bailey & Cho, 2010). Further, they do not cast light on the noncognitive factors that may influence student success in college.

Emerging Practices in Assessment and Placement

Colleges and college systems are seeking ways to improve entry assessments while minimizing costs and administrative challenges. Based on recent research on assessment practices (Bracco et al., 2014; Duffy, Schott, Beaver, & Park, 2014), options include employing alternative measures, the use of multiple measures, and broader conceptions of placement. As outlined in Table 7.1, we propose the following framework for considering these alternatives.

Measures

Colleges have options beyond commonly available placement tests to assess students' readiness to take college-level courses and the likelihood that they would benefit from supportive services.

Table 7.1 Options for Course Placement

Measures	*Systems or Approaches*	*Placement Types*
Administered by College 1 Traditional placement tests 2 Alternative placement tests 3 Noncognitive assessments 4 Writing assessments 5 Computer skills assessments 6 Questionnaire items *Obtained from Outside of College* 1 High school GPA 2 Other high school transcript information (courses taken, course grades) 3 Standardized test results (e.g., ACT, SAT, Smarter Balanced, PARCC)	• Placement based on results of single assessment • Waiver system • Decision bands • Placement formula • Decision rules • Directed self-placement	• Placement into traditional courses • Placement into alternative coursework • Placement into support services

Some of these are commercially available, while others may be developed by a particular college. The selection or development process involves both identifying an appropriate instrument and establishing cut scores that can be used in decision making. Cut score decisions are generally guided by a review of prior research, analysis of concordance tables showing relationships between previously used measures and the proposed measure, and/or by analyzing historical data associated with students at the college when available. Some examples of alternative measures follow.

Alternative Placement Tests

While most colleges continue to use traditional placement tests, some have selected or developed alternative tests in an effort to align the knowledge and skills measured with the specific courses they offer. Colleges may also seek diagnostic assessments that guide students into particular entry points in a developmental curriculum. Both Virginia and North Carolina have developed assessment systems that place students into specific developmental education modules (Hodara et al., 2012).

Alternative placement tests have the advantage of being customizable to each college's standards and introductory coursework. They can also have more diagnostic value than standardized instruments (see, for example, Reddy & Harper, 2013). However, test development and validation is complex and costly—and may result in instruments with questionable reliability and validity (Hughes & Scott-Clayton, 2011).

Noncognitive Assessments

There is increasing recognition among postsecondary educators that success in college depends on more than students' content knowledge (Hughes & Scott-Clayton, 2011). Noncognitive assessments seek to measure students' psychosocial characteristics, such as motivation, learning strategies, academic tenacity, or sense of belonging (Lipnevich, MacCann, & Roberts, 2013). Examples of noncognitive tests include SuccessNavigator (offered by the Education Testing Service), Engage (offered by ACT), the Learning and Study Strategies Inventory (offered by H&H publishing), and the College Student Inventory (offered by Noel Levitz). In addition, colleges may incorporate the use of short scales, such as the Grit Scale or Adult Hope Scale, into existing surveys or tests.

Noncognitive tests allow colleges to gather information about students that might lead to improved course placement and can help place students into supports and services. However, the evidence base for their use in placement is thin. Research conducted on SuccessNavigator suggests that it has some value as a measure when used in conjunction with a placement test to move students just below a cut score into a higher level math course (Rikoon, Liebtag, Olivera-Aguilar, Robbins, & Jackson, 2014). A study on an early version of Engage suggests that its Academic Discipline scale is predictive of student success in initial college level courses (Robbins, Allen, Casillas, & Peterson, 2006). Additional information on noncognitive assessments can be found in Gaertner and Roberts (2017).

Writing Assessments

In many colleges, students are assessed via a performance task, most commonly writing a short essay, in addition to a standardized assessment. For example, some colleges in the University of Wisconsin System use a faculty-scored essay in addition to the Wisconsin Placement Test; student essays are scored based on the first-year composition learning outcomes used across the system. Research conducted by two faculty members found that the proportion of at-risk students who remained in good standing at the end of their fall semester grew from 59% in 2006, just before the introduction of the writing assessment, to 73% in 2009 (Duffy et al., 2014).

However, colleges typically have to assess large numbers of incoming students within a short period of time, at low cost. While writing assessments may provide more complete and nuanced information on which to base placement decisions, they typically require added staff time to score (Rodríguez, Bowden, Belfield, & Scott-Clayton, 2015), although this may be ameliorated when they are graded using automated systems.

Computer Skills Assessments

Some colleges want to make sure that students have the basic computer skills needed to succeed in college courses. For example, the College of Western Idaho (CWI Assessment and Testing, n.d.) and Richland Community College in Texas (RCC Computer Skills Placement, n.d.) administer short computer skills assessments to all or selected incoming students. Other colleges use assessments to determine students' readiness to succeed in online coursework. Students lacking skills may be placed into appropriate courses or workshops. However, testing students and providing them with counseling based on results will add cost.

Questionnaire Items

Colleges may ask incoming students to respond to selected questions about their prior experiences with learning certain kinds of material or their confidence about mastering future material, most commonly math (Venezia, Bracco, & Nodine, 2010). A study at one college found that students' responses to questions about their high school academic history improved placement accuracy when considered in addition to placement test scores (Gordon, 1999). However, there is limited evidence that responses to these kinds of questions are good predictors of future success in college coursework.

High School GPA and Other Transcript Data

A growing body of research indicates that high school GPA is a strong predictor of success in college courses. Other items from the high school transcript may also be utilized, especially coursework in the subject area related to the placement decision. For example, math courses taken and math grades earned may be indicative of likely student success in future math courses. As an example, North Carolina's placement system considers students college ready in math if they have an overall high school GPA of at least 2.6 and have completed four approved high school math courses (North Carolina Community College System, 2015).

While high school transcript data can be valuable for placement purposes, many colleges and state systems find it difficult to obtain this information in a timely manner. It is seldom available to colleges from state data systems, and it may not be in place when decisions need to be made. Alternatively, students can be asked to submit high school transcripts, a process that has gone smoothly in some locales and been challenging in others. Student self-report of high school GPA may also be used; research suggests that students' reports tend to be accurate (Sanchez & Buddin, 2015).

Standardized Test Results

Many college placement systems take into account student scores on the SAT and ACT or other 11th-grade standardized tests, such as those associated with the Common Core State Standards. Some of the impetus for using test results in college placement systems is a desire to align college-readiness standards across K–12 and postsecondary education (Bracco et al.,

2014). There is considerable research on the extent to which the SAT and ACT predict success in first college-level courses in math and English, with both being modestly predictive (ACT, 2014; Mattern, Patterson, & Kobrin, 2012). However, as with high school transcripts, it can be difficult to obtain scores in a timely manner. They are seldom routinely available to colleges from state data systems.

System or Approach to Using Assessment Results

Most colleges require entering students to take placement tests and use the scores as the sole determinant of whether students are ready for college-level coursework. However, there is increasing awareness of the limitations of using single tests for placement and a growing interest in employing multiple measures. We define multiple-measures placement as a system that combines two or more measures to place students into appropriate courses and/or supports. We have identified five approaches that permit measures to be combined for placement purposes: a waiver system, decision bands, placement formula, decision rules, and directed self-placement. These methods may, in some instances, be used in combination.

All placement systems require a decision on what constitutes college readiness. While selecting a cut score on a single measure is relatively straightforward, the process is more complex when more than one measure is involved. These decisions can be based on the research literature or on analyses of prior data associated with either single measures or measures used in combination. Typically, such analyses involve predicting the probability of student success in a college-level course using available administrative data from a college or state system (e.g., Scott-Clayton, 2012). The information derived may be presented to college faculty, who set a minimum probability of student success in a given course, taking into account the tradeoffs between the proportion of students placing into a college-level course and the proportion of students expected to pass the course.

Placement rules can also vary according to a student's intended major and the associated requirements in math or English. Increasingly, math course sequences are differentiated according to student goals and may involve different placement criteria; similarly, students entering technical programs may be placed based on the math and English requirements of jobs for which they are preparing.

Waivers

In a waiver system, one or more criteria are used to waive placement testing requirements and allow students to place directly into college-level courses. At some colleges, students with a specified high school GPA or standardized test score are exempt from placement testing. In Ohio, legislation requires that students be considered college ready (or "remediation-free") if they meet predefined scores on widely used assessments such as the ACT, SAT, and ACCUPLACER, or less commonly administered assessments, such as ALEKS, Place U., and MapleSoft T.A. (Ohio Department of Higher Education, 2016).

Decision Bands

Colleges may determine that students with placement test scores that fall within a specified range be further evaluated using additional criteria. For instance, students who score just below a college-level placement test cut score could be further assessed using high school GPA or the results of a noncognitive assessment. Alternatively, a decision band system could start with a range on the high school GPA. In the state of Washington, when students' placement test scores fall just below a certain threshold, added measures can be considered in determining their placement (Bracco et al., 2014).

Placement Formula

In a placement formula system, historical data are used to predict the influence of varied measures on success in college-level courses. Using the results, a placement formula is developed that weights and combines these measures, resulting in a placement score for each student. The placement formula can be integrated into the existing testing system if desired. Such an approach has been employed in research underway with several State University of New York (SUNY) community colleges to assess its impact on student outcomes (Center for the Analysis of Postsecondary Readiness, 2014).

Decision Rules

Decision rules generally consist of a series of "if-then" statements and may be hierarchical. Typically, a type of branching system is used that distinguishes between different categories of students and also takes into account the varied evidence that may be available to assess any given enrollee. A common distinction is between students matriculating directly from high school and those entering college one or more years after high school graduation. In the example shown in Table 7.2, students are assessed on their readiness to take specific math courses with those right out of high school (direct matriculants) assessed using 11th-grade GPA, final high school math course taken, and course grades, while later enrollees (nondirect matriculants) are assessed using 12th-grade information. In this example, test scores are not taken into account.

Directed Self-Placement

With directed self-placement, students may be permitted to place themselves into the course level of choice, usually informed by the results of placement testing, a review of their high school performance, and/or information about college-level expectations in math and English. Florida has instituted this policy across its colleges based on legislation passed in 2013. Early descriptive data from Florida indicate that directed self-placement leads to much higher

Table 7.2 California Decision Rules for Science, Technology, Engineering, and Mathematics (STEM) Directed Courses in Mathematics (RP Group, 2016)

Level (Minimal final high school course level required for placement)	*Direct Matriculants* (Up through 11th grade)	*Non-Direct Matriculants*
Calculus I Passed Precalculus or Trigonometry (or better)	11th-grade GPA $\geq$ 3.6 11th-grade GPA $\geq$ 3.2 and Precalculus C (or better)	12th-grade GPA $\geq$ 3.1 and took Calculus 12th-grade GPA $\geq$ 3.5
Precalculus Passed Algebra II (or better)	11th-grade GPA $\geq$ 3.4 11th-grade GPA $\geq$ 2.6 and took Calculus	12th-grade GPA $\geq$ 3.3 12th-grade GPA $\geq$ 3 and Algebra II California Standards Test $\geq$ 340 12th-grade GPA $\geq$ 3 and Calculus C (or better)
Trigonometry Passed Algebra II (or better)	11th-grade GPA $\geq$ 3.4 11th-grade GPA $\geq$ 3 and Precalculus C+ (or better) 11th-grade GPA $\geq$ 3 and Algebra II B (or better)	12th-grade GPA $\geq$ 3.3 12th-grade GPA $\geq$ 2.8 and Precalculus C (or better)
College Algebra Passed Algebra II (or better)	11th-grade GPA $\geq$ 3.2 11th-grade GPA $\geq$ 2.9 and Precalculus C (or better)	12th-grade GPA $\geq$ 3.2 12th-grade GPA $\geq$ 3.0 and Precalculus or Statistics with C (or better)

enrollment rates in introductory college-level courses in English and math but lower pass rates for these courses. However, the sheer number of students passing a gateway course has increased over time (Hu et al., 2016).

Types of Placement

For the most part, colleges assess incoming students for math, writing, and reading course placement purposes. However, some colleges are also concerned with other kinds of placement—most commonly, into specific course types or into supports or services.

For colleges involved in a developmental education reform such as corequisite courses[2] or changes to course sequences and pathways (as discussed in Leahy & Landel, 2017),[3] the placement process may be used to inform decisions about which options are most appropriate for which students. For example, a college using a decision band system for placement may decide that students within a certain band will be placed into corequisite English courses, while those below the band will take developmental English and those above will take college-level English. At another college, students placing close to the college-ready level are encouraged to take an accelerated developmental education course, in which two semesters of material are compressed into one (see Colorado Community College System, 2009).

Some colleges also use the assessment and placement process to make sure that students receive appropriate supports. Low community college graduation rates, even among students deemed college ready, suggest that students need well-conceived, targeted assistance (Karp, 2011). Further, it is important that the help begin early (Lu, 1994; Mallinckrodt & Sedlacek, 1987). Most colleges offer a range of supports but typically meet the needs of limited numbers of students. Especially with more time-intensive options, it can be difficult to make sure that supports are optimally matched with the students who would most benefit from them. An assessment system, especially one that incorporates noncognitive assessments, may lead to better targeting and use of supports.

Emerging Issues Affecting Assessment and Placement

Reform Movements

A great deal of reform is currently taking place in higher education, motivated by concerns about graduation rates, equity, and the costs and benefits of a college education (Bailey et al., 2015). Changes in assessment and placement practices intersect with other initiatives in ways that can increase both opportunities and challenges.

Developmental Education Reform

Following years of concern about the effectiveness of developmental education, colleges are undertaking major reforms. There is a growing consensus that developmental sequences are too long, with multiple opportunities for students to run aground before becoming eligible to enter a college course. In addition, colleges are revising developmental education content and pedagogy to promote student engagement and better learning outcomes. Changes to course content, sequences, and expected prerequisite knowledge mean that assessment methods will need to change accordingly.

Math Pathways

Partly due to the number of students who fail traditional algebra courses and partly due to questions about the relevance of algebra to many students' goals, math course sequences are changing (this topic is discussed in detail in Leahy & Landel, 2017). Some would argue that, while all students should possess numeracy skills, many would gain more from quantitative reasoning or statistics courses than from traditional college algebra (Burdman, 2015).

Guided Pathways and Meta-Majors

Numerous colleges have decided to restructure their curriculum offerings in ways that encourage students to choose a curricular pathway and stick with it over time. The rationale is that students will complete a credential in a timely way if they pick at least a broad focus area at the beginning of their college career. Math and English course requirements often differ depending on the pathway chosen.

Technology

Individualized Assessment and Instruction

As more refined technology-assisted learning tools become available, assessment and instruction can be intertwined and tailored to the individual student. For example, students may undergo an initial math assessment using an online tool and then be placed into computer-based modules in which they work through material designed to address their specific deficiencies. Such systems may come to replace traditional assessment and developmental education in some colleges.

State Data System Improvements

As these systems improve, opportunities increase to combine data from K–12 and higher education in a timely way in order to make placement decisions.

Policy Issues

Equity

Different approaches to assessment and placement are likely to have differential impact, with the potential to reduce or exacerbate existing inequities. For example, Scott-Clayton et al. (2012) studied a large urban system and found that African-American students would be somewhat more likely to be placed in English (but not math) remedial courses if evaluated based on both high school GPA and test score. Thus, it is important for colleges to take measures to evaluate and reduce negative effects of changes in assessment and placement systems.

Local versus State Control

The more decentralized the policy decisions about assessment and placement, the more likely that there will be diverse ways of thinking about and measuring college readiness. Different definitions of college readiness can lead to confusing messages for K–12 educators and students (Venezia & Jaeger, 2013; also see Mattern & Gaertner, 2017). On the other hand, local decision-making can ensure that assessments and courses at particular colleges are well aligned.

Opportunities to Promote College Readiness in High School

When there are clear standards for college readiness and information about whether students are on track to college readiness in 11th grade, the senior year can be used to help students meet college-readiness standards. Close relationships between colleges and feeder high schools can support this work (Barnett, 2016).

Implications for Policy, Practice, and Research

The use of multiple measures for placement has the potential to enable more students to enter the most appropriate level of coursework and increase their likelihood of success. However, as Bracco et al. (2014) commented, "The choice to broaden placement policy to include multiple measures beyond a single standardized test score involves trade-offs, including potential trade-offs between precision and cost, test validity and face validity, and local policy variation and uniform statewide implementation" (p. iv). Careful consideration is required to create systems that work well for both institutions and students.

Decision-making in this arena is hampered by a lack of high-quality research on the strategies discussed here and by others. First, more information is needed on the extent to which existing measurement tools—alone and in combination—predict success in initial college courses; currently, decisions typically have to be made with a paucity of evidence of their predictive validity. In addition, the field would benefit from high quality evaluations of varied assessment and placement approaches that permit insights into their efficacy, implementation requirements, costs and benefits, and differential impact on varied student populations. Finally, research is needed on ways to bypass current approaches to assessment and placement altogether in favor of alternative ways of onboarding students.

Notes

1 The research reported here was undertaken through the Center for the Analysis of Postsecondary Readiness and supported by the Institute of Education Sciences, US Department of Education, through Grant R305C140007 to Teachers College, Columbia University. The opinions expressed are those of the authors and do not represent views of the Institute or the US Department of Education.
2 In the corequisite model of developmental education, students enroll in college-level English or math and an accompanying support course (see, e.g., Accelerated Learning Program, n.d.).
3 There is widespread discussion of changes to the types of math that students need for different life and career paths (see Dana Center Mathematics Pathways, n.d. and Carnegie Math Pathways, n.d.).

References

Abraham, A. A., Jr. (1987). *A report on college-level remedial/developmental programs in SREB states.* Atlanta, GA: Southern Regional Education Board.
Accelerated Learning Program. (n.d.). *What is ALP?* Retrieved from http://alp-deved.org/what-is-alp-exactly.
ACT. (2014). *Technical manual.* Iowa City, IA: ACT.
Attewell, P., Lavin, D., Domina, T., & Levey, T. (2006). New evidence on college remediation. *The Journal of Higher Education, 77*(5), 886–924.
Bailey, T., & Cho, S.-W. (2010). *Issue brief: Developmental education in community colleges.* New York: Columbia University, Teachers College, Community College Research Center.
Bailey, T., Jaggars, S. S., & Jenkins, D. (2015). *Redesigning America's community colleges: A clearer path to student success.* Boston, MA: Harvard University Press.
Barnett, E. (2016). *Building momentum from high school into college.* Boston, MA: Jobs for the Future.
Belfield, C., & Crosta, P. M. (2012). *Predicting success in college: The importance of placement tests and high school transcripts* (CCRC Working Paper No. 42). New York: Columbia University, Teachers College, Community College Research Center.
Boylan, H. R. (2002). *What works: Research-based practices in developmental education.* Boone, NC: Continuous Quality Improvement Network with the National Center for Developmental Education, Appalachian State University.

Bracco, K. R., Dadgar, M., Austin, K., Klarin, B., Broek, M., Finkelstein, N., ... & Bugler, D. (2014). *Exploring the use of multiple measures for placement into college-level courses: Seeking alternatives or improvements to the use of a single standardized test.* San Francisco, CA: WestEd.

Burdman, P. (2015). *Degrees of freedom: Probing math placement policies at California colleges and universities [Report 3 of a 3-part series].* Oakland, CA: Learning Works.

Byrd, K. L., & Macdonald, G. (2005). Defining college readiness from the inside out: First-generation college student perspectives. *Community College Review, 33*(1), 22–37.

Carnegie Math Pathways. (n.d.). Retrieved from https://www.carnegiefoundation.org/in-action/carnegie-math-pathways/.

Center for the Analysis of Postsecondary Readiness. (2014). *Research on alternative placement systems and student outcomes [Fact Sheet].* New York: Community College Research Center, Teachers College, Columbia University.

Cohen, A. M., Brawer, F. B., & Kisker, C. B. (2014). *The American community college* (6th ed.). San Francisco, CA: Jossey-Bass.

Colorado Community College System. (2009). *Remedial math tracking project.* Denver, CO: Community College of Denver.

Crisp, G., & Delgado, C. (2014). The impact of developmental education on community college persistence and vertical transfer. *Community College Review, 42*(2), 99–117.

CWI Assessment and Testing. (n.d.). Retrieved from http://cwidaho.cc/current-students/computer-skills-assessment-csa.

Dana Center Mathematics Pathways. (n.d.). Retrieved from http://www.utdanacenter.org/higher-education/dcmp/.

Duffy, M., Schott, A., Beaver, J. K., & Park, E. (2014). *Tracing the development of multiple measures for college placement across states and systems: Analysis of three state systems – Phase 1 report.* Philadelphia, PA: Research for Action.

Fields, R., & Parsad, B. (2012). *Tests and cut scores used for student placement in postsecondary education: Fall 2011.* Washington, DC: National Assessment Governing Board.

Fonte, R. (1997). Structured versus laissez-faire open access: Implementation of a proactive strategy. *New Directions for Community Colleges, 1997*(100), 43–52.

Gaertner, M. N., & Roberts, R. D. (2017). More than a test score: Defining and measuring personal qualities. In K. L. McClarty, K. D. Mattern, & M. N. Gaertner (Eds.), *Preparing students for college and careers: Theory, measurement, and educational practice.* New York: Routledge.

Gordon, R. J. (1999, January). *Using computer adaptive testing and multiple measures to ensure that students are placed in courses appropriate for their skills.* Paper presented at the North American Conference on the Learning Paradigm, San Diego, CA.

Hodara, M., Jaggars, S. S., & Karp, M. M. (2012). *Improving developmental education assessment and placement: Lessons from community colleges across the country* (CCRC Working Paper No. 51). New York: Columbia University, Teachers College, Community College Research Center.

Hu, S., Park, T., Woods, C., Richard, K., Tandberg, D., & Jones, T. B. (2016). *Probability of success: Evaluation of Florida's developmental education redesign based on cohorts of first-time-in-college students from 2009–10 to 2014–15.* Tallahassee: Florida State University, Center for Postsecondary Success.

Hughes, K. L., & Scott-Clayton, J. (2011). Assessing developmental assessment in community colleges. *Community College Review, 39*(4), 327–351.

Jencks, C. (1998). Racial bias in testing. In C. Jencks & M. Phillips (Eds.), *The black-white test score gap* (pp. 55–85). Washington, DC: Brookings Institution.

Karp, M. M. (2011). *Toward a new understanding of non-academic student support: Four mechanisms encouraging positive student outcomes in the community college* (CCRC Working Paper No. 28). New York: Columbia University, Teachers College, Community College Research Center.

Leahy, F. F., & Landel, C. (2017). Multiple mathematics pathways to college, careers, and beyond. In K. L. McClarty, K. D. Mattern, & M. N. Gaertner (Eds.), *Preparing students for college and careers: Theory, measurement, and educational practice.* New York: Routledge.

Lipnevich, A. A., MacCann, C., & Roberts, R. D. (2013). Assessing non-cognitive constructs in education: A review of traditional and innovative approaches. In D. H. Saklofske, C. R. Reynolds, & V. Schwean (Eds.), *Oxford handbook of psychological assessment of children and adolescents* (pp. 750–772). Cambridge, MA: Oxford University Press.

Lu, L. (1994). University transition: Major and minor stressors, personality characteristics and mental health. *Psychological Medicine, 24*(1), 81–87.

Mallinckrodt, B., & Sedlacek, W. E. (1987). Student retention and the use of campus facilities by race. *NASPA Journal, 24*(3), 28–32.

Mattern, K. D., & Gaertner, M. G. (2017). Mixed messages: When different assessments yield different results. In K. L. McClarty, K. D. Mattern, & M. N. Gaertner (Eds.), *Preparing students for college and careers: Theory, measurement, and educational practice.* New York: Routledge.

Mattern, K. D., Patterson, B. F., & Kobrin, J. L. (2012). *The validity of SAT scores in predicting first-year mathematics and English grades.* New York: College Board.

National Center for Public Policy and Higher Education & Southern Regional Education Board. (2010). *Beyond the rhetoric: Improving college readiness through coherent state policy.* Atlanta, GA: Southern Regional Education Board.

North Carolina Community College System. (2015). *NCCCS policy using high school transcript GPA and/ or standardized test scores for placement (Multiple measures for placement).* Retrieved from https:// www.southwesterncc.edu/sites/default/files/testing/Multiple%20Measures%20Revised%202015.pdf.

Ohio Department of Higher Education. (2016). *Uniform statewide standards for remediation-free status.* Retrieved from https://www.ohiohighered.org/sites/ohiohighered.org/files/uploads/college-readiness/ 2016_UNIFORM_STATEWIDE_REMEDIATION_FREE_STANDARDS.pdf.

RCC Computer Skills Placement (n.d.). Retrieved from https://richlandcollege.edu/test-center/ computer-skills-placement.

Reddy, A. A., & Harper, M. (2013). Mathematics placement at the University of Illinois. *PRIMUS: Problems, Resources, and Issues in Mathematics Undergraduate Studies, 23*(8), 683–702.

Rikoon, S., Liebtag, T., Olivera-Aguilar, M., Robbins, S., & Jackson, T. (2014). *A pilot study of holistic assessment and course placement in community college: Findings and recommendations* (ETS RM–14–10). Princeton, NJ: Educational Testing Service.

Robbins, S. B., Allen, J., Casillas, A., & Peterson, C. H. (2006). Unraveling the differential effects of motivational and skills, social, and self-management measures from traditional predictors of college outcomes. *Journal of Educational Psychology, 98*(3), 598–616.

Rodríguez, O., Bowden, B., Belfield, C., & Scott-Clayton, J. (2015). *Calculating the costs of remedial placement testing* (CCRC Analytics). New York: Columbia University, Teachers College, Community College Research Center.

Rounds, J. C., & Anderson, D. (1985). Placement in remedial college classes: Required vs. recommended. *Community College Review, 13*(1), 20–27.

RP Group. (2016). *Multiple measures high school variables model summary—Phase 2—Updated.* Retrieved from http://rpgroup.org/system/files/StateWideDecisionRules_3.31.16.pdf.

Sanchez, E., & Buddin, R. (2015). *How accurate are self-reported high school courses, course grades, and grade point average?* (WP-2015-03). Iowa City, IA: ACT.

Scott-Clayton, J. (2012). *Do high-stakes placement exams predict college success?* (CCRC Working Paper No. 41). New York: Columbia University, Teachers College, Community College Research Center.

Scott-Clayton, J., Crosta, P. M., & Belfield, C. R. (2012). *Improving the targeting of treatment: Evidence from college remediation* (NBER Working Paper No. 18457). Cambridge, MA: National Bureau of Economic Research.

Scott-Clayton, J., & Rodriguez, O. (2015). Development, discouragement, or diversion? New evidence on the effects of college remediation policy. *Education Finance and Policy, 10*(1), 4–45.

Venezia, A., Bracco, K. R., & Nodine, T. (2010). *One-shot deal? Students' perceptions of assessment and course placement in California's community colleges.* San Francisco, CA: WestEd.

Venezia, A., & Jaeger, L. (2013). Transitions from high school to college. *The Future of Children, 23*(1), 117–136.

Woods, J. E. (1985). *Status of testing practices at two-year postsecondary institutions.* Washington, DC: American Association of Community and Junior Colleges & American College Testing Program.

Zis, S., Boeke, M., & Ewell, P. (2010). *State policies on the assessment of student learning outcomes: Results of a fifty-state inventory.* Boulder, CO: National Center for Higher Education Management Systems.

8 Fairness Issues in the Assessment of College and Career Readiness[1]

Rebecca Zwick

Although it is generally agreed that today's high school graduates should be "college and career ready," controversies abound concerning the meaning of readiness and the best way of measuring it. What kinds of tasks should be used to assess students' readiness? Should personal qualities, in addition to academic skills, be measured? How do various groups differ in their opportunities to acquire the needed skills and characteristics? Each of these questions has fairness implications, especially if readiness indicators are to be used in screening individuals for college or for jobs. This chapter will consider these issues and their impact on various student groups.

As described in the earlier chapters of this book, definitions of college and career readiness (CCR) vary widely, as do the current methods for measuring readiness. In 2014, the College and Career Readiness and Success Center at American Institutes for Research provided a useful review of the definitions then in effect for 36 states and the District of Columbia (Mishkind, 2014). Of the 37 "states," 33 used a single definition for both college and career readiness. Twenty-one definitions listed "concrete knowledge, skills, and dispositions" that students must master in order to be considered ready for the postsecondary world (Mishkind, 2014, pp. 2–3). The categories of capabilities that were mentioned most often were academic content knowledge (19 states), critical thinking or problem solving (14), social and emotional learning, collaboration, or communication (14), grit, resilience, or perseverance (8), and citizenship or community involvement (8) (Mishkind, 2014). Among the college success criteria that have been proposed are exemption from remedial classes, grades in specific courses, first-year grade-point average, persistence, and graduation (Camara, 2013). Few criteria for career success have emerged, although satisfactory completion of career training programs is frequently mentioned (Camara, 2013; Mishkind, 2014).

There are two broad purposes for CCR assessment and analysis. One is to make inferences about groups, such as all students in Georgia, all 11th graders in the United States, or all African-American students in the Chicago area. Analyses of groups of students can be used to inform educational policy decisions about program development and resource allocation and to track progress over time. Findings of group-based analyses can help to determine what kinds of institutional supports should be offered to middle school, high school, and college students to improve readiness. To maximize accuracy, research on the readiness of student groups should be based on rich prediction models that include academic measures, demographic characteristics, students' personal qualities, and institutional factors. In their study of 8th-grade participants in the National Education Longitudinal Study of 1988 (NELS), Gaertner and McClarty (2015) used 140 variables in 6 categories to predict college readiness, which was defined as a composite of SAT score, ACT score, and high school grade-point average. Academic achievement variables explained the largest percentage of readiness variance (17%), followed by motivation (15%), behavior (14%), family circumstances (12%), school characteristics (7%), and social engagement (4%). Clearly, using academic variables alone would have resulted in a much weaker prediction model.

Different considerations apply, however, in the second major application of CCR analyses, which, as presently conceived, has as its purpose the classification of individual students as ready or not ready. In this situation, we must examine the consequences of identifying a student as ready or unready and meticulously evaluate the fairness of the measures and procedures used to make these designations. In this chapter, I focus on the application of CCR standards to individual students. In particular, I discuss fairness issues associated with test-based systems of making CCR determinations. CCR standards have been defined for the assessments developed by the Partnership for Assessment of Readiness for College and Careers (PARCC) and the Smarter Balanced Assessment Consortium, the two groups of states that developed tests as part of the Common Core State Standards effort. However, Achieve, Inc. reported that in selecting tests for evaluating CCR in the 2014–2015 school year, most states relied instead on the SAT or ACT (Achieve, 2016). Because of the prominence of these two tests and their associated benchmarks, I will devote much of my discussion to them. Also, I will focus primarily on college rather than career readiness, reflecting the substance of both the public conversation and the education literature.

ACT, Inc. describes the ACT benchmarks as follows:

> The ACT College Readiness Benchmarks are the minimum ACT® college readiness assessment scores required for students to have a high probability of success in credit-bearing college courses—English Composition, social sciences courses, College Algebra, or Biology... Students who meet a Benchmark on the ACT ... have approximately a 50 percent chance of earning a B or better and approximately a 75 percent chance of earning a C or better in the corresponding college course or courses.
>
> (ACT, 2013, pp. 1–2)

The benchmark on the ACT English test is associated with performance in English composition courses, the Reading test with social science courses, the Math test with college algebra courses, and the Science test with biology courses. In the ACT score reports, the students' scores on these four tests, which constitute the mandatory portion of the ACT, appear on bar displays along with the corresponding college-readiness benchmark. On a separate bar, the ACT composite score appears, along with an indication of the location of three "Progress Toward Career Readiness" levels, labeled bronze, silver, and gold. Evaluation of test-takers' career-readiness status is based on a linkage that has been established between the composite score on the ACT and ACT National Career Readiness Certificate (NCRC) level, a credential of workplace skills (ACT, 2016).

On the SAT, a single set of benchmarks, described as follows, is used for both college and career.

> The new college and career readiness benchmarks are based on actual student success in entry-level college courses. Benchmarks are set at the section level (Math, Evidence-Based Reading and Writing) ... The **SAT benchmark scores** represent a 75% likelihood of a student achieving at least a C grade in a first-semester, credit-bearing college course in a related subject.
>
> The **SAT Math benchmark** is the SAT Math section score associated with a 75% chance of earning at least a C in first-semester, credit-bearing, college-level courses in algebra, statistics, precalculus, or calculus.[2]
>
> The **SAT Evidence-Based Reading and Writing benchmark** is the SAT Evidence-Based Reading and Writing section score associated with a 75% chance of earning at least a C in first-semester, credit-bearing, college-level courses in history, literature, social science, or writing.
>
> (College Board, 2016a, p. 1, emphases in original)

On the score report, Math and Evidence-Based Reading and Writing scores appear along with the relevant benchmarks. Green, yellow, and red are used to indicate whether the student meets or exceeds the benchmark, is "approaching" the benchmark, or needs to "strengthen skills," respectively.

Ideally, the current focus on readiness of individual students would be a boon to education: in late middle school or early high school, students would receive highly accurate reports about their readiness level for various kinds of colleges and careers. The results would be used to determine the type and level of instructional support and counseling they would receive during the remainder of their schooling. By the end of high school, all students would emerge with clear and realistic plans for attaining their educational and occupational goals. But several factors stand in the way of this utopian outcome:

- Commonly used CCR benchmarks do not take high school coursework or grades into account, limiting predictive accuracy.
- Some factors may increase predictive accuracy but perpetuate disadvantage.
- "Not ready" designations may depress teacher and student expectations and, ultimately, student achievement.
- Members of groups that are underrepresented in higher education may be particularly disadvantaged by a "not ready" label.

I discuss each of these points in further detail in the following sections.

Commonly Used CCR Benchmarks Do Not Take High School Course Work or Grades into Account, Limiting Predictive Accuracy

In the ACT and SAT benchmark systems, admissions test scores alone are applied to produce CCR designations. This use of admissions tests differs sharply from their role in the admissions context itself, where test scores are considered along with high school record and other factors, as recommended by both ACT and the College Board. The accuracy of college-readiness judgments that are made in the absence of information about students' high school coursework and grades is, by definition, limited. This is most obviously true in the case of colleges that have specific requirements in terms of high school coursework.[3]

Not surprisingly, there is evidence that CCR conclusions based on coursework can be quite different from those based on test scores. For example, Achieve reports that in Hawaii, only 14% of those who graduated from high school in 2014 had completed a college- and career-ready curriculum, according to state standards. However, 45% of students met the ACT benchmark in English, 30% in Reading, and 29% in Math in 2014–2015. (The ACT participation rate was 93%.) In other states, the reverse pattern held. In Kentucky, for example, the percentages meeting the ACT benchmarks in English, Reading, and Math were 60, 39, and 32 (with a 100% participation rate), while 88% of the cohort graduating in 2014 was reported to have completed a CCR course of study (Achieve, 2016).

For the high school class of 2015, ACT reported that 28% of test-takers had exceeded all four of its benchmarks, and the College Board reported that 41.9% had met the CCR standard on the SAT (Adams, 2015).[4] In contrast, a recent study conducted by the Education Trust found that only 6% of the graduating class had taken a CCR curriculum and attained a GPA of at least 2.5 (Education Trust, 2016). The comparison between the admissions test results and the Education Trust study is not straightforward because the samples are very different. The ACT and SAT results are based on the students who took the tests in 2015—about 1.9 million for the ACT and 1.7 million for the SAT. These students took the test because they planned to apply to college or because they were administered the test as part of an accountability program. The Education Trust research was based on a nationally representative sample of high school graduates of 2013 from the High School Longitudinal Study. Nevertheless, the disparate results from Achieve, the Education Trust, ACT, and the College Board, combined with consistent research findings verifying the importance of high school GPA in predicting both college grades and college graduation, suggest that assessing individual students' CCR status in the absence of any information about high school record is a risky venture.

This practice is especially questionable when the tests that are used are not intended to measure mastery of high school coursework. The portions of the ACT and SAT on which the benchmarks are based do not tell us whether students can write an essay or a short story or whether they know anything about world history, physics, calculus, music, or art. And yet, these might be the very areas in which some test-takers hope to specialize in their schooling or in their work. How can their test scores tell us if they are ready?

ACT and SAT scores are also used, indirectly, to make predictions about younger students. In the case of the ACT, researchers initially determined readiness benchmarks for ACT Explore, taken in 8th or 9th grade, and for ACT Plan, taken in 10th grade, by linking these tests to the ACT (ACT, 2013). In 2014, ACT Explore and ACT Plan were replaced by ACT Aspire, a system of assessments taken by students from grade 3 through early high school. A concordance study based on an equipercentile approach was conducted to link Aspire scores (which range from 400 to 460 across all grades and subjects) to scores on the 1–36 scale used for the ACT. According to the ACT Aspire technical manual,

> the ACT Readiness Benchmarks for grades 8 through 10 were derived from the [resulting] concordance tables. The corresponding concorded ACT Aspire scale scores for the ACT College Readiness Benchmarks were taken as the ACT Readiness Benchmarks on the ACT Aspire scale. The grade 8 ACT Readiness Benchmarks [for English, math, reading and science] were then used to obtain the ACT Readiness Benchmarks for grades 3–7 using a z-score backmapping procedure[5] … Students at or above the benchmark are on target to meet the corresponding ACT College Readiness Benchmarks in grade 11.
>
> (ACT, 2016, p. 131)

The same ACT to Aspire concordance, along with backmapping, is also used to provide "Progress toward Career Readiness" designations for students in grades 8–10 who take the Aspire assessment. This career-readiness evaluation builds on the earlier linkage established between ACT NCRC and the ACT composite. (See Camara, Allen, & Moore, 2017, for further details on ACT's CCR benchmarks.)

Setting the benchmarks on the three versions of the PSAT—the PSAT/NMSQT, the PSAT 10, and the PSAT 8/9—was achieved by "observing how students grow from year to year and by adjusting the SAT benchmark using the average rate of progress" (College Board, 2016b, p. 5). The SAT benchmarks themselves depend on a linkage between tests, because the original benchmark research, which investigated the relationship between SAT scores and college grades, was based on the pre-2016 SAT. A concordance between the two SAT versions was used to determine the benchmarks on the current SAT scale (College Board, 2016a).

Because they depend on multiple linkages and, in some cases, are determined well in advance of high school completion, readiness designations for students who take ACT Aspire or the PSAT/NMSQT are likely to be substantially less accurate in their predictions of college performance than results based directly on ACT or SAT scores that students receive late in high school.

It is interesting that, according to an early College Board report on readiness, SAT benchmarks were not originally intended to be applied to individuals. According to Wyatt, Kobrin, Wiley, Camara, and Proestler (2011, p. 8),

> these benchmarks are intended to provide information on the college readiness of groups of students (e.g., aggregated by school, district, state, or nation). In considering the college readiness of individual students, many factors should be considered in addition to test scores. These may include high school GPA (HSGPA), completed course work, recommendations, and noncognitive factors.

Concerns about the accuracy of readiness estimates are amplified in the case of career readiness. Whereas there are decades of research evidence about the value of admissions test scores in predicting college grades, we know little about the degree to which these tests can predict performance in the workplace.

Some Factors May Increase Predictive Accuracy But Perpetuate Disadvantage

Although CCR systems that rely solely on test scores can be faulted for adopting a narrow definition of readiness, a single-minded focus on improving predictive accuracy would lead to unfortunate results. More specifically, factors that would improve the strength of prediction could perpetuate the disadvantages already experienced by members of some student groups. (See Zwick, 2017, Chapters 3 and 6 for related discussions.) Race and family income, for example, have consistently been found to be predictive of college grades and graduation rates, with White, Asian, and high-income students performing better than other groups (e.g., see Lauff, Ingels, & Christopher, 2013; Rothstein, 2004). If we were to combine these factors with a test score to determine readiness, the strength of prediction would improve. However, through no action of their own, Black, Latino, American Indian, and low-income students would have lower readiness scores than their White, Asian, and high-income counterparts who share the identical test score. Similar arguments apply to institutional factors, such as the ethnic composition or student-teacher ratio in the student's school.

It is not only demographic and institutional factors, which are clearly outside the student's control, that present troubling situations. Factors like grit and perseverance, used by some states in their readiness definitions, may be predictive of college and work performance, but using such characteristics in CCR evaluations could have unintended consequences. Even grit's greatest promoter, Angela Duckworth, concedes that measuring personal qualities of this kind is complex and that attempting to do so to make educational decisions is extremely challenging. Efforts to use student or teacher questionnaires for measuring these so-called noncognitive factors can be affected by interpretation errors, widely varying frames of reference, and deliberate distortions. Performance tasks constructed to measure these personal qualities are likely to be expensive and may not generalize well to real-life situations (Duckworth & Yeager, 2015).

In addition, it is not clear that the personal qualities of most interest are malleable. In an extensive review of the current state of knowledge on noncognitive factors, Farrington et al. (2012) noted that

> much of the recent attention to noncognitive factors focuses on the idea of developing students' 'grit' or perseverance in challenging work. However, despite the intuitive appeal of this idea, there is little evidence that working directly on changing students' grit or perseverance would be an effective lever for improving their academic performance.

(pp. 6–7)

Cementing this point, the authors note elsewhere that "to date there is little conclusive research showing grit to be a malleable factor" (p. 24).

If these qualities are more appropriately considered dispositions rather than behaviors, we need to consider the implications of labeling students as unready for college because they have "the wrong personality." Critics have also raised the concern that the current emphasis on grit and similar qualities blames victims of poverty for failing to overcome the harsh environments they have experienced (Zernike, 2016). Put differently, it may be much easier to persevere in some milieus than in others.

Further compounding this situation, research described in the following sections suggests that lower readiness scores could themselves dampen achievement and that groups that are underrepresented in higher education are the least likely to obtain the support they need to improve their readiness. In short, maximizing prediction may mean perpetuating disadvantage, especially in the absence of good support systems.

"Not Ready" Designations May Depress Teacher and Student Expectations and, Ultimately, Student Achievement

Some policymakers and researchers have suggested that CCR indicators could be used as an early warning system to determine if students in lower grades "are 'on track' to be CCR by the end of high school" (see Camara, 2013, p. 16; Gaertner & McClarty, 2015). If this could be done reliably, and if early identification of problems led to an increase in support, this type of warning system might have some advantages. But the literature on student tracking holds lessons on the possible dangers of this type of classification: a designation of "not ready," whether well-founded or not, may lead to reduced expectations and correspondingly reduced outcomes, rather than improved support.

In their study of curriculum tracking, based on NELS data, Kelly and Carbonaro (2012) focused on high school students who were simultaneously in more than one track. For example, a student might be in the "regular" track in math and the "academic" track in English. The researchers then used within-student models to examine whether teachers' college expectations for these students depended on the track to which the students were assigned, net of other factors. They analyzed differences in teacher expectations for the same student, after adjusting for teacher and student background factors and student behavior and academic performance. The researchers concluded that teacher expectations were heavily based on track location *per se*. Students in the regular track were judged to be much less likely to go to college than those in the academic and honors/advanced tracks, after adjusting for other factors. The researchers noted that labeling students as low performing can reduce incentives for future achievement. These students may instead become "less ... engaged in school in an effort to preserve a positive sense of self-worth" (p. 273).

Karlson (2015) studied the impact of track placement on students' educational expectations of themselves and on their subsequent achievement. Like Kelly and Carbonaro (2012), Karlson used data from NELS, focusing on the track placement of participants when they were in 8th and 10th grades. Students' educational expectations were measured in terms of the years of schooling they expected to acquire, based on their questionnaire responses. Using a differences-in-differences model, Karlson found greater changes in expectations among students whose tracking situation had changed between 8th and 10th grade. Moving to a higher track was associated with a substantial increase in expectations, after taking account of other factors. He concluded that "adolescents view track placement as a signal about their academic abilities" and modify their expectations in response (p. 115). Karlson further speculated that tracking produces self-fulfilling prophecies: "Labeled a high-track or low-track student, an adolescent is likely to change goal orientation, in turn possibly leading to behavioral changes that will tend to conform to these labels." Thus, he argues, tracking is likely to perpetuate existing differences in achievement. In addition, "because track placement correlates with socioeconomic background, tracking in high schools is likely to reinforce preexisting socioeconomic inequalities in educational expectations and consequent educational attainment" (p. 136).

Findings like these raise the possibility that labeling students as not ready for college may serve to reduce their own educational expectations, as well as those of their teachers, and ultimately lead to reduced achievement. This is of particular concern for two reasons. First, especially for younger students, the accuracy of any CCR designation is questionable. Second, a "not ready" designation may not lead to an increase in support. Related findings are described in the following section.

Members of Groups That Are Underrepresented in Higher Education May Be Particularly Disadvantaged by a "Not Ready" Label

How likely is it that students who are, in fact, unready for college or career will receive the support they require? Will these students find the academic counseling and the course offerings they need to remedy the situation? According to a survey of 165,000 US high school students conducted between 2010 and 2015 by the nonprofit group YouthTruth, "students are by and large not taking advantage of support services to prepare them for future goals" (YouthTruth, n.d., p. 4). While 87% of high schoolers state they wanted to go to college, only 60% believe they have the skills and knowledge needed for college-level classes, and only 46% believe their school helped them identify realistic career possibilities. Perhaps this is not surprising, given the finding by the 2013–2014 Civil Rights Data Collection (CRDC), a survey of all public schools in the United States, that 21% of high schools nationwide do not have access to any school counselors (US Department of Education, 2016). The CRDC also reveals the degree to which academic preparation opportunities vary across student groups. For example, 33% of schools with high Black and Latino enrollment offer calculus, compared to 56% of schools with low Black and Latino enrollment. Schools with high Black and Latino enrollment are also less likely to offer physics, chemistry, and Algebra II. In schools where these courses are offered, enrollment rates vary across groups. This is particularly true of calculus, in which Black and Latino students, as well as students with disabilities and English learners, tend to be substantially underrepresented (US Department of Education, 2016). The CRDC also found that Black, Latino, and American Indian or Alaska Native students are more likely than White or Asian students to attend schools with substantial percentages of teachers who are in their first year of teaching.

It would be a grim scenario indeed if students deemed unready were disadvantaged through lowered expectations and also lacked the opportunity to improve their readiness. Research suggests that the student groups that are at risk for this outcome are those that are already underrepresented in selective postsecondary institutions.

Implications for Policy, Practice, and Research

Making sure that high school graduates are prepared for college or for the workplace is a worthwhile educational goal, and research that explores the current state of readiness and the best ways to improve it is a key component of this effort. The practice of labeling individual students as ready or unready, however, can be problematic, particularly if this is done on the basis of test scores alone.

In other contexts, educators and test-makers have cautioned against the overinterpretation of test scores, pointing out the inevitable presence of measurement error and the importance of using multiple measures to assess students' capabilities. At present, though, scores on tests, including the ACT and SAT, as well as the PARCC and Smarter Balanced assessments, provide for the assignment of readiness labels to students without consideration of their high school records. This practice reflects a severely limited perspective on college readiness, particularly in the case of tests that are not designed to assess curriculum mastery.

A further problem is that the variability in requisite skills across the nation's many post-secondary institutions and programs of study is not taken into account. Can the same math benchmark apply to both a student who wants to major in physics at MIT and one who plans to complete a bookkeeping degree at a community college? Can the same language benchmark apply to a student who seeks a two-year degree in business communication as well as one who hopes to study comparative literature at Harvard? Applying the same readiness standards across the vast array of possible careers is even more questionable.

And yet, the information imparted by a readiness designation does not distinguish among academic programs or jobs. A student who fails to exceed a readiness benchmark is seemingly being labeled as unready for any college or any post-high-school occupation. And if CCR designations are taken seriously by students, parents, and educators, they could have a substantial impact on students' educational futures. From that perspective, applying readiness labels based on a single test score to individual test-takers may be inconsistent with Standard 12.10 of the *Standards for Educational and Psychological Testing*, which says that "in educational settings, a decision or characterization that will have a major impact on a student should take into consideration not just scores from a single test but other relevant information" (American Educational Research Association, American Psychological Association, & National Council on Measurement in Education, 2014, p. 198).

The precision of readiness designations is further compromised by dichotomization, which has an insidious effect. While reducing the accuracy of prediction by discarding information, dichotomization paradoxically conveys an increased sense of certainty: the message is that a "college-ready" student is qualitatively different from an "unready" one, even though their scores may differ by a psychometrically negligible amount. Imposition of a largely arbitrary benchmark has the effect of converting a test score to a student label, which is likely to be regarded as much more definitive than it is. Even if information on the standard error of measurement at the cut point, along with data on decision consistency, is available, educators, parents, and students are unlikely to grasp the implications.

Broadening the models used to determine the readiness of individual students by including demographic or institutional factors presents difficulties as well, given that these factors are not under the students' control and will lead to more pessimistic designations for students from lower-scoring schools, ethnic groups, or income brackets than for their academically equivalent counterparts from higher-scoring schools and groups. Incorporating noncognitive variables can have pitfalls too, given the measurement challenges involved and the fact that these qualities may not, in fact, be malleable.

The literature on student tracking reveals the difficulties that student labeling can initiate, possibly leading to a downward spiral in educational expectations and achievement. Compounding the problem, research shows that groups that are underrepresented in selective colleges and universities—Black, Latino, American Indian, and Alaska Native students, as well as students with disabilities and English learners—are least likely to get the resources they need to improve their readiness in high school.

It is important to recognize that improving readiness for high school students does not require individual labels. Information about the readiness of groups, such as schools or districts, could be used to target remediation. Research on the readiness of groups of students could rely on matrix sampling of anonymous students, avoiding the necessity of testing each student. For these group-based assessments, richer prediction models could be used.

In any case, previous research has already told us a great deal about the kinds of questions that need to be addressed as part of any effort to improve readiness: Do students have the information they need about college life? This can be a particular issue with students who are the first in their family to apply to college. Do they need information about possible careers and how to pursue them? Do they have access to high-quality instruction and materials? Do they need tutoring or counseling to succeed? Do they need information about how to apply for admissions and financial aid? Are students registering for the courses they will need to be ready to embark on a college degree or to pursue their desired occupation? Do they know that to even be considered for college admission, they may need to complete a set of required courses? Past research conducted at the University of California showed that the primary reason for ineligibility for UC admission was failure to complete the required high school coursework (see Zwick, 1999).

Any individual characterizations of students' readiness status should include consideration of their high school records. The impact of including any nonacademic factors in a readiness assessment should be carefully evaluated. Dichotomization of readiness conclusions should be avoided (see Maruyama, 2012), and comprehensible cautions should be attached to any readiness scores. Finally, sufficient resources must be devoted to student support. In particular, the availability of college preparatory courses, tutoring, and academic counseling must be increased. Above all, it is important to dispel the notion that college readiness status is deterministic or static. Even if all the measurement and prediction challenges could be overcome, any such designation would still represent only a snapshot in time.

Notes

1 I am grateful to Brent Bridgeman, Neil Dorans, Shelby Haberman, Michael Kane, and the three volume editors for their perceptive reviews of this chapter. The opinions I have expressed in this chapter are my own and not necessarily those of Educational Testing Service.
2 As a reviewer pointed out, actual benchmarks would presumably differ across the courses considered. For example, the benchmark corresponding to a 75% probability of obtaining at least a C in calculus would be higher than the benchmark for algebra. Similar considerations apply to the Reading and Writing benchmarks.
3 The College Board developed an academic rigor index (ARI) for use in assessing college readiness. Although the ARI was found to be predictive of college enrollment (Wyatt, Wiley, Camara, & Proestler, 2011), subsequent research found that, in predicting first-year college GPA, "incremental validity was not increased by adding the ARI to HSGPA and SAT scores" (Mattern & Wyatt, 2012).
4 The SAT test, reporting scale, and benchmarks have changed since 2015.
5 Let z represent the difference between the grade 8 benchmark and the grade 8 mean in within-grade standard deviation units. The benchmarks for grades 3–7 were set so that they, too, differed from their respective grade-level means by z within-grade standard deviation units. A different procedure was used for the writing scale and for benchmarks that were set for STEM and English Language Arts. In addition to indicating whether students have reached a benchmark, results for grades 3–10 are also reported in terms of four readiness levels (ACT, 2016).

References

Achieve. (2016, March). *The college and career readiness of U.S. high school graduates.* Retrieved from http://www.achieve.org/files/CCRHSGrads-March2016.pdf.
ACT. (2013, September). *What are the ACT College Readiness Benchmarks?* (ACT Information Brief). Retrieved from http://www.act.org/content/dam/act/unsecured/documents/benchmarks.pdf.
ACT. (2016). *Summative technical manual* (2016 Version 1). Retrieved from https://www.discoveractaspire.org/act-aspire-technical-manual/.
Adams, C. J. (2015, September 9). 2015 SAT, ACT scores suggest many students aren't college-ready. *Education Week.* Retrieved from http://www.edweek.org/ew/articles/2015/09/09/2015-sat-act-scores-suggest-many-students.html.
American Educational Research Association, American Psychological Association, & National Council on Measurement in Education. (2014). *Standards for educational and psychological testing.* Washington, DC: American Educational Research Association.
Camara, W. (2013). Defining and measuring college and career readiness: A validation framework. *Educational Measurement: Issues and Practice, 32,* 16–27.

Camara, W., Allen, J., & Moore, J. (2017). Empirically-based college-and career-readiness cut scores and performance levels. In K. L. McClarty, K. D. Mattern, & M. N. Gaertner (Eds.), *Preparing students for college and careers: Theory, measurement, and educational practice*. New York: Routledge.

College Board. (2016a). *The college and career readiness benchmarks for the SAT suite of assessments.* (College Board K-12 educator brief). Retrieved from https://collegereadiness.collegeboard.org/pdf/educator-benchmark-brief.pdf.

College Board. (2016b). *PSAT/NMSQT: Understanding scores 2015.* (College Board brief, updated May 2016). Retrieved from https://collegereadiness.collegeboard.org/pdf/2015-psat-nmsqt-understanding-scores.pdf.

Duckworth, A. L., & Yeager, D. S. (2015). Measurement matters: Assessing personal qualities other than cognitive ability for educational purposes. *Educational Researcher, 44*, 237–251.

Education Trust. (2016, April). *Meandering toward graduation: Transcript outcomes of high school graduates.* Retrieved from https://edtrust.org/wp-content/uploads/2014/09/MeanderingTowardGraduation_EdTrust_April2016.pdf.

Farrington, C. A., Roderick, M., Allensworth, E., Nagaoka, J., Keyes, T. S., Johnson, D. W., & Beechum, N. O. (2012). *Teaching adolescents to become learners. The role of noncognitive factors in shaping school performance: A critical literature review.* Chicago, IL: University of Chicago Consortium on Chicago School Research.

Gaertner, M. N., & McClarty, K. L. (2015). Performance, perseverance, and the full picture of college readiness. *Educational Measurement: Issues and Practice, 34*, 20–33.

Karlson, K. B. (2015). Expectations on track? High school tracking and adolescent educational expectations. *Social Forces, 94*, 115–141.

Kelly, S., & Carbonaro, W. (2012). Curriculum tracking and teacher expectations: Evidence from discrepant course taking models. *Social Psychology of Education, 15*, 271–294.

Lauff, E., Ingels, S. J., & Christopher, E. (2013). *Education Longitudinal Study of 2002 (ELS:2002): A first look at 2002 high school sophomores 10 years later* (NCES 2014–363). U.S. Department of Education. Washington, DC: National Center for Education Statistics. Retrieved from http://nces.ed.gov/pubsearch.

Maruyama, G. (2012). Assessing college readiness: Should we be satisfied with ACT or other threshold scores? *Educational Researcher, 41*, 252–261.

Mattern, K. D., & Wyatt, J. N. (2012). *The validity of the academic rigor index (ARI) for predicting FYGPA.* (College Board Info to Go 2012-05). Retrieved from https://research.collegeboard.org/publications/validity-academic-rigor-index-ari-predicting-fygpa.

Mishkind, A. (2014). *Overview: State definitions of college and career readiness.* Washington, DC: American Institutes for Research.

Rothstein, J. M. (2004). College performance and the SAT. *Journal of Econometrics, 121*, 297–317.

U.S. Department of Education (2016). *2013–14 Civil Rights Data Collection: A first look.* (Office for Civil Rights Report). Retrieved from http://www2.ed.gov/about/offices/list/ocr/docs/2013-14-first-look.pdf.

Wyatt, J., Kobrin, J., Wiley, A., Camara, W. J., & Proestler, N. (2011). *SAT benchmarks: Development of a college readiness benchmark and its relationship to secondary and postsecondary school performance.* (Research Report 2011-5). New York: College Board.

Wyatt, J. N., Wiley, A., Camara, W. J., & Proestler, N. (2011). *The development of an index of academic rigor for college readiness.* (College Board Info to Go 2011-11). Retrieved from https://research.collegeboard.org/taxonomy/term/239.

YouthTruth (n.d.). *Most high schoolers feel unprepared for college and careers.* Retrieved from http://www.youthtruthsurvey.org/wp-content/uploads/2016/01/YouthTruth-Learning-From-Student-Voice-College-and-Career-Readiness-2016.pdf.

Zernike, K. (2016, February 29). Testing for joy and grit? Schools nationwide push to measure students' emotional skills. *New York Times.* Retrieved from http://www.nytimes.com/2016/03/01/us/testing-for-joy-and-grit-schools-nationwide-push-to-measure-students-emotional-skills.html?_r=0.

Zwick, R. (1999, December). Eliminating standardized tests in college admissions: The new affirmative action? *Phi Delta Kappan*, 320–324.

Zwick, R. (2017). *Who gets in? Strategies for fair and effective college admissions.* Cambridge, MA: Harvard University Press.

9 Mixed Messages

When Different Assessments Yield Different Results

Krista D. Mattern and Matthew N. Gaertner

In 1983, *A Nation at Risk* shined a bright light on the US educational system, highlighting systemic deficiencies with existing practices and policies (Gardner, Larsen, Baker, Campbell, & Crosby, 1983). The report argued that the educational system was failing to adequately prepare students for college or a career because so many students were passing through the K–12 system only to be placed in remedial coursework once in college. In short, a high school diploma did not signal proficiency in any useful sense, as many high school graduates lacked the knowledge and skills necessary to perform college-level work. In response, the US government has supported various educational reforms over the last 34 years, with an eye toward standards-based education. President Clinton's reauthorization of the Elementary and Secondary Education Act (ESEA) and President George W. Bush's introduction of No Child Left Behind (NCLB) were part of this movement. The Common Core State Standards (CCSS) Initiative and the Every Student Succeeds Act (ESSA) represent current thinking on standards-based educational reform.

The US is inarguably interested in improving students' college and career readiness and has devoted significant resources to this cause. For example, for fiscal year 2016, the US Department of Education budget provided $70.7 billion in discretionary funding, representing a 5.4% increase from 2015 (US Department of Education, 2016). Yet, despite a demonstrated enthusiasm for

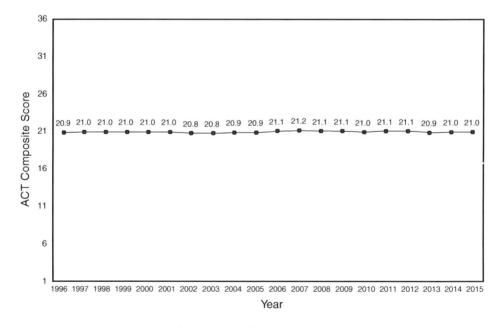

Figure 9.1 Average ACT Composite for the National Graduating Cohort from 1996 to 2015

improving student progress, the United States appears to have hit an educational plateau. Over the last 20 years, the average ACT composite score has remained virtually unchanged, fluctuating minimally from a low of 20.8 to a high of 21.2 (Figure 9.1). Similar patterns are evident in other national measures of student learning, such as the SAT and NAEP (College Board, 2015; US Department of Education, 2015). We contend that the lack of progress is, in part, a function of variations across governing bodies in their implementation of educational reform.

All states should adopt rigorous standards that put students on a path toward college and career readiness. In fact, that was the CCSS Initiative's fundamental goal. The execution, however, has been inconsistent. States vary widely in their definitions of college and career readiness, as highlighted by sizable differences between individual states' test results and national indicators of college and career readiness. Even the states that have adopted the CCSS maintain discretion to augment the Standards in alignment with local curriculum. These varying definitions of college and career readiness hamper US efforts to evaluate and improve educational attainment and send mixed messages to learners, their parents, their educators, and the general public about students' level of academic preparedness.

Proliferation of Tests and Accountability Models: How Many Ways Are Students Assessed to Evaluate Their Level of Mastery?

Students receive feedback on their level of academic preparation through a variety of separate channels. Though many forms of feedback ostensibly provide information on a student's standing in a particular content area, results often provide conflicting information. Let's consider mathematics. One source of information about students' levels of mathematics knowledge is their mathematics course grades. Even though this seems like a reliable source of information, the courses students take, particularly in high school, vary considerably with respect to content and academic rigor. For example, only 6% of the 2015 ACT-tested graduating class reported taking calculus in high school (ACT, 2015). Even among courses with the same titles, some courses are specified as honors, advanced, and dual enrollment, and therefore, should vary in their level of rigor and breadth of material covered—meaning that a B in Algebra II may not mean the same level of mathematics knowledge as a B in an honors version of an Algebra II class. Advanced Placement (AP) is another illustrative example; students receive grades in their AP courses based on their teacher's grading system, as well as a score on the standardized end-of-course assessment. It is reasonable to suspect that even within individual courses, students may receive conflicting information about their level of academic mastery.

Owing to variations in grading policies and class compositions, it is difficult to draw inferences from comparisons of mathematics GPAs across students, courses, and schools. Confusion mounts when alternate sources of information such as state assessments, NAEP, SAT/ACT, Partnership for Assessment of Readiness for College and Careers (PARCC), Smarter Balanced Assessment Consortium (SBAC), and placement tests are introduced. As the number of sources of information increases, the likelihood that conflicting information will be provided increases, especially when the assessments vary on important dimensions such as:

- constructs assessed,
- intended uses,
- cut scores and performance levels,
- populations, and
- consequences.

We elaborate on each of these issues in the following.

Constructs Assessed

Valid comparison across multiple measures requires construct consistency. Constructs that are measured in the classroom should be similar to those assessed on standardized tests. However, a comparison of the feedback students receive from an ACT score report versus high school grades highlights the potential for conflicting information. Students have flexibility in the courses they take in high school, thereby varying the degree of construct overlap between grades and test scores across students.[1] Moreover, it is generally accepted that grades are not pure measures of academic proficiency but also reflect other personal characteristics, such as working hard, showing up for class, and completing homework (Kautz, Heckman, Diris, ter Weel, & Borghans, 2014). Research examining discrepant high school grade point average (HSGPA) and standardized admission test score performance supports this proposition (Mattern, Shaw, & Kobrin, 2011).

Continuing with the example of assessing mathematics proficiency, we can compare students' reported high school math grades and their ACT mathematics test scores. Even though the two measures are highly correlated, ACT mathematics scores vary considerably for students with the same math course grades. Likewise, students who earn similar ACT mathematics scores may vary considerably in terms of their math grades. Table 9.1 highlights this variability, presenting the distribution of math grades by ACT Mathematics scores.[2] While the overall trend indicates higher ACT mathematics test scores are generally associated with higher math grades in high school, it is also clear that a substantial proportion of students earn high grades but low ACT scores and vice versa. Interestingly, among students with low math grades (<2.00), there is less variability in the distribution of test scores: 95% of those students do not meet the ACT College-Readiness Benchmark in mathematics (a score of 22 or better; Allen, 2013). That is, for this subgroup, both measures provide a consistent message: the student is not academically prepared in mathematics.

The variance in test scores among students with a high math grades is much larger. For example, among students who have near perfect math grades (3.9 or higher), 23% do not meet the ACT College-Readiness Benchmark. That is, many students who are receiving positive feedback (high grades) in math courses will receive quite another message from standardized tests.

Researchers and psychometricians are generally attuned to the many differences (in both assessment methods and construct representation) between standardized test scores and grades. However, do students perceive these differences and use that information to contextualize the feedback they receive? Moreover, which feedback will a student attend to and trust if different sources provide conflicting information? How does this trust (or distrust) affect the credibility of various academic performance measures and thereby public confidence in those measures?

Table 9.1 Distribution of High School Mathematics GPAs and ACT Mathematics Scores for 2015 ACT-Tested Graduating Cohort

High School Math Grades	ACT Mathematics								
	1–12	*13–15*	*16–18*	*19–21*	*22–24*	*25–27*	*28–30*	*31–33*	*34–36*
0.0–1.9	2.7	43.1	41.7	7.7	3.6	1	0.1	0	0
2.0–2.3	1.8	29.9	44.7	12.7	7.7	2.8	0.5	0.1	0
2.4–2.7	1.1	20.4	42.9	16.5	12.2	5.4	1.2	0.2	0
2.8–3.1	0.7	14.2	36	18.4	16.9	10.1	2.8	0.6	0.2
3.2–3.4	0.3	6.2	25.3	18.8	22.2	17.8	6.8	1.9	0.7
3.5–3.8	0.2	4.1	17.7	15.5	22	22.9	11.5	4.2	1.9
3.9+	0.2	2.9	9.9	9.9	17.4	24.9	18.3	9.3	7.3

* Rows sum to 100%.
N = 1,604,694.

Intended Uses

Another factor to consider when comparing results across assessments is the intended uses of those assessments. In particular, the intended uses of a given test should dictate that test's development process. Tests that are designed for different uses (e.g., college admissions, placement, or accountability) will undoubtedly vary in content and statistical specifications. It may not be appropriate to compare results across different assessments developed for different purposes. However, even when limiting comparisons to tests that claim to assess college and career readiness and that are used for accountability purposes, construct-coverage differences persist. Although most assessments of college and career readiness focus on English language arts (ELA) and math, some cover additional domains. For example, ACT has a science test along with English, reading, and mathematics tests, whereas the most recent SAT includes only two sections: (1) evidenced-based reading and writing and (2) math. Moreover, the original intent of the ACT and SAT was for use in college admissions. Both assessments were therefore developed to predict college outcomes. State assessments, on the other hand, have been developed historically to cover state-specific standards and gauge what students know and are able to do relative to those standards. Although the SAT and ACT were developed to support college admissions decisions, multiple states have adopted these assessments for accountability purposes. It is unclear whether the ACT and SAT are appropriate for the accountability uses for which they are being deployed. This issue demands careful, state-by-state analysis.

The likelihood of conflicting information naturally increases when states include measures focused on a broader set of constructs (e.g., both cognitive and noncognitive). This practice will likely become more pervasive under ESSA, which encourages the adoption and use of "multiple measures." Specifically, in addition to academic indicators, states are required to include a nonacademic indicator such as school climate or student engagement under ESSA (Vitale, 2016). States are also given much more latitude in how they design their accountability systems, which includes the choice of which nonacademic measure to implement. If different criteria are being used to classify students as college and career ready across states, then the results from different assessment systems will not support meaningful comparisons.

Cut Scores and Performance Levels

Even among tests with similar content and statistical specifications—in fact, even on the same test—using different methods to set cut scores and performance levels will introduce mixed messages (Camara, 2013; Camara & Quenemoen, 2012). States now have a variety of viable standard-setting methods from which to choose. Historically, states have relied on content-based standard-setting approaches to set cut scores and performance levels for their accountability tests. This class of methodologies relies on the expertise of subject-matter experts (SMEs). For college admissions tests, a different approach has been adopted. The originating purpose of the SAT and ACT was to determine whether a student is likely to succeed in college, so these tests' developers use empirical methods to set college-readiness thresholds based solely on the statistical relationship between test scores and first-year grades, with no input from SMEs (Allen, 2013; Wyatt, Kobrin, Wiley, Camara, & Proestler, 2011). Increased focus on readiness (rather than status) in K–12 accountability systems has generated yet another approach—evidence-based standard setting—where SMEs are presented with criterion-related data, yet still provide their expert judgment to set cut scores (McClarty, Way, Porter, Beimers, & Miles, 2013).

Even if two states were to adopt the same basic methodology to set their own cut scores, differences would still probably arise. For the purely empirical methods, decisions need to be made prior to running any statistical models, and human judgment will influence those decisions.

Specifically, if a state is interested in identifying the cut score associated with a certain level of success, it first needs to define what it means by success. In particular, the state will need to specify and operationalize an outcome. If that outcome is college success, it may be measured via course grades, first-year grade point average (FYGPA), graduation, or some other metric. Once the outcome is determined, the "success" threshold must be specified. For example, if success is defined in terms of course grades, should students be considered successful if they earn a B or higher, C or higher, or some other grade? Finally, states will need to predefine the probability that proficient students will achieve the desired outcome. For example, should the cut score be based on a 50% probability that a student will earn at least a C in a corresponding college course? Do we want to be more confident, say 65%? (See Camara, Allen, & Moore, 2017, for a more detailed description of the empirical standard-setting method.)

Clearly, human judgment will influence cut scores, even for fully empirical standard-setting methods. The ACT and SAT College-Readiness Benchmarks provide a useful example. The SAT benchmark was derived based on estimating the SAT composite score associated with a 65% probability of earning an FYGPA of at least 2.67 (i.e., a B-). ACT instead developed subject-specific cut scores based on a 50% probability of earning a B or higher in the first-year college course in the same content area.[3] In sum, these two assessment programs both set empirically derived cut scores, but made quite different decisions along the way. Their benchmarks target different outcomes (FYGPA versus grades in corresponding college courses), success thresholds (B- versus B), and probabilities (65% versus 50%).

Populations

Different students take different tests, and different examinee groups are not randomly equivalent. Thus, examinee populations are another source of variability that can confound cross-test comparisons (Achieve, 2015; Mattern & Lacina, 2014). If examinees are self-selected or state results do not generalize to the larger population of interest, comparisons should be heavily qualified, if they are made at all. For example, state assessments and NAEP were developed to gauge educational progress for all students within a state. National tests like the SAT and ACT were traditionally taken by self-selected groups of college-bound students who were usually better prepared than the average student.

Though many states are administering the ACT or SAT to all high school juniors, self-selection still confounds statewide generalizations in most states. To wit, research suggests a negative relationship between ACT/SAT participation rate and average ACT/SAT test scores (Clark, Rothstein, & Schanzenbach, 2009). Specifically, and intuitively, states that test a larger percentage of students tend to have lower average SAT or ACT scores. SAT- or ACT-based comparisons across states are therefore not appropriate, yet they are still made on a regular basis. Furthermore, the "opt-out" phenomenon is not random across the academic performance distribution, and it therefore diminishes the generalizability of statewide assessment results to the statewide populations (Croft, 2015).

Consequences

Finally, one should consider the consequences associated with an assessment and whether it is appropriate to compare assessment results when the assessments in question have different stakes attached. College- and career-readiness tests' consequences can run the gamut from high-stakes (admissions decisions based on admission tests) to low- or no-stakes (national trends derived from NAEP). Whether students are equivalently motivated to perform well on low-stakes and high-stakes tests is an important question for researchers, practitioners, and policymakers. In consequence, there is a growing body of literature examining the impact of motivation on test performance in the context of low-stakes assessments. For example, in an experiment examining the effect of monetary incentives on 12th-grade NEAP reading scores, researchers found that incentivizing students to try harder by paying them for right answers significantly improved their performance (Braun, Kirsch, & Yamamoto, 2011). Results were similar for a low-stakes assessment used to track learning outcomes in higher education (Liu, Bridgeman, & Adler, 2012); students who were randomly assigned to personally motivating conditions had higher scores than their peers in the control condition. The findings suggest that motivation can be heightened for low-stakes tests by framing the purpose and use of such assessments. A note of caution is warranted: motivational interventions become another factor that can compromise cross-state comparisons. If there is variability in the extent to which states attempt to manipulate motivation and how effectively they do so, comparisons across states may be biased.

Multiple Sources of Bias

Comparing students' academic progress across states and time becomes more challenging when the assessments in question differ on two or more of the factors listed before. In these cases, identifying the source of the discrepancy is particularly difficult. In a recent report, Mattern and Lacina (2014) illustrate this issue by comparing three different sources of assessment data: ACT, NAEP, and state assessments. State assessment and NAEP results are intended to be representative of all students within a state, whereas ACT results are based on the subsample of students who choose to take the ACT. The percentage of students taking the ACT varies considerably across states; in some states, the percentage is small (<20%), whereas others test the majority of students (>90%). To test whether differences in results across these three assessment programs is due to population differences or some other source, Mattern and Lacina examined the degree to which NAEP, state assessment, and ACT results converged as ACT participation rates increased. If differences were solely a function of differences in tested populations, we would expect that ACT results would converge with NAEP and state assessment results for states where the ACT participation rate is high.

The authors found that the 2013 NAEP 8th-grade proficiency rates in mathematics were similar to the percentage of students who met the ACT mathematics benchmark in 2014 for states with high ACT participation rates (Figure 9.2).[4] For states that administered the ACT statewide, the difference in percentages of students considered ready in mathematics ranged from −4 to 6 percentage points, with a mean difference of 1 percentage point. For states with low ACT participation rates, ACT results suggest that a larger percentage of students are ready in mathematics as compared to NAEP results, supporting the self-selection bias hypothesis. In sum, the results indicate that the performance levels for NAEP and ACT are similar and that divergences appear to be a function of differences in populations.

A comparison of ACT results to 8th-grade state assessment results leads to a different conclusion. As shown in Figure 9.3, compared to the ACT results, state assessment results tend to suggest a much higher percentage of students are proficient in mathematics (this is indicated by negative values on the *y*-axis). Differences between ACT- and state-assessment-based results grow more stark (i.e., negative values are more common) as ACT participation rates increase. On average, ACT mathematics readiness rates were 12 percentage points lower than state results, with differences ranging from −46 to +47 percentage points. Even among states where there is ACT-census testing, we see much more variability in the ACT-versus-state assessment comparisons than in the ACT-versus-NAEP comparison. For example, state test results for Mississippi, where ACT is administered statewide, indicated that 67% of their 2013 8th grades were proficient in mathematics. Only 21% of the 2014 ACT-tested graduating cohort met the ACT mathematics benchmark. These results echo an earlier report by Achieve (2015), which noted that more than half of states reported proficient rates 30 percentage points higher on their state assessments as compared to their NAEP results. Put simply, cut scores matter. Even when assessment results are based on the same student population and the assessments in question measure a similar construct, results can still diverge as a function of proficiency thresholds.

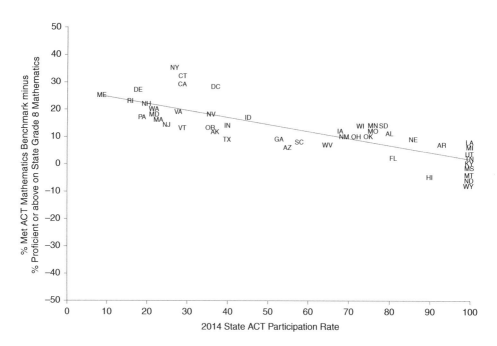

Figure 9.2 Consistency between 2014 ACT and 2013 NAEP Mathematics Performance by ACT Participation

Source: Reproduced from Mattern, K., & Lacina, C. (2015). *Different assessments, different results: A cautionary note when interpreting state test results* (ACT Issue Brief). Iowa City, IA: ACT, Inc.

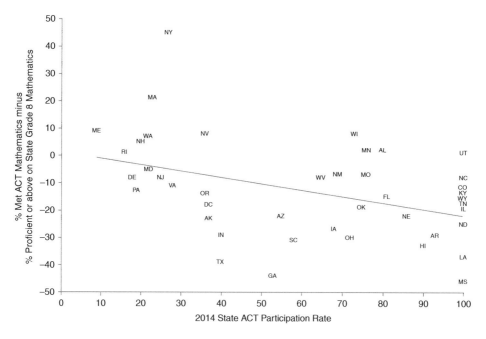

Figure 9.3 Consistency between 2014 ACT and 2013 State Test Mathematics Performance by ACT Participation

Source: Reproduced from Mattern, K., & Lacina, C. (2015). *Different assessments, different results: A cautionary note when interpreting state test results* (ACT Issue Brief). Iowa City, IA: ACT, Inc.

Consequences of Mixed Messages

The first part of this chapter illustrated not only the possibility but the near-certainty that students will receive mixed messages about their level of postsecondary readiness throughout their K–12 educational careers. What is the impact of these inconsistent messages across measures, states, and time? For one, variation in definitions of college and career readiness hampers US efforts to evaluate and improve readiness levels over time. Without a common yardstick to evaluate college and career readiness, it is quite difficult to evaluate whether changes to the educational system are having a positive impact on student learning. Substantial resources are being allocated to educational reform; collecting metrics that support evaluation of these reforms' efficacy should be considered as one requirement attached to funding.

There is a clear argument in favor of standardizing how we evaluate college and career readiness across entities and over time. Still, inconsistencies in our college- and career-readiness definitions continue to plague research and practice. If the benefits of standardization are clear, why have things not changed? Part of the problem may be traced to "local control"—that is, the policy argument that states, not the federal government or any other national entity, should maintain full discretion over their curricula, standards, and assessments. It is an appealing idea that may nonetheless generate unintended consequences. Given states' focus on measuring college and career readiness for accountability purposes rather than to support individual students' development, incentives to game the system and set lower proficiency thresholds are unavoidable (Achieve, 2015). Under the guise of local control, states can give the impression that their educational system is doing a good job preparing students, even when many students are graduating high school ill-prepared for postsecondary endeavors. Large inequities across states are masked by variability in performance levels on state assessments.

Variability in performance-level thresholds is neither unimportant nor benign; it promotes inefficiencies and suboptimal allocation of resources. If the percentage of students passing grade-level standards is more a function of cut-score placement than actual student learning, how do we know where to devote resources? Moreover, if states with the highest success rates are evaluated as case studies to find out what works in education, conclusions will be spurious if passing rates are only tangentially related to what students are learning in the classroom. In other words, variability across states in what it means to be college and career ready can hamper scientific knowledge as it relates to pedagogy and student learning.

Another potential consequence of mixed messages is confusion among consumers of educational metrics and thereby distrust in test results. If different assessments provide different results, students, parents, and policymakers may question those assessments' validity and reliability. Moreover, when presented with conflicting information, which source of information will consumers attend to and trust, and which one will they discredit? For example, imagine a student is presented with multiple pieces of information about her level of mathematics proficiency; one piece of information says she is proficient and one says she is not. Is she more likely to believe the favorable or unfavorable evaluation, even if the unfavorable evaluation result is more valid? Social-psychological research on self-evaluation provides some insights (Dunning, Heath, & Suls, 2004). For skills and abilities that are ill-defined, individuals are more likely to attend to the feedback that reinforces positive self-appraisals (Dunning, Perie, & Story, 1991). That is, when presented with conflicting information, most students will trust the favorable evaluation of their mathematics readiness.

Students may prefer receiving favorable feedback, but feedback that exaggerates academic preparation is a disservice. Research clearly shows that providing feedback to students regarding whether they are on track for college and career readiness at the end of high school is too late to effect change (ACT, 2008; Gaertner & McClarty, 2015). Along these lines, if the feedback students receive throughout their K–12 educational career provides no indication that they are in need of remediation, students may coast through high school with confidence, unknowingly ill-prepared for what lies ahead.

In response to the significant percentage of students entering college unprepared for college-level work, higher education institutions have expanded remedial coursework (Sparks & Malkus, 2013). Unfortunately, research on college remediation indicates that students who start in remediation are at high risk of noncompletion (Attewell, Lavin, Domina, & Levey, 2006; NCES, 2004). Instead, providing feedback—early and empirically linked to future outcomes—will help students better calibrate their college and career expectations and take proactive steps to address their academic weaknesses (Mattern et al., 2014).

Current State of Affairs: Have We Made Progress?

One of the main outcomes of the CCSS Initiative was the development of two assessment consortia dedicated to measuring student progress relative to the new standards. The US Department of Education awarded hundreds of millions of dollars for PARCC and SBAC to develop new assessments in math and ELA. Now that these new assessments are being administered operationally, research studies can be designed and executed to evaluate not only whether PARCC and SBAC tests are well suited (in terms of both reliability and predictive validity) for identifying which students are college and career ready, but also whether the new assessments represent an improvement over the "50 tests for 50 states" paradigm of the past 15 years.

Early research on this topic has generated some surprising conclusions. In the spring of 2015, the PARCC exam was administered in 11 states and the District of Columbia. Massachusetts was one of the participating states. Once the data were available, Massachusetts commissioned Mathematica to evaluate whether the PARCC exam provided a better indication of which students were college ready as compared to their existing state assessment, the Massachusetts Comprehensive Assessment System (MCAS) (Nichols-Barrer, Place, Dillon, & Gill, 2015). The results indicated that the PARCC exam and MCAS were equally predictive of college grades and enrollment status in remedial courses; however, students who were classified as college ready on the PARCC exam were twice as likely to earn grades of B or higher in college mathematics courses, compared to students who were classified as proficient on the MCAS.[5] In essence, the exams diverged in their mathematics performance proficiency thresholds; the PARCC exam had a higher cut score.

The findings from the Mathematica study raise important questions: Was the development of new college- and career-readiness exams a judicious use of resources? Would that money and time have been better spent aligning feedback rather than assessments? More specifically, should states adopt the new assessments, or would it be more worthwhile to evaluate how performance levels compare across assessments and states? The Mathematica study suggests that Massachusetts does not necessarily need a new exam, just a higher cut score. We contend that as long as states continue to vary in their definitions of college and career readiness (i.e., cut scores, performance-level descriptors, and constructs), mixed messages will remain a problem. We hope that attention and resources will be directed at the root of the problem: performance standards. The Mathematica findings suggest that quite a bit of money was devoted to the development of a new assessment that predicts college outcomes no better than its predecessor.

Implications for Policy, Practice, and Research

If we want to improve the feedback students receive so that it is consistent and reflective of their true level of academic preparation, the educational testing community should work with states to align assessments and readiness diagnoses, both with each other and with national frameworks. To accomplish this goal, one line of research should focus on conducting alignment studies to determine whether different assessments cover the same content specifications. To support a national blueprint of content specifications, researchers should continue to refine the set of knowledge and skills that are most relevant to college and career readiness.

Another way to ensure stakeholders receive consistent feedback is through concordance and linking studies. Concordance and linking studies are extremely valuable, as they provide information about how performance on one test relates to performance on another test across the score scale. More importantly, researchers should continue to evaluate the comparability of cut scores across assessments; it is common practice in the context of college admissions (Dorans, 2004). Concordance studies relating performance on the SAT and ACT help ensure that regardless of the exam a student takes, the student will be evaluated on a common yardstick for admission decision purposes. Similar studies should be designed to evaluate assessments states adopt for their accountability systems. Of course, students residing in one state (e.g., Arkansas) will likely not be sitting for another state's accountability assessment (MCAS), but the problem is not methodologically insurmountable. With common assessments across states (i.e., PARCC, SBAC, SAT, or ACT), state assessments can be linked to a common scale. For example, Phillips (2016) compared the 4th- and 8th-grade reading and mathematics performance standards on SBAC, PARCC, and ACT Aspire by linking each test to a common metric—NAEP. The common scale supported an examination of discrepancies in performance standards across national assessments.

Going forward, we would prefer to use student-level data to support true concordances or linking studies that identify the score on one assessment that corresponds with the cut score on another. Such research designs could build on existing studies comparing aggregate outcomes (e.g., Achieve, 2015; Mattern & Lacina, 2014; Phillips, 2016) as well as studies limited to individual states (Nichols-Barrer et al., 2015). States should be free to develop their own assessments and their own performance standards, but documenting the relationships between scale scores across states would foster more candid dialogue about the educational progress of US students.

We are not suggesting that standardized tests are the first and final word in measuring student performance. There is great value in other sources of information, such as course grades and noncognitive skills. But, for the purposes of accountability and tracking educational progress across state lines and over time, standardized metrics give meaning to our comparisons. On the other hand, when the focus is on student development, guidance, and advising, diverse data are preferable (Mattern et al., 2014). More nuanced and personalized information can help individual students align their interests, skills, and abilities with a college, a major, and a career. As with any problem, it is important to first define the use case and then design an effective solution that best addresses users' most pressing priorities. For the problem of tracking college and career readiness, we argue that standardized metrics and consistent readiness thresholds are the best course.

Notes

1 For example, the ACT mathematics section includes the following reporting categories: number and quantity, algebra, functions, geometry, statistics and probability, integrating essential skills, and modeling.
2 These data are based on the 2015 ACT-tested graduating cohort.
3 For example, the ACT College Readiness Benchmark in mathematics was derived based on course grades in College Algebra.
4 Note that this comparison is between middle school proficiency rates and high school college readiness rates. Therefore, to obtain comparable results across the two assessments, the assumption that cut scores are similarly distributed across grade levels must hold true in addition to the other factors identified.
5 The differences for ELA tests were not statistically significant.

References

Achieve. (2015, May 14). *Proficient versus prepared: Disparities between state tests and the National Assessment of Educational Progress (NAEP)*. Washington, DC: Achieve, Inc.

ACT. (2008). *The forgotten middle: Ensuring that all students are on target for college and career readiness before high school*. Iowa City, IA: ACT.

ACT. (2015). *ACT profile report – National graduating class 2015*. Iowa City, IA: ACT.

Allen, J. (2013). *Updating the ACT college readiness benchmarks* (ACT Research Report 2013–6). Iowa City, IA: ACT, Inc.

Attewell, P., Lavin, D., Domina, T., & Levey, T. (2006). New evidence on college remediation. *Journal of Higher Education, 77*(5), 886–924.

Braun, H., Kirsch, I., & Yamamoto, K. (2011). An experimental study of the effects of monetary incentives on performance on the 12th grade NAEP reading assessment. *Teachers College Record, 113*(11), 2309–2344.

Camara, W. (2013). Defining and measuring college and career readiness: A validation framework. *Educational Measurement: Issues and Practice, 32*(4), 16–27.

Camara, W., Allen, J., & Moore, J. (2017). Empirically-based college- and career-readiness cut scores and performance levels. In K. L. McClarty, K. D. Mattern, & M. N. Gaertner (Eds.), *Preparing students for college and careers: Theory, measurement, and educational practice*. New York: Routledge.

Camara, W. J., & Quenemoen, R. (2012). *Defining and measuring CCR and informing the development of performance level descriptors*. Retrieved from http://www.parcconline.org/files/40/Technical%20 Advisory%20Committee/48/Defining-Measuring-CCR-Camara-Quenemoen.pdf.

Clark, M., Rothstein, J., & Schanzenbach, D. W. (2009). Selection bias in college admission test scores. *Economics of Education Review, 28*, 295–307.

College Board. (2015). *2015 College-bound seniors total group profile report*. New York: College Board.

Croft, M. (2015). *Opt-outs: What is lost when students do not test* (ACT Issue Brief). Iowa City, IA: ACT, Inc.

Dorans, N. J. (2004). Equating, concordance, and expectation. *Applied Psychological Measurement, 28*(4), 227–246.

Dunning, D., Heath, C., & Suls, J. M. (2004). Flawed self-assessment implications for health, education, and the workplace. *Psychological Science in the Public Interest, 5*, 69–106.

Dunning, D., Perie, M., & Story, A. L. (1991). Self-serving prototypes of social categories. *Journal of Personality and Social Psychology, 61*(6), 957–968.

Gaertner, M. N., & McClarty, K. L. (2015). Performance, perseverance, and the full picture of college readiness. *Educational Measurement: Issues and Practice, 34*, 20–33.

Gardner, D. P., Larsen, Y. W., Baker, W., Campbell, A., & Crosby, E. A. (1983). *A nation at risk: The imperative for educational reform*. Washington, DC: United States Department of Education.

Kautz, T., Heckman, J., Diris, R., ter Weel, B. T., and Borghans, L. (2014). Fostering and Measuring Skills: Improving Cognitive and Non-Cognitive Skills to Promote Lifetime Success. NBER Working Paper Series 20749. Retrieved from: www.nber.org/papers/w20749.pdf.

Liu, O. L., Bridgeman, B., & Adler, R. M. (2012). Measuring learning outcomes in higher education: Motivation matters. *Educational Researcher, 41*(9), 352–362.

Mattern, K., Burrus, J., Camara, W., O'Connor, R., Hanson, M. A., Gambrell, J., … Bobek, B. (2014). *Broadening the definition of college and career readiness: A holistic approach* (ACT Research Report No. 2014–5). Iowa City, IA: ACT, Inc.

Mattern, K., & Lacina, C. (2014). *Different assessments, different results: A cautionary note when interpreting state test results* (ACT Issue Brief). Iowa City, IA: ACT, Inc.

Mattern, K. D., Shaw, E. J., & Kobrin, J. L. (2011). An alternative presentation of incremental validity discrepant SAT and HSGPA performance. *Educational and Psychological Measurement, 71*(4), 638–662.

McClarty, K. L., Way, W. D., Porter, A. C., Beimers, J. N., & Miles, J. A. (2013). Evidence based standard setting: Establishing a validity framework for cut scores. *Educational Researcher, 42*(2), 78–88.

National Center for Education Statistics. (2004). *The condition of education 2004* (NCES 2004–077). Washington, DC: US Department of Education, Office of Educational and Research Improvement.

Nichols-Barrer, I., Place, K., Dillon, E., & Gill, B. (2015). *Predictive validity of MCAS and PARCC: Comparing 10th grade MCAS tests to PARCC Integrated Math II, Algebra II, and 10th grade English language arts tests.* Cambridge, MA: Mathematica Policy Research.

Phillips, G. W. (2016). *National benchmarks for state achievement standards.* Washington, DC: American Institutes for Research.

Sparks, D., & Malkus, N. (2013). *First-year undergraduate remedial coursetaking: 1999–2000, 2003–04, 2007–08* (Statistics in Brief. NCES 2013–013). Washington, DC: National Center for Education Statistics.

U.S. Department of Education. (2016, February 9). President Obama's 2017 Budget Seeks to Expand Educational Opportunity for All Students [Press Release]. U.S. Department of Education.

U.S. Department of Education, Institute of Education Sciences, National Center for Education Statistics, National Assessment of Educational Progress (NAEP), 1992, 1994, 1998, 2000, 2002, 2003, 2005, 2007, 2009, 2011, 2013 and 2015 Reading Assessments.

Vitale, D. (2016). *Including measures of student behavioral skills in accountability systems* (ACT Issue Brief). Iowa City, IA: ACT, Inc.

Wyatt, J., Kobrin, J., Wiley, A., Camara, W. J., & Proestler, N. (2011). *SAT benchmarks: Development of a college readiness benchmark and its relationship to secondary and postsecondary school performance.* (College Board Research Report 2011–5). New York: The College Board.

Part 3

Improving College and Career Readiness

10 Early Intervention in College and Career Readiness

The GEAR UP Model and its Implications for 21st-Century Education Policy

Chrissy Tillery and Brent Duckor

Student affluence prevails as a marker of college success as indicated by postsecondary enrollment rates of 45.5% for low-income, recent high school graduates, as compared to 78.5% for high-income, high school graduates (Digest of Education Statistics, 2013). With a delta of 33 percentage points, that leaves too many students in need without an opportunity to advance their education. College placement examination results often provide college- and career-readiness benchmarks and are a marker for where a student enrolls, if they do indeed enroll. In the US, results often indicate that students are not adequately prepared.

These trends are particularly troubling for low-income students. ACT (2016) reports that low-income students are especially vulnerable; only 11% of low-income students met all four college- and career-readiness benchmarks, and 50% did not meet any benchmarks. If test preparation alone was a cure for this increasing issue, test preparation programs would be the answer (Domingue & Briggs, 2009). However, a more holistic, service-oriented approach aimed at students most in need is a better solution. Gaining Early Awareness and Readiness for Undergraduate Programs (GEAR UP) is a federal program that has been designed to address such holistic issues for minority, low-income, and first-generation students in low-income schools and communities across the country. Through practices aimed at enhancing academic readiness and social supports, GEAR UP can bolster a large number of these at-risk students.

Historical Expansion of College Access

College access is a vital part of college and career readiness. With a focus on early intervention services and strategies, college access is an educational movement that assists students, particularly low-income and underrepresented students, in their endeavor to enroll, persist, and graduate from postsecondary institutions through strategic programming interventions that take place in middle and high school. Several factors have contributed to the evolution of college access for underserved students within the United States. Among the first were the Morrill Land Grant Acts of 1862 and 1890 that supported the creation of land-grant colleges, many of which are still landmark postsecondary institutions today. Land grants and subsequent colleges were a response to the industrial revolution and provided an opportunity for minority students and those from lower social classes to attend postsecondary institutions. Additionally, the 1944 G.I. Bill of Rights benefited 7.8 million veterans of World War II through federal payouts for college expenses, training programs, and monthly stipends (Mettler, 2005). An additional 55,000 veterans have received benefits under the Post-9/11 Veterans Educational Assistance Act; these benefits have been used at more than 6,500 colleges across the country (Sander, 2012).

Furthermore, legislation passed in the 1950s and 1960s led to new postsecondary opportunities for minority, low-income, and first-generation students who had previously been excluded in a segregated society. In 1954, the Supreme Court's ruling in *Brown v. Board of Education* declared state laws establishing separate public schools for black and white students uncon-stitutional. A decade later, the Civil Rights Act of 1964, in conjunction with the Economic Opportunity Act of 1964, promoted greater inclusion of minorities in the educational and economic life of America. Additionally, the Higher Education Act (HEA) of 1965 was intended "to strengthen the educational resources of our colleges and universities and to provide finan-cial assistance for students in postsecondary and higher education" (Higher Education Act of 1965, Public Law 89–329, p. 1). The Higher Education Opportunity Act (HEOA) of 2008 reauthorized the HEA of 1965, further strengthening the federal college access agenda. Each of these decisions has underscored the ideal that every US student should have access to a college education. With the publication of *A Nation at Risk* (Gardner, Larsen, Baker, Campbell, & Crosby, 1983), policymakers set out to reform middle and secondary schools with a series of initiatives aimed at better student preparation for college and career. The 1996 New American High School initiative, under the direction of the US Secretary of Education Riley, represented the federal government's efforts to showcase schools throughout the country that represent a broad range of educational approaches serving the needs of at-risk youth.

Federal programs have been put in place over the last 50 years to assist low-income students in their attainment of higher education. Many of these programs are supported through funds that are funneled to states through discretionary federal grant projects. One of those, the US Department of Education's GEAR UP initiative, aims to increase the number of students successfully prepared to enter college. GEAR UP serves either priority students[1] or cohorts of students[2] starting no later than the 7th grade in schools where at least 50% of the stu-dents are eligible for free or reduced-price lunch. States and local partnerships are funded and serve students continuously through the end of high school or first year of college, depending on the fiscal year they were funded and the program structure. Created to help overcome educational disparities by providing resources and services to students and families from low-income communities, GEAR UP's mission is to prepare students to enter and succeed in postsecondary education. GEAR UP has three global performance measures as outlined in the following:

1   To increase the academic performance and preparation for postsecondary education of participating students;
2   To increase the rate of high school graduation and participation in postsecondary education of participating students; and
3   To increase educational expectations for participating students and increase student and family knowledge of postsecondary education options, preparation, and financing.

Preparing for college is a lifelong journey and one that does not begin during a student's senior year of high school (ACT, 2008). For low-income students, the journey may be particularly fraught (Dougherty, 2014). The GEAR UP program is intended as a vehicle to provide early interventions to students and families in broad-based school settings, in communities most in need.

GEAR UP Program Components

GEAR UP has traditionally been a college access program; however, in 2011, there was a shift allowing grantees to serve students in their first year of postsecondary education (US Department of Education, 2011). While the GEAR UP program aims for students to enroll and succeed in college, the primary goal is to serve them in middle and high school to get them pre-pared to enter and succeed in college. GEAR UP offers many service interventions to students and families, as guided by the HEOA and outlined in Table 10.1.

Table 10.1 GEAR UP Student and Parent/Family Services

GEAR UP Student Services	GEAR UP Parent/Family Services
1. Supportive Services (Required) 2. Rigorous Academic Curricula (Required) 3. Comprehensive Mentoring (Required) 4. Financial aid counseling/advising (Required) 5. Counseling/advising/academic planning/career counseling (Required) 6. College visit/college student shadowing 7. Tutoring/homework assistance 8. Job site visit/job shadowing 9. Summer programs 10. Educational field trips 11. Workshops	1. Workshops on college preparation/ financial aid 2. Counseling/advising 3. College visits 4. Family events

Note: Sourced from the U.S. Department of Education's Annual Performance Report for Partnership and State Projects.

The GEAR UP service areas span noncognitive and academic domains that complement research findings in the field. GEAR UP components draw on a growing body of research examining strategies for getting students to and through college, including college match and fit (Byndloss & Reid, 2013), summer melt (Castleman, Arnold, & Wartman, 2012), and text messaging to increase postsecondary access (Castleman, Owen, Page, & Stephany, 2014). Parent engagement, for example, is a large component of GEAR UP service delivery. In low-income communities, parent involvement has been shown to increase student readiness in social, emotional, and behavioral areas (Kingston, Huang, Calzada, Dawson-McClure, & Brotman, 2013).

In addition, counseling—one of the most frequently provided services for GEAR UP—has been found to positively increase postsecondary enrollment (Tillery, 2013). Bryan, Moore-Thomas, Day-Vines, and Holcomb-McCoy (2011) also found that counseling supports for students increased the submission of college applications. GEAR UP provides personnel supports and full-time or part-time GEAR UP coordinators or college coaches in school districts to complement and enhance the school counselor's work with the goal of increasing application and enrollment.

GEAR UP Effectiveness

Educational practitioners and policymakers seek answers on how to best assist students, especially those from low-income schools, in their postsecondary endeavors. Federal and private dollars are invested in myriad college access and readiness programs across the country, and we continuously pursue evidence about how well these programs work for students, their families, and our national economy. Since its inception in 1998, there have been three national evaluations of the GEAR UP program. In 1999, the year after GEAR UP was created, the US Department of Education contracted with Westat, Inc. to conduct a national evaluation of GEAR UP (US Department of Education, 2003). Survey results from intervention and comparison middle schools provided a descriptive overview of how GEAR UP programs are implemented across the nation and found that attending a GEAR UP school was positively associated with student and parent knowledge. A follow-up study by Standing, Judkins, Keller, and Shimshak (2008) found that attending a GEAR UP middle school was positively associated with parents' and students' postsecondary knowledge, parent involvement, parent aspirations for their children to attend college, and students taking above grade-level science courses. Terenzini, Cabrera, Deil-Amen, and Lambert (2005), funded through the Institute of

Education Sciences, also provided a comprehensive analysis of the GEAR UP program. Results indicated the "reach" or percent of eligible students that participated in targeted services had a significant positive impact on awareness and that parent engagement had a positive impact on increasing students' social capital. Each study provided insight into the effectiveness of the GEAR UP program, yet none spanned the full spectrum of the six- or seven-year program services and examined postsecondary outcomes. There remains a pressing need for comprehensive and longitudinal evaluations that follow GEAR UP students through the program and through college completion, as well as an examination of the service interventions that are particularly impactful for GEAR UP students.

In 2011, a group of state GEAR UP grantees came together to form the College and Career Readiness Evaluation Consortium (CCREC), bringing together leaders across the country serving almost 100,000 students. Led by the National Council for Community and Education Partnerships (NCCEP) and in partnership with ACT and the National Student Clearinghouse Research Center, CCREC aims to better evaluate the effectiveness of the GEAR UP program by conducting longitudinal research and evaluation from middle school through postsecondary completion. CCREC adopted common data definitions and research questions and developed a longitudinal research and evaluation plan. Baseline data show that in the GEAR UP and non-GEAR UP comparison group, about two-thirds of students in each group plan to obtain a bachelor's or graduate degree, despite the fact that about 40% of students have parents or guardians with no college experience and most students are not on track to be academically ready for college by the time they graduate from high school (based on 8th-grade assessments) (Cruce & Burkum, 2015). GEAR UP therefore serves students who have great need yet high educational aspirations. Rich longitudinal data allow GEAR UP to focus on interventions that can best meet the student's needs—whether that is in academic support, through tutoring or homework assistance, or social support, through providing family engagement on topics related to college. The CCREC has two research strands—one a longitudinal study of the effectiveness of GEAR UP on the academic achievement, college going, and college retention of low-income students using a matched non-GEAR UP comparison group, and the other a longitudinal evaluation of the effectiveness of GEAR UP interventions in attaining key secondary and postsecondary outcomes.

Because GEAR UP grants end after either high school or the first year of postsecondary education, there are limited resources to address questions about postsecondary success and longitudinal impact. As Ward, Stambler, and Linke (2013) point out, their Yale-Bridgeport Schools partnership grant will preclude them from evaluating the program beyond the six-year award period and into students' first year of college. They are seeking other ways, through partnerships, to perform this critical evaluation. Program sustainability (after funding ends) is another key concern; as Ward (2006) also indicates, sustainability is particularly an issue for high-poverty school districts.

GEAR UP Studies Focused on College Knowledge and Readiness

Several studies have shown increased postsecondary preparedness for GEAR UP students. Bausmith and France (2012) conducted a quasi-experimental study on College Board assessment data of 173 GEAR UP schools compared to non-GEAR UP low-income schools and found that the GEAR UP program showed positive evidence for increasing college readiness. Studying four cohorts of students, researchers found that the third and fourth cohorts had increased scores in SAT reading and mathematics compared to students in the non-GEAR UP comparison schools, suggesting that GEAR UP students were better prepared for postsecondary education. Similarly, ACT (2007a,b) conducted a longitudinal study of 250 GEAR UP schools compared to non-GEAR UP low-income schools and found positive results in reading, English, the percent of students taking core high school coursework, and postsecondary aspirations.

Yampolskaya, Massey, and Greenbaum (2006) conducted a matched comparison study in an urban setting and found that increased time in GEAR UP-related academic interventions led to increased grade-point averages (GPAs) and that students who spent time in behavior-related interventions had fewer disciplinary problems. Yampolskaya et al. also found enhanced social competence for students participating in GEAR UP. Additionally, GEAR UP students had higher aspirations and college knowledge (Watt, Huerta, & Lozano, 2007), while a follow-up study found that students participating in either Advancement Via Individual Determination (AVID) or GEAR UP had additional college knowledge, preparation, and support as compared to a comparison group (Lozano, Watt, & Huerta, 2009). GEAR UP students who received academic mentoring also had higher Algebra I, Algebra II, and state mathematics assessment performance compared with non-GEAR UP students (Fetsco, Kain, Soby, Olszewski, & Crites, 2011).

Stack, Alexander, Doyle, and Kamin (2012) conducted a quasi-experimental study using retrospective data to assess student outcomes after a GEAR UP summer transition program. Findings indicate that students who received the summer transition program had higher 9th-grade passing rates in Algebra I and were more likely to be on track to graduate; there were no statistically significant differences in attendance and GPA.

GEAR UP Studies Focused on Student Service Interventions

The core of GEAR UP is the required and permissible service interventions provided to students and families. College advising is a widely used intervention tool for preparing GEAR UP students. In a 2014 NCCEP survey of GEAR UP projects, 41% of respondents reported using near-peers as their primary college advising strategy (NCCEP, 2014). Often from similar backgrounds as the target population, near-peers can speak to younger high-need students from personal experience regarding the academic, financial, and social components of preparing, enrolling, and succeeding in college. Prickett (2004) illustrates an early use of near-peer advising or mentoring as a cost-effective and beneficial means to assist students in GEAR UP schools in their postsecondary endeavors. The study also points out the great need to have teachers and students who understand the problems faced by underrepresented students. Other studies have found that strategic academic advisors significantly improve outcomes for GEAR UP middle school students in core academic courses (Van Kannel-Ray, Lacefield, & Zeller, 2008). Summer programs are another service intervention used by GEAR UP to increase college preparedness. Beer, Le Blanc, and Miller (2008) studied summer learning camps in the rural south and found that students who attended a GEAR UP summer program had more academic awareness after summer camp than before. Results also showed significant increases in these students' ACT Explore mathematics scores.

GEAR UP Studies Focused on Family/Parent Service Interventions

Parent involvement is central to GEAR UP students' success (Terenzini et al., 2005). However, even with the requirement to serve parents and the knowledge that their involvement is critical, GEAR UP struggles to find ways to reach parents in low-income communities and as such, lacks data on parental involvement and outcomes. One study with adequate data (Stack, 2010) examined the relationship between parent involvement and student success in the Chicago GEAR UP Alliance. Stack found a statistically significant relationship between parent involvement and 9th-grade GPA and ACT Plan composite scores, but did not find a significant relationship between parent involvement and postsecondary aspirations. Gibson and Jefferson (2006) examined GEAR UP and non-GEAR UP comparison groups and found that increased parental involvement, even if perceived, led to increased self-concept for students.

GEAR UP Studies Focused on Postsecondary Outcomes

Postsecondary enrollment, persistence, and graduation are the intended outcome of GEAR UP nationally; however, we still know relatively little about GEAR UP's influence on these outcomes. Building strong evidence requires comparison groups and either experimental or quasi-experimental designs. These designs, in turn, require longitudinal data, and some grantees have found ways to track student-level outcomes beyond the grant terms. The Kentucky Council on Postsecondary Education (2013), for example, found that students from their 2005–2011 state grant graduated high school at comparable rates to matched non-GEAR UP students, but enrolled at significantly higher rates (44% compared to non-GEAR UP postsecondary enrollment of 36%). Rhode Island's GEAR UP program, College Crusade, tracked high school graduating classes from 2006 to 2010 and found that 68% of the 1,508 students enrolled in college and that 49% did so immediately after high school (Fogg & Harrington, 2013); they also found that these students had an 84% postsecondary persistence rate. Mann (2012) conducted an evaluation of the Washington State GEAR UP program and found that among a cohort of 769 GEAR UP postsecondary students, they were more likely than comparison peers to enroll in (84% compared to 59%), persist in (83% compared to 74%), and complete a degree or certificate (38% compared to 32%). The majority of postsecondary credentials in both groups were four-year degrees.

GEAR UP Studies Focused on Service Interventions and Postsecondary Outcomes

A gap in our understanding of the GEAR UP program is evaluating linkages between service interventions and postsecondary outcomes. In order to conduct such analyses, data must be collected and linked across datasets and across years. Without a federal requirement and associated training, many programs do not conduct such comprehensive analyses, which is why the CCREC was formed and is carrying out longitudinal analyses and sharing best practices for evaluation. Some grantees have also developed an infrastructure for housing data long-term and linking data from multiple sources. An evaluation of GEAR UP North Carolina linked service intervention data to postsecondary enrollment and found that select student (counseling/advising and college visits) and parent/family (workshops, college visits, and family events) services led to significantly higher postsecondary enrollment rates (Tillery, 2013). While Tillery did not find parent services had an aggregate impact on postsecondary enrollment, the study did show that those services where parents are most likely to self-initiate had positive impacts on student enrollment. Furthermore, Dais, Dervarics, and Fowler (2013) found positive relationships between taking Advanced Placement (AP) courses, taking a GEAR UP project-specific course, FAFSA completion, and postsecondary enrollment. Dais et al. found that, overall, 81% of GEAR UP students who had enrolled in postsecondary education persisted. In addition, 91% of students who enrolled in AP courses and 82% of students who had GEAR UP-targeted tutoring returned for a second year of college, though there was little correlation between years in GEAR UP and persistence to a second year of college. These findings begin to establish the importance of specific GEAR UP interventions, noting that just being a GEAR UP student may not be as impactful as receiving targeted GEAR UP interventions.

Making Valid Inferences with GEAR UP Data

Across the fields of secondary and postsecondary education, there is an increasing focus on development of the whole child and how to best prepare students for the demands of college and career. Researchers have established a positive correlation between academic achievement outcomes and so-called affective or noncognitive indicators (Hein, Smerdon, & Sambolt, 2013).

GEAR UP has played a role in gauging and augmenting noncognitive outcomes, which have an influence on students' ability to learn, be successful, and contribute to society.

We agree with our colleagues that the research is clear on the association between noncognitive indicators and academic achievement (Farrington et al., 2012). Research on the impact of GEAR UP programs on acceptance, college going, and, to a lesser extent, persistence is still emerging. But the grain size of these research findings is too large for stakeholders—those who deliver GEAR UP program services—to make sensible use of the data as educators. In both academic and noncognitive domains, we would like students, teachers, school counselors, and staff affiliated with GEAR UP to know which "data-driven" practices really make a difference, for their students and local contexts.

GEAR UP has a complex and multipronged theory of action, as do many college- and career-readiness interventions. Evaluations of these theories of action, particularly as related to the use and interpretation of noncognitive data, would benefit from a close reading of the *Standards for Educational and Psychological Testing* (American Educational Research Association, American Psychological Association, & National Council on Measurement in Education, 2014). Determining the overall effectiveness of GEAR UP programs requires a multifaceted research program, and the results of any study will depend in part on the quality of the metrics used to gauge success. A complicating factor in the evaluation of GEAR UP programs is that the uses of any data (e.g., levels of perseverance, academic mindset, and so forth) for making decisions must be clearly specified for a given population. GEAR UP stakeholders want to use the data generated by studies, reports, and evaluation tools. The challenge at hand is validating the data for particular intended uses.

In this volume, we argue for a closer examination of the *Standards* (2014). To guide the collection of validity and reliability evidence for examining particular claims about, for example, a noncognitive score result or intervention designed to boost "levels of engagement," we must first consult the evidence-based framework outlined by the *Standards*. When proposing a particular use of data, the *Standards* call for credible lines of evidence regarding: content coverage, response processes, internal structure, relations to other variables, relations to criteria, and consequences.

While a GEAR UP researcher, data provider, or evaluator may decide to focus on claims made at the item or total test score level, they all should utilize the *Standards* to evaluate the "network of inferences" leading from the [task] score to statements and decisions (Kane, 1992). The plausibility of an interpretation based on GEAR UP metrics depends on evidence supporting the proposed interpretation and on the evidence refuting competing interpretations of results. We should expect that different types of validity and reliability evidence will be relevant to different parts of an argument for use of any GEAR UP measure, depending on contexts, programs, and student populations. If GEAR UP program providers, for example, use ACT Engage (or other instruments that have been validated to evaluate summative outcomes) to make diagnostic decisions that have consequences for placement or services provided to these vulnerable student populations, it might be cause for concern.

Messick (1989) further reminds us that validity is not a property of the instrument itself but refers to score interpretation. Validation, from this perspective, is an ongoing process and a matter of degree. There is no such thing as a valid GEAR UP instrument that the experts have vetted for all times and places. Rather, validity will pertain to an instrument's evolving uses and contexts for GEAR UP programs. Kane (2013) adds to this conception of validity the idea that researchers and practitioners must carefully examine the kinds of claims that instrument developers can warrant to guide the appropriate use(s) of data. Thus, it is important for both policymakers and stakeholders in the GEAR UP community to understand the nature of the scores, points, and other metrics used in their programs and how data can inform (and impede) progress for at-risk students.

Important questions on data use emerge from the extant GEAR UP studies, reports, and non-peer reviewed literature: Is the GEAR UP data primarily intended for diagnostic, formative, or summative use? By whom? What are the specific warrants and evidence for any or all of those uses? For example, can diagnosing a GEAR UP student's level of "grit" lead to formative interventions that provide *positive, nonjudgmental, timely, specific,* or *actionable* feedback (Duckor, 2017)? The research on classroom-based formative evaluation emphasizes that effective feedback is subject to instructional intervention and change (Hattie & Timperley, 2007; Heritage, 2017; Linquanti, 2014). GEAR UP data must be formative if a change in students' perceptions, behaviors, and skills development is to occur.

Implications for Policy, Practice, and Research

To advance GEAR UP research, evaluation, and measurement, and college- and career-readiness research more broadly, we offer several recommendations. The CCREC has started some of this work through uniformly defining GEAR UP service interventions and outcome measures, as well as using a relational database where systematic, longitudinal data are housed. For federal policy interventions such as GEAR UP that attempt comparisons across multiple states and programs, reliable postsecondary data (e.g., from the National Student Clearinghouse) is imperative. Moreover, the ability to use data in more formative, data-driven delivery systems at an appropriate grain size would greatly benefit students and their mentors, counselors, and teachers. So far, these databases, while ripe for data mining for policymakers, are not educative for service providers on the ground.

Despite the technological advances in integrating academic test results, noncognitive measures, and school climate indicators into reporting mechanisms, the challenge of linking effective formative and summative uses of data for local GEAR UP stakeholders is substantial. GEAR UP has worked with providers in the private and public sector to improve data delivery and reporting tools largely for program evaluation purposes. Stakeholders—such as teachers, parents, after-school providers, principals, and school staff—will likely require more timely, specific, intervention-oriented feedback to aid in instructional decision-making and program service delivery in their local contexts (Gheen, Smerdon, Hein, & Lebow, 2012; Hyslop, 2011).

In addition to practical challenges in communicating the purposes and uses of data within the GEAR UP community, there are psychometric issues that warrant continued attention. For example, over the last decade, policymakers and evaluators have increasingly looked to noncognitive variables as predictors of postsecondary school success (Hein et al., 2013; National Research Council, 2012). At the federal level, under the Every Student Succeeds Act (ESSA), noncognitive outcomes have received increased emphasis as part of college and career readiness.

Regardless of the domain, we must carefully distinguish the grain size and appropriate use of data for program evaluation, policy studies, and accountability mechanisms. The *Standards* must be consulted if GEAR UP data are integrated with secondary learning outcomes in schools. These *Standards* guide the profession toward responsible use of educational data and the limits of permissible inference from scores. To the extent GEAR UP data are folded into decision-making for educational leaders interested in "multiple measures," we will need to hold those *Standards* close for guidance and advice.

A final note: we might now consider moving beyond the top-down model of research and evaluation that delivers reports and charts to distal stakeholder groups. For outcomes to shift and engagement with proximal stakeholders—students, parents, teachers, and school counselors—to occur, we will need state and federal investment in advancing research related to the allocation of funds for practitioner training, formative uses of GEAR UP data, and professional development that supports collaboration between researchers and practitioners. With the push to elevate evidence-based interventions, it is imperative for a practitioner-based program like GEAR UP to be able make such transitions with the help of engaged researchers. With public investment and leadership from educational researchers who work across both academic and affective domains, we can pioneer solutions that honor the growth and "coachability" of GEAR UP students on their journey to college and careers.

Notes

1 Priority students are defined as any student in secondary school who is eligible to be counted under the Elementary and Secondary Education Act of 1965, eligible for Title IV assistance, eligible for assistance under the McKinney-Vento Homeless Assistance Act, or otherwise considered to be a disconnected student.
2 The cohort or whole-grade model involves providing services to all students in the participating grade levels, rather than a selected group of students. A cohort must start no later than the 7th grade, and services must be provided to the students in the cohort through the 12th grade.

References

ACT. (2007a). *Using EPAS to evaluate school-based intervention programs: GEAR UP.* Iowa City, IA: ACT.

ACT. (2007b). *Using EXPLORE and PLAN to evaluate GEAR UP programs.* Iowa City, IA: ACT.

ACT. (2008). *The forgotten middle: Ensuring that all students are on target for college and career readiness before high school.* Iowa City, IA: ACT.

ACT. (2016). *The condition of college and career readiness.* Iowa City, IA: ACT.

Alexander, J., Stack, W., Doyle, S., & Kamin, C. (2012). The Effects of a Summer Transition Program on 9th Grade Outcomes: A Retrospective Study. *Funded through U.S. Department of Education and Research Triangle International.* Retrieved from http://tinyurl.com/gu-summer-transition-wp.

American Educational Research Association, American Psychological Association, & National Council on Measurement in Education. (2014). *Standards for educational and psychological testing.* Washington, DC: Author.

Bausmith, J. M., & France, M. (2012). The impact of GEAR UP on college readiness for students in low income schools. *Journal of Education for Students Placed at Risk, 17*(4), 234–246.

Beer, G., Le Blanc, M., & Miller, M. J. (2008). Summer learning camps: Helping students to prepare for college. *College Student Journal, 42*(3), 930–938.

Bryan, J., Moore-Thomas, C., Day-Vines, N. L., & Holcomb-McCoy, C. (2011). School counselors as social capital: The effects of high school college counseling on college application rates. *Journal of Counseling & Development, 89*(2), 190–199.

Byndloss, D. C., & Reid, C. (2013). *Promoting college match for low-income students: Lessons for practitioners.* New York: MDRC.

Castleman, B. L., Arnold, K., & Wartman, K. L. (2012). Stemming the tide of summer melt: An experimental study of the effects of post-high school summer intervention on low-income students' college enrollment. *Journal of Research on Educational Effectiveness, 5*(1), 1–17.

Castleman, B. L., Owen, L., Page, L. C., & Stephany, B. (2014). *Using text messaging to guide students on the path to college* (Working Paper No. 33). Center for Education Policy and Workforce Competitiveness. Charlottesville, VA: University of Virginia Charlottesville.

Cruce, T., & Burkum, K. (2015). *Core research program: Student baseline data.* Iowa City, IA: ACT.

Dais, R., Dervarics, C., & Fowler, M. (2013). *Following GEAR UP students to college: The Massachusetts data utilization project.* Boston, MA: Massachusetts State GEAR UP.

Digest of Education Statistics. (2013). *Percentage of recent high school completers enrolled in 2-year and 4-year colleges, by income level: 1975 through 2013.* Retrieved from https://nces.ed.gov/programs/digest/d13/tables/dt13_302.30.asp.

Domingue, B., & Briggs, D. C. (2009). Using linear regression and propensity score matching to estimate the effect of coaching on the SAT. *Multiple Linear Regression Viewpoints, 35*(1), 12–29.

Dougherty, C. (2014). *Catching up to college and career readiness: The challenge is greater for at-risk students.* Iowa City, IA: ACT.

Duckor, B. (2017). Got grit? Maybe...*Phi Delta Kappan, 98*(7), 61–66.

Farrington, C. A., Roderick, M., Allensworth, E., Nagaoka, J., Keyes, T. S., Johnson, D. W., & Beechum, N. O. (2012). *Teaching adolescents to become learners. The role of noncognitive factors in shaping school performance: A critical literature review.* Chicago, IL: University of Chicago Consortium on Chicago School Research.

Fetsco, T. G., Kain, D. L., Soby, B., Olszewski, T., & Crites, T. (2011). *Mentoring for math success.* Phoenix, AZ: GEAR UP, Northern Arizona University.

Fogg, N. P., & Harrington, P. E. (2013). *Freshman-year retention rates of college crusaders who graduated between 2006 and 2010.* Philadelphia, PA: College Crusade Research Brief, Drexel University, Center for Labor Market and Policy.

Gardner, D. P., Larsen, Y. W., Baker, W., Campbell, A., & Crosby, E. A. (1983). *A nation at risk: The imperative for educational reform.* Washington, DC: United States Department of Education.

Gheen, M., Smerdon, B., Hein, V., & Lebow, M. (2012). *Outcomes and measures for college and career success: How do we know when high school graduates meet expectations?* Washington, DC: National High School Center, American Institutes for Research.

Gibson, D. M., & Jefferson, R. M. (2006). The effect of perceived parental involvement and the use of growth-fostering relationships on self-concept in adolescents participating in GEAR UP. *Adolescence, 41*(161), 111–125.

Hattie, J., & Timperley, H. (2007). The power of feedback. *Review of Educational Research, 77*(1), 81–112.

Hein, V., Smerdon, B., & Sambolt, M. (2013). *Predictors of postsecondary success.* Washington, DC: College and Career Readiness and Success Center, American Institutes for Research.

Heritage, M. (2017). Changing the assessment relationship to empower teachers and students. In K. L. McClarty, K. D. Mattern, & M. N. Gaertner (Eds.), *Preparing students for college and careers: Theory, measurement, and educational practice.* New York: Routledge.

Higher Education Act of 1965. Public Law 89–329 (1965). Retrieved from https://www.gpo.gov/fdsys/pkg/STATUTE-79/pdf/STATUTE-79-Pg1219.pdf.

Hyslop, A. (2011). *Data that matters: Giving high schools useful feedback on grads' outcomes.* Washington, DC: Education Sector.

Kane, M. (1992). An argument-based approach to validation. *Psychological Bulletin, 112,* 527–535.

Kane, M. (2013). Validation as a pragmatic, scientific activity. *Journal of Educational Measurement, 50*(1), 115–122.

Kentucky Council on Postsecondary Education. (2013). *GEAR UP Kentucky II: Comprehensive Report.* Frankfort, KY: Kentucky Council on Postsecondary Education.

Kingston, S., Huang, K. Y., Calzada, E., Dawson-McClure, S., & Brotman, L. (2013). Parent involvement in education as a moderator of family and neighborhood socioeconomic context on school readiness among young children. *Journal of Community Psychology, 41*(3), 265–276.

Linquanti, R. (2014). Supporting Formative Assessment for Deeper Learning: A Primer for Policymakers. *Formative Assessment for Students and Teachers/State Collaborative on Assessment and Student Standards.* Washington, DC: Council of Chief State School Officers.

Lozano, A., Watt, K. M., & Huerta, J. (2009). A comparison study of 12th grade Hispanic students' college anticipations, aspirations, and college preparatory measures. *American Secondary Education, 38*(1), 92–110.

Mann, C. (2012). *Making the dream a reality: Positive outcomes in college enrollment, persistence, and employment of GEAR UP alumni.* Social and Economic Sciences Research Center, Washington State University.

Messick, S. (1989). Validity. In R. L. Linn (Ed.), *Educational measurement* (3rd ed., pp. 13–103). New York: Macmillan.

Mettler, S. (2005). *Soldiers to citizens: The G.I. Bill and the making of the greatest generation.* New York: Oxford University Press, Inc.

National Council for Community and Education Partnership (NCCEP). (2014). *Implementing near-peer and college fit services across the GEAR UP community and recommendations for expansion.* Washington, DC.

National Research Council. (2012). *Education for life and work: Developing transferable knowledge and skills for the 21st century.* Washington, DC: The National Academies Press.

Prickett, C. (2004). And college for all: Revisited. *Principal Leadership, 5*(4), 28–31.

Sander, L. (2012). *The post-911 GI Bill, explained.* The Chronicle of Higher Education.

Stack, W. M. (2010). *The relationship of parent involvement and student success in GEAR UP communities in Chicago* (unpublished doctoral dissertation). Antioch University.

Standing, K., Judkins, D., Keller, B., & Shimshak, A. (2008). *Early outcomes of the GEAR UP program: Final report.* U.S. Department of Education, Office of Planning, Evaluation and Policy Development, Policy and Program Studies Service.

Terenzini, P. T., Cabrera, A. F., Deil-Amen, R., & Lambert, A. (2005). *The dream deferred: Increasing the college preparation of at-risk student. Year 4: Final report* (Grant #R305T0101667). Washington, DC: U.S. Department of Education.

Tillery, C. Y. (2013). *The summative impact of college access interventions: An evaluation of GEAR UP North Carolina* (unpublished doctoral dissertation). Appalachian State University, Boone, NC.

U.S. Department of Education (2003). *National evaluation of GEAR UP: A summary of the first two years.* Policy and Program Studies Service. Washington, DC: U.S. Department of Education.

U.S. Department of Education (2011). *FY 2011 Application for grants under the Gaining Early Awareness & Readiness for Undergraduate Programs (GEAR UP).* Washington, DC: U.S. Department of Education.

Van Kannel-Ray, N., Lacefield, W. E., & Zeller, P. J. (2008). Academic case managers: Evaluating a middle school intervention for children at-risk. *Journal of Multidisciplinary Evaluation, 5*(10), 21–29.

Ward, N. L. (2006). Improving equity and access for low-income and minority youth into institutions of higher education. *Urban Education, 41*(1), 50–70.

Ward, N. L., Strambler, M. J., & Linke, L. H. (2013). Increasing educational attainment among urban minority youth: A model of university, school, and community partnerships. *The Journal of Negro Education, 82*(3), 312–325.

Watt, K. M., Huerta, J., & Lozano, A. (2007). A comparison study of AVID and GEAR UP 10th-grade students in two high schools in the Rio Grande valley of Texas. *Journal of Education for Students Placed at Risk, 12*(2), 185–212.

Yampolskaya, S., Massey, O. T., & Greenbaum, P. E. (2006). At-risk high school students in the Gaining Early Awareness and Readiness Program (GEAR UP): Academic and behavioral outcomes. *The Journal of Primary Prevention, 27*(5), 457–475.

11 Multiple Mathematics Pathways to College, Careers, and Beyond

Francesca Fraga Leahy and Carolyn Landel

All students deserve the opportunity to attain an excellent mathematics education and readiness for college, careers, and beyond. However, at a time when mathematics is more important to success in school, work, and life than ever before, mathematics coursework remains a barrier for too many students. Multiple mathematics pathways represent a comprehensive approach to addressing these challenges and transforming mathematics education into a ladder, rather than a barrier, to upward mobility. A well-designed mathematics pathway results in a structured and intentional student learning experience, more coherent and effective than taking discrete mathematics courses designed in isolation. This chapter draws on data and case studies from initiatives embodying the multiple mathematics pathways approach, with a special focus on the Dana Center Mathematics Pathways (DCMP).

Modern Goals for Mathematics Education

American higher education is broadly seen as one of our society's greatest achievements because of its contributions to the economy and upward mobility. Beginning in the latter half of the 20th century, education policy and reform initiatives focused on enrolling more students in the courses necessary for college access, including algebra-based mathematics course sequences. Over the last three decades, this concentrated effort led to steady growth in high school calculus enrollment, contributing to a 10.4 million student increase since 1970 in total undergraduate enrollment at degree-granting institutions (Cahalan & Perna, 2015).

Although the achievements of this era are laudable, ensuring equal access to college-preparatory mathematics courses and resources still remains a challenge (Handwerk, Tognatta, Coley, & Gitomer, 2008). In addition, critical shifts in our economy, society, and academia have increased the urgency of achieving our nation's ambitious goals for students and mathematics education. These goals include a shift in emphasis from equal to equitable education and from access alone to access and completion of a rigorous education relevant to the modern world of work and citizenship.

Applications of mathematics and statistics are now normative practice in the social sciences and a wide variety of other fields. Higher education degree attainment is more critical to economic opportunity now than it was at the end of the 20th century. Furthermore, college major matters. Quantitative knowledge and skills are now common characteristics of high-labor-market-value credentials and are prerequisite to many professional advancement opportunities (Carnevale, Cheah, & Hanson, 2015; US Department of Education, 2015). Finally, numeracy or quantitative literacy is more critical than ever to personal finance, health care, and citizenship (OECD, 2016; Reyna, Nelson, Han, & Dieckmann, 2009; Steen & National Council on Education and the Disciplines, 2001).

Given these shifts, ensuring all students have the capacity, confidence, and willingness to engage in quantitative practices and thinking is essential to supporting equitable opportunities for upward mobility. Key outcomes indicating achievement of this goal are:

- College readiness—Mastery of mathematical knowledge and skills necessary for success in college credit-bearing courses aligned to students' intended programs of study;
- Career readiness—Timely attainment of mathematics credits relevant to students' academic and career aspirations and completion of credentials with labor market value;
- Civic readiness—Mastery and confident application of quantitative knowledge and skills in diverse, nonacademic contexts.

Current State of College, Career, and Civic Readiness Goals

College-readiness deficits surface in a broad swath of undergraduate mathematics education programs. Among beginning postsecondary students in 2003–2004, 59% starting in public two-year and 33% in public four-year institutions took a remedial mathematics course. Among them, 50% and 42% (respectively) did not complete all of the remedial mathematics courses in which they enrolled (Chen, 2016). Equally worrisome, among 2003–2004 first-time postsecondary students, the percentage of college-level mathematics credits attempted, but not earned, ranged from 38% in two-year colleges to 46% in four-year colleges (Radford & Horn, 2012). The abundance of evidence shows low-income and minority students are disproportionately represented in developmental courses and experience high rates of failure in college-level mathematics courses, which highlights how critical these issues are to addressing equity gaps (Fernandez, Barone, & Klepfer, 2014; Sparks & Malkus, 2013).

Failure to succeed in remedial and in college-level mathematics courses is correlated with non-completion and employment disappointment. Across the country, 36% of all students beginning college in 2009 had not completed a degree or certificate within six years of enrolling and were no longer enrolled in postsecondary education; almost half (46%) of students starting in public two-year colleges did not complete a degree (Wei & Horn, 2013). Among students taking at least one remedial course, only 28% went on to complete a college credential within 8.5 years (Attewell, Lavin, Doimina, & Levey, 2006).

Complete College America estimates that students seeking bachelor's degrees spend an average of $68,153 in additional tuition, fees, and living expenses, plus forgone income, every additional year enrolled in college (CCA, 2014). Not only are students not earning the credentials they need for employment, but they are also going into debt, further diminishing return on investment and the value of their degree relative to their personal income.

Furthermore, early failure in undergraduate mathematics courses is correlated with STEM attrition and low enrollment in higher-level mathematics courses (Chen & Soldner, 2013). Over half of the students in two-year and 21% in four-year institutions did not earn a college-level mathematics credit while enrolled (Chen, 2016). This evidence suggests that students are not being adequately supported in attaining degrees, knowledge, and skills of value in the workforce.

Finally, attention to civic readiness is critical to preparing students for successful futures, and this is especially relevant for mathematics education. Despite having higher-than-average levels of educational attainment, adults in the US have below-average basic numeracy skills, or ability to use, access, interpret, and communicate mathematical information and ideas (OECD, 2016). Unsurprisingly, despite improvements over the last three decades, the 2015 National Assessment of Educational Progress (NAEP) scores show only 40% of 4th-grade students and 33% of 8th-grade students perform at or above the Proficient level in NAEP mathematics, with Black and Hispanic students scoring less than half as well as White and Asian students

(US Department of Education, 2015). Furthermore, six in ten Americans report having difficulty when faced with applying mathematics in everyday situations. Three in ten report they are not good at mathematics and one in five feels frustrated or anxious doing mathematics (Change the Equation, 2010).

Barriers to Achieving Modern College, Career, and Civic Readiness Goals

Misalignment of Mathematics Education Programs with Students' Futures

Students' success in their first year of college is shaped in large part by the learning experiences they receive in high school. However, a 2013 National Center on Education and the Economy report found that the mathematics most needed by community college students is elementary and middle school mathematics that is not taught in high school and is not learned well enough by many students because of the rush to cover additional algebra-based content (NCEE, 2013). Other experts find mathematics standards do not adequately equip students with the knowledge and skills required for effective citizenship, such as applications of statistics that help students make sense of concepts from student debt to tax reform (Packer, 2016).

Statements from associations of mathematicians demonstrate a professional consensus that failure rates can be partly attributed to misalignment of developmental and college-level course content with students' intended academic and career goals (Saxe & Braddy, 2015). Traditionally, entry-level mathematics coursework consists of a one-size-fits-all algebra sequence designed to prepare students for calculus, which is necessary in algebra-intensive STEM fields. However, workforce data indicate that, for students entering postsecondary education in 2003–2004, just 20% of associate's degree and about 28% of bachelor's degree students entered an algebra-intensive STEM field (Chen & Soldner, 2013). Students in social science, liberal arts, and fine arts would be better served by more relevant preparation in statistics or quantitative reasoning. Traditional entry-level sequences are doubly problematic—they lower student success and completion, and they do not adequately prepare students for the quantitative needs of most majors.

A Conference Board of the Mathematical Sciences study showed 91% of students enrolled in mathematics coursework at two- and four-year postsecondary institutions were enrolled in algebra-intensive mathematics coursework (Blair, Kirkman, & Maxwell, 2013). However, only one-fifth of jobs require more than 8th-grade mathematics skills, and less than 25% of all majors require preparation for calculus (Handel, 2016). Knowing that quantitative literacy is critical to citizenship and that mathematics content knowledge has high labor market value, this suggests too many students lack both strong foundations in and experience with applying mathematics concepts. Indeed, some argue that the lack of alignment between mathematics sequences and job requirements has too often led to students with postsecondary credentials landing a job interview, but not having the skills to secure gainful employment (Treisman & Taylor, 2015). STEM graduates from top universities have also spoken out about their sense of lack of preparation for the workforce, asserting their preparation focused too much on theorems, definitions, and proofs, and lacked real-world applications, interdisciplinary links, and data-based examples (Transforming Post-Secondary Education in Mathematics, 2015a).

Ineffective Systemic Practices of Mathematics Remediation

Too many students are labeled "underprepared" and required to repeat course content they have taken previously in order to advance. Though intended to support students in advancing along the traditional algebra-based sequence from 7th to 12th grade, repeating algebra in high school is not a successful remediation practice. A 2010 study investigating mathematics placement in

San Francisco schools found nearly 65% of students who took Algebra I in 8th grade repeated it in 9th grade, even though 42% met or exceeded proficiency levels on standardized tests (Waterman, 2010). Another study of 24 California school districts found students were repeating Algebra in grades 9 and 10, and fewer than 9% became proficient on their second attempt in grade 10 (Finkelstein, Fong, Tiffany-Morales, Shields, & Huang, 2012). A 2014 Department of Education report showed repeating algebra had statistically significant positive impacts on students who were the least prepared; however, this practice had statistically significant negative effects on more prepared students (Fong, Jaquet, & Finkelstein, 2014).

Repeating calculus in college is similarly not a successful remediation strategy. Bressoud (2015) found that the majority of students who take calculus in their first year of college have already taken it in high school and were advised or deemed unprepared to enroll in Calculus II in college. Calculus is not required for most students' programs of study; moreover, there are struggling students for whom repeating a traditional college calculus course is not an effective strategy for content mastery (Bressoud & Rasmussen, 2015). Many of these students become disheartened when they get to college and perform poorly in a course in which they succeeded in high school. Several studies indicate that first-year calculus courses negatively affect the mathematics identities and persistence of women, first-generation students, and underrepresented minority students (Cribbs, Hazari, Sonnert, & Sadler, 2015; Ellis, Fosdick, & Rasmussen, 2016).

In postsecondary remedial mathematics education, half of the students in two-year and 42% of students in four-year institutions do not complete all of the remedial mathematics courses in which they enroll. Remedial students at public two-year institutions take about three remedial courses, while those at public four-year institutions take two remedial courses (Chen, 2016). Long course sequences have high attrition rates (Bailey, Jeong, & Cho, 2010; Wlodkowski, Mauldin, & Campbell, 2002). The percentage of students who complete the remedial sequence is inversely related to the number of remedial levels that students must complete before reaching the college-level mathematics course (Hayward & Willett, 2014). This phenomenon is attributed to the number of exit points in the sequence (Edgecombe, 2011). In addition to those students who do not pass the course, other students fail to enroll in the next course or drop out between courses.

Ineffective Placement, Transfer, and Applicability Policies

In secondary mathematics, a combination of the traditional algebra sequence and ineffective placement policies leads to some students repeating algebra and students in both advanced and remedial courses failing to demonstrate deep understanding (Bressoud, 2015; Clotfelter, Ladd, & Vigdor, 2012; Loveless, 2013; Stein, Kaufman, Sherman, & Hillen, 2011; Williams, Haertel, & Kirst, 2011). Experts recommend course sequences involving key "decision points" at grades 11 and 12; but, ultimately, districts must choose when and how to offer separate mathematics pathways to which groups of students (Brown, Look, Finkelstein, Dinh, & Clerk, 2014; San Francisco Unified School District, 2014). Equity issues complicate this process, including concerns about fairness, fears of tracking, and hopes of providing accelerated opportunities for the most underrepresented student populations (Daro, 2014; Loveless, 2015).

In higher education, placement, transfer, and applicability policies and practices reinforce misalignment and remediation barriers by defaulting to algebra-based developmental course sequences for students, regardless of academic or career aspirations. Default placement practices too often lead to adverse equity outcomes, especially for STEM fields (Couturier & Cullinane, 2015). See Barnett and Reddy (2017) for further discussion on placement practices.

Currently, 45% of all US undergraduates are enrolled in the 1,108 community colleges across the country, and more than one-third of college students transfer at some point before earning a degree (American Association of Community Colleges, 2016). Transfer students face credit mobility problems when a receiving institution does not accept their course credits and when it accepts courses as elective credits, rather than credits applying to a degree program. Both transfer and applicability credit losses extend students' time to degree, increase their expenses, and lower the likelihood of bachelor's degree attainment.

Outdated Curriculum Design and Pedagogical Practices

Most states have shifted their K–12 mathematics standards to reflect a greater emphasis on depth, rather than breadth, of understanding (Garland, 2016; Korn, Gamboa, & Polikoff, 2016). A large body of research, much of which serves as the foundation for these standards, provides evidence that curriculum design providing opportunities for students to both develop deep understanding and gain an appropriate breadth of content knowledge enhances student readiness and future success at all levels of education (Conley, 2008, 2015; National Research Council, 2001; Schwartz, Sadler, Sonnert, & Tai, 2008). However, many districts are struggling with how to both support all students in attaining deep understanding and respond to pressure to accelerate some students so that they can demonstrate to colleges the greater breadth of their content exposure (Daro, 2014; Heitin, 2015; Texas Association of School Administrators, 2014). On the other end of the traditional algebra sequence, over 30 years of calculus reforms have aimed to enhance students' depth of understanding and make calculus a pump rather than a filter (Bressoud, Mesa, & Rasmussen, 2015). However, many postsecondary mathematics advocates find that on-the-ground curriculum design and pedagogy have yet to live up to ambitious reform goals.

Ineffective pedagogical practices can prevent students from feeling as though they belong in quantitative environments and from confidently applying quantitative knowledge and skills outside the classroom. Teacher-centered strategies, such as traditional lecture-based instruction, often promote surface-level awareness building, rather than deep understanding and critical skill-building (Freeman et al., 2014; National Education Association, 2014). Too many mathematics courses, particularly in postsecondary education, lack meaningful knowledge application opportunities involving real-world problems and settings (Perin, 2011; Rathbun, 2015). When abstraction is not appropriately balanced with application, learning is disconnected from meaning and becomes a compliance activity, rather than a path to content mastery. Finally, separating in-class instruction and associated learning supports, such as student learning centers, adversely affects the quality and coherence of academic support.

In addition, traditional pedagogy rarely addresses strategies to help students develop skills as learners. Pintrich (2003) demonstrated the importance of motivational beliefs and classroom contexts as factors significantly moderating students' conceptual change in understanding their content coursework. Other research reveals that lack of self-regulated learning strategies (e.g., assessing confidence, reviewing strategy use, correcting conceptual errors) limits students' ability to accurately assess their abilities and to succeed on course examinations (Zimmerman, Moylan, Hudesman, White, & Flugman, 2011). Learning strategies that focus on changing student perceptions of their ability to learn, rather than achieving a specific grade, are critical for student success.

Overcoming Barriers through Mathematics Pathways

Mathematics pathways represent a strategy that coherently combines targeted methods to address key structural, curricular, and pedagogical barriers to college, career, and civic readiness through mathematics.

Program Coherence from K–12 through Postsecondary Education

Mathematics pathways approaches redesign mathematics education by beginning with the end in mind. For example, entry-level mathematics courses should align with the needs of programs of study; high school mathematics courses should align with entry-level college courses. This alignment is accomplished by defining the specific quantitative learning objectives required by programs of study and identifying the entry-level mathematics course best suited to those objectives. Given students' diverse needs for their quantitative preparation, alternatives to the traditional algebra sequence are now seen as more appropriate for many programs of study (Burdman, 2015). These alternatives include a greater emphasis on statistics, modeling, computer science, and quantitative reasoning. The Mathematical Association of America's Committee on the Undergraduate Program in Mathematics (CUPM) supports this view, asserting that mathematics departments should consider students' career paths and colleges' particular field-of-study agreements (Mathematical Association of America & Barker, 2004).

At the institutional level, mathematics pathways alignment is a relatively mature reform effort that remains largely focused on lower-division postsecondary education. National advocacy efforts and state-level activities are expanding their focus to K–12 alignment. Mathematics task forces in six states have identified a need for increased consideration of state-based or Common Core standards and dual enrollment as potential starting points. These states' recommendations also underscore that state and institutional definitions of college readiness are not constrained exclusively to completion of intermediate algebra. In addition, a 2013 Texas law created high school graduation "endorsements"—similar to a college meta-major—and allow students to build their mathematics sequences around their chosen endorsement. The legislation also requires that districts partner with institutions of higher education to offer a course for entering 12th graders who are not yet ready for college-level mathematics as another way to create more coherence at the K–12 to higher education transition.

Until recently, there has been little focus on mathematics pathways for upper-division college courses, particularly in non-STEM programs of study. However, one of the strategic priorities of Transforming Post-Secondary Education in Mathematics is promoting "Routes with Relevance"—upper-division postsecondary mathematics pathways providing broader and more relevant training for all undergraduates by offering courses or other learning experiences valuable in the workplace (2015b). According to the TPSE Mathematics strategic plan:

> While there have always been some upper-division service courses in mathematics, such as complex analysis, other topics are growing in importance, including probability, game theory, algorithms, applied linear algebra, mathematics of networks, data analytics and machine learning. Mathematics majors also can benefit from acquiring some of these skills.
>
> (2015b, p. 21)

Replacing Extended Developmental Sequences with Accelerated and Corequisite Pathways

To address ineffective remediation practices, mathematics pathways approaches redesign course structures and placement policies through acceleration and corequisite strategies. These approaches operate under a principle that all students can succeed in higher-level mathematics with the right support structures. The goal is to ensure more students advance toward their academic and career goals and to provide differentiated levels of support. When corequisite strategies have been used in lower-division mathematics, few students required additional support.

Methods for structuring and sequencing courses vary across mathematics pathways approaches. Several initiatives have developed models combining acceleration and alignment to programs of study for students referred to developmental mathematics. These initiatives fall into two categories: one-semester models and one-year models. DCMP curriculum offers a two-semester developmental and college-level mathematics sequence for the most underprepared students and supports institutions with implementing corequisite strategies for most students. City University of New York's model allows developmental students to directly enroll in college-level statistics courses, thus allowing them to complete a college-level course in one semester. Ivy Tech's mathematics pathways model allows students to co-enroll in a revised developmental mathematics course and college-level quantitative reasoning course in the same semester. Finally, the Carnegie Foundation's Statway program integrates the developmental education course into a year-long college-level statistics course (Rutschow, 2016).

Offering the "Right" Mathematics and Assuring Its Broad Acceptance

Rather than placing students into college algebra by default, the mathematics pathways approach enacts policies and structures placing students into the mathematics course indicated for their intended program of study. Indeed, eight of nine state mathematics task forces studied point explicitly to the need for training advisors on new and emerging mathematics pathways to prevent default placement of students into college algebra (Massey & Cullinane, 2015). Some task forces establish multiple measures or modify placement policies instead of using cut scores alone. Nevada revised placement policies through the use of a combination of placement exams, high school GPA, course selection, performance in grade 12, and intended postsecondary program of study. Almost all task forces highlight the importance of aligning mathematics pathways across two- and four-year institutions to preserve mathematics credits for students when they transfer across institutions. To address credit applicability concerns, states recommend developing common learning outcomes, identifying common course numbers, adding multiple entry-level mathematics courses to the general education curriculum, and identifying the majors (or creating meta-majors) that align with different mathematics pathways.

Modernizing Mathematics Curriculum Design and Pedagogy

Common characteristics of redesigned curricula developed by mathematics pathways approaches include mathematics and statistics presented in context and with connections to other disciplines. In addition, curricula incorporate the use of discipline-specific terminology, language constructs, and symbols to intentionally build mathematical and statistical understanding. Mathematics pathways curricula also support the development of problem-solving skills, and students apply previously learned skills to solve nonroutine problems. These courses are designed to actively involve students in doing mathematics and statistics, analyzing data, constructing hypotheses, solving problems, reflecting on their work, and making connections. Class activities generally provide opportunities for students to actively engage in discussions and tasks using various instructional strategies (e.g., small groups, class discussions, interactive lectures). Math pathways curricula also incorporate embedded strategies to help students develop skills as learners, such as productive persistence.

Mathematics pathways approaches provide professional learning support, often connected to the curriculum. Supports include increased professional learning opportunities, strengthened communication, pairing faculty with master instructors, and financial assistance. Increasingly, professional associations are advocating for the adoption of evidence-based practices, including mathematics pathways approaches. The Conference Board for Mathematical Sciences,

TPSE Mathematics, the American Mathematical Association for Two-Year Colleges, and the National Council for Teachers of Mathematics have all directed their members to professional learning support to update their skills in alignment with mathematics pathways efforts.

Case Study

The DCMP Approach

DCMP leads a national movement that is "faculty-driven, administrator-supported, policy-enabled, and culturally-reinforced." The Dana Center supports institutions to implement the DCMP model, grounded in four principles. Structural and policy changes to align content and shorten course sequences are made quickly and at scale. Mathematics pathways are structured so that:

- Principle 1: All students, regardless of college readiness, enter directly into mathematics pathways aligned to their programs of study.
- Principle 2: Students complete their first college-level mathematics requirement in their first year of college.

The DCMP model also supports institutions and departments to engage in a deliberate and thoughtful process of continuous improvement to ensure high-quality, effective instruction. Students engage in high-quality learning experiences in mathematics pathways designed so that:

- Principle 3: Strategies to support students as learners are integrated into courses and are aligned across the institution.
- Principle 4: Instruction incorporates evidence-based curriculum and pedagogy.

The Dana Center works at multiple levels of the system to support meaningful and sustainable change. The DCMP works within institutions to engage, mobilize, and coordinate the actions of individuals with different roles. DCMP also works at the regional, state, and national levels to coordinate the actions of institutions and organizations working in different sectors and address critical issues, such as placement and transfer and applicability policies. The Dana Center offers a suite of tools, resources, and technical assistance services to support this work.

(DCMP, 2016)

Evidence of the Effectiveness of Mathematics Pathways

Multiple mathematics pathways initiatives at the lower-division level have measurably improved student success and timely progress toward completion. Importantly, research suggests that a majority of students can succeed in college-level mathematics courses with appropriate support. In some instances, course success rates decrease as access to the course is expanded, but evidence shows there is still an increase in the overall percentage and number of underprepared students who complete the entry-level course.

Success rates in all three gateway courses increased when, in 2014, The University of Texas at Arlington began shifting student enrollment out of college algebra and into quantitative reasoning and statistics courses (Getz, Ortiz, Hartzler, & Leahy, 2016). Also, students in the New

Mathways Project statistics pathway experienced higher engagement than those in traditional algebra-intensive mathematics courses (Rutschow & Diamond, 2015).

The national developmental-to-gateway mathematics course completion rate for underprepared students is 20% over three years (Bailey et al., 2010). But student success rates in one-year mathematics pathways range from 23% to 51%—double the traditional completion rate. When one-year models are appropriate, their success is greatly increased when the first and second semesters are linked through back-to-back mathematics. Furthermore, one-semester corequisite remediation has even higher completion rates: 51%–64%. Underprepared students can clearly succeed in college-level mathematics courses at higher rates and in less time than students enrolled in traditional developmental sequences (Bailey et al., 2010; Hayward & Willett, 2014; Rutschow & Diamond, 2015; Sowers & Yamada, 2015).

Implications for Policy, Practice, and Research

Equitable access to high-quality mathematics education opens doors for students—preparing them for success in college and careers. All students, regardless of background or prior mathematics preparation, deserve a rigorous mathematics education and support for timely completion of degrees, certificates, or licenses of academic and labor market value. However, system misalignment, ineffective remedial structures, and outdated curricular and pedagogical strategies have been persistent barriers to student success.

Multiple mathematics pathways represent a systemic approach to ensuring a rigorous and relevant mathematics education for all. The approach works at multiple educational levels and across multiple sectors to drive large-scale, sustainable reform. Mathematics pathways are improving student success in the first two years of college. Efforts to expand mathematics pathways to K–12 and upper-division postsecondary mathematics programs are quickly gaining traction and should receive additional support to move to implementation at scale.

Further success will require continued engagement with state policy agencies to build their capacity, development of technical assistance tools and services to support practitioners in continuous improvement processes, and research on which strategies best serve which populations of students in order to support institutions in making the best use of limited funds.

References

American Association of Community Colleges. (2016). *AACC 2016 Fact Sheet*. Retrieved from www.aacc.nche.edu/AboutCC/Documents/AACCFactSheetsR2.pdf.

Attewell, P. A., Lavin, D. E., Domina, T., & Levey, T. (2006). New evidence on college remediation. *Journal of Higher Education, 77*(5), 886–924.

Bailey, T., Jeong, D. W., & Cho, S.-W. (2010). Referral, enrollment, and completion in developmental education sequences in community colleges. *Economics of Education Review, 29*(2), 255–270.

Barnett, E., & Reddy, V. (2017). College placement strategies: Evolving considerations and practices. In K. L. McClarty, K. D. Mattern, & M. N. Gaertner (Eds.), *Preparing students for college and careers: Theory, measurement, and educational practice.* New York: Routledge.

Blair, R. M., Kirkman, E. E., & Maxwell, J. W. (2013). *Statistical abstract of undergraduate programs in the mathematical sciences in the United States: Fall 2010 CBMS survey.* Providence, RI: AMS.

Bressoud, D. (2015). Insights from the MAA national study of college calculus. *Mathematics Teacher, 109*(3), 179–185.

Bressoud, D., Mesa, V., & Rasmussen, C. (2015). *Insights and recommendations from the MAA national study of college calculus. MAA Notes.* Washington, DC: The Mathematical Association of America.

Bressoud, D., & Rasmussen, C. (2015). Seven characteristics of successful calculus programs. *Notices of the American Mathematical Society, 62*(02), 144–146.

Brown, K., Look, S. C., Finkelstein, N., Dinh, T., & Clerk, G. (2014). *Acceleration, access, and equity: Pathways for success in the Common Core.* Presented at the Curtis Center Mathematics and Teaching Conference. Retrieved from http://curtiscenter.math.ucla.edu/sites/default/files/curtis_conf_2014/Brown.pdf.

Burdman, P. (2015). *Probing math placement policies at California colleges and universities.* Stanford: Policy Analysis for California Education, PACE.

Cahalan, M., & Perna, L. (2015). *Indicators of higher education equity in the United States.* Washington, DC: Pell Institute for the Study of Opportunity in Higher Education.

Carnevale, A. P., Cheah, B., & Hanson, A. R. (2015). *The economic value of college majors.* Washington, DC: Georgetown University Center on Education and the Workforce.

Change The Equation. (2010). *In a new survey, Americans say, "We're not good at math."* Retrieved from http://changetheequation.org/press/new-survey-americans-say-%E2%80%9Cwe%E2%80%99re-not-good-math%E2%80%9D.

Chen, X. (2016). *Remedial coursetaking at U.S. Public 2- and 4-Year institutions.* Washington, DC: National Center for Education Statistics.

Chen, X., & Soldner, M. (2013). *STEM attrition: College students' paths into and out of STEM fields.* Washington, DC: National Center for Education Statistics.

Clotfelter, C. T., Ladd, H. F., & Vigdor, J. L. (2015). The aftermath of accelerating algebra. *Journal of Human Resources, 50*(1), 159–188.

Complete College America. (2014). *Four-Year Myth.* San Francisco, CA: Retrieved from http://completecollege.org/wp-content/uploads/2014/11/4-Year-Myth.pdf.

Conley, D. T. (2015). Breadth vs. depth: The deeper learning dilemma. *Education Week.* Retrieved from http://blogs.edweek.org/edweek/learning_deeply/2015/10/breadth_vs_depth_the_deeper_learning_dilemma.html.

Couturier, L., & Cullinane, J. (2015). *A call to action to improve mathematics placement policies and processes.* Boston, MA: Jobs for the Future.

Cribbs, J. D., Hazari, Z., Sonnert, G., & Sadler, P. M. (2015). Establishing an explanatory model for mathematics identity. *Child Development, 86*(4), 1048–1062.

Dana Center Mathematics Pathways Model. (2016). *DCMP.* Retrieved from https://dcmathpathways.org/dcmp/dcmp-model.

Daro, P. (2014). *Oakland and San Francisco create course pathways through Common Core mathematics.* Washington, DC: Strategic Education Research Partnership.

Edgecombe, N. (2011). *Accelerating the academic achievement of students referred to developmental education* (CCRC Brief Number 55). Community College Research Center.

Ellis, J., Fosdick, B. K., & Rasmussen, C. (2016). Women 1.5 times more likely to leave STEM pipeline after calculus compared to men: Lack of mathematical confidence a potential culprit. *PLoS One, 11*(7), e0157447.

Fernandez, C., Barone, S., & Klepfer, K. (2014). *Developmental education and student debt.* TG. Retrieved from https://www.tgslc.org/pdf/Developmental-Education-and-Student-Debt.pdf.

Finkelstein, N., Fong, A., Tiffany-Morales, J., Shields, P., & Huang, M. (2012). *College bound in middle school & high school? How math course sequences matter.* San Francisco, CA: Center for the Future of Teaching and Learning at WestEd.

Fong, A. B., Jaquet, K., & Finkelstein, N. (2014). *Who repeats Algebra I, and how does initial performance relate to improvement when the course is repeated?* San Francisco, CA: REL West.

Freeman, S., Eddy, S. L., McDonough, M., Smith, M. K., Okoroafor, N., Jordt, H., & Wenderoth, M. P. (2014). Active learning increases student performance in science, engineering, and mathematics. *Proceedings of the National Academy of Sciences, 111*(23), 8410–8415.

Garland, S. (2016). In Texas, new math standards look a whole lot like Common Core. *Hechinger Report.* Retrieved from http://hechingerreport.org/texas-new-math-standards-look-whole-lot-like-common-core/.

Getz, A., Ortiz, H., Hartzler, R., & Leahy, F. F. (2016). *The case for mathematics pathways.* Austin, TX: Charles A. Dana Center. Retrieved from https://dcmathpathways.org/resources/making-case-math-pathways.

Handel, M. J. (2016). What do people do at work? A profile of U.S. jobs from the survey of workplace skills, technology, and management practices. *Journal for Labour Market Research, 49*(2), 177–197.

Handwerk, P., Tognatta, N., Coley, R. J., & Gitomer, D. H. (2008). *Access to success: Patterns of advanced placement participation in U.S. high schools* (Policy Information Report). Princeton, NJ: Educational Testing Service.

Hayward, C., & Willett, T. (2014). *Curricular redesign and gatekeeper completion.* Sacramento, CA: California Acceleration Project, RP Group.

Heitin, L. (2015). Common Core seen falling short in high school math. *Education Week.* Retrieved from www.edweek.org/ew/articles/2015/02/25/common-core-seen-falling-short-in-high.html.

Korn, S., Gamboa, M., & Polikoff, M. (2016). *Just how common are the standards in Common Core states?* Center on Standards, Alignment, Instruction, and Learning. Retrieved from http://c-sail.org/resources/blog/just-how-common-are-standards-common-core-states.

Loveless, T. (2013). *The resurgence of ability grouping and persistence of tracking.* Washington, DC: Brown Center on Education Policy at Brookings.

Loveless, T. (2015). *High achievers, tracking, and the Common Core* (The Brown Center Chalkboard Series). Washington, DC: Brookings.

Massey, K., & Cullinane, J. (2015). *Momentum for improving undergraduate mathematics: Progress from state mathematics task forces.* Austin, TX: Dana Center Mathematics Pathways.

Mathematical Association of America, & Barker, W. (Eds.). (2004). *Undergraduate programs and courses in the mathematical sciences: CUPM curriculum guide 2004.* Washington, DC: Mathematical Association of America.

National Center on Education and the Economy. (2013). *What does it really mean to be college and career ready?* Retrieved from http://ncee.org/college-and-work-ready/.

National Education Association. (2014). *Preparing 21st century students for a global society: An educator's guide to the "Four Cs."* Washington, DC: Author.

National Research Council. (2001). *Adding it up: Helping children learn mathematics.* Washington, DC: The National Academies Press.

OECD. (2016). *Skills matter: Further results from the survey of adult skills.* Paris: OECD Publishing.

Packer, A. (2016). Creating informed citizens should be education's goal. *Education Week.* Retrieved from www.edweek.org/ew/articles/2016/03/16/creating-informed-citizens-should-be-educations-goal.html.

Perin, D. (2011). *Facilitating student learning through contextualization* (CCRC Brief Number 53). New York: Community College Research Center.

Pintrich, P. R. (2003). A motivational science perspective on the role of student motivation in learning and teaching contexts. *Journal of Educational Psychology, 95*(4), 667–686.

Radford, A. W., & Horn, L. (2012). *An overview of classes taken and credits earned by beginning postsecondary students.* Washington, DC: National Center on Education Statistics.

Rathburn, M. K. (2015). Building connections through contextualized learning in an undergraduate course on scientific and mathematical literacy. *International Journal for the Scholarship of Teaching and Learning, 9*(1), Article 11.

Reyna, V. F., Nelson, W. L., Han, P. K., & Dieckmann, N. F. (2009). How numeracy influences risk comprehension and medical decision making. *Psychological Bulletin, 135*(6), 943–973.

Rutschow, E. Z. (2016). *Memo to CAPR annual meeting attendees.* New York: CAPR.

Rutschow, E. Z., & Diamond, J. (2015). *Laying the foundations: Early findings from the New Mathways Project.* New York: MDRC.

San Francisco Unified School District. (2014). *From middle school to high school: Mathematics course sequence for the CCSS-M.* Retrieved from http://www.sfusdmath.org/uploads/2/4/0/9/24098802/sfusd_course_sequence_recommendation.pdf.

Saxe, K., & Braddy, L. (2015). *A common vision for undergraduate mathematical science programs in 2025.* Mathematical Association of America.

Schwartz, M. S., Sadler, P. M., Sonnert, G., & Tai, R. H. (2008). Depth versus breadth: How content coverage in high school science courses relates to later success in college science coursework. *Science Education, 93*(5), 798–826.

Sowers, N., & Yamada, H. (2015). *Pathways impact report.* Stanford, CA: Carnegie Foundation for the Advancement of Teaching.

Sparks, D., & Malkus, N. (2013). *First-year undergraduate remedial coursetaking: 1999–2000, 2003–04, 2007–08.* (Statistics in Brief). Washington, DC: National Center on Education Statistics.

Steen, L. A., & National Council on Education and the Disciplines. (Eds.). (2001). *Mathematics and democracy: The case for quantitative literacy.* Princeton, NJ: NCED.

Stein, M. K., Kaufman, J. H., Sherman, M., & Hillen, A. F. (2011). Algebra: A challenge at the crossroads of policy and practice. *Review of Educational Research, 81*(4), 453–492.

Texas Association of School Administrators. (2014). *Implementation of revised TEKS: Issues and concerns.* Retrieved from www.tasanet.org/cms/lib07/TX01923126/Centricity/shared/images/tasadaily/pdfs/teks.pdf.

Transforming Post-Secondary Education in Mathematics. (2015a). *Report of a meeting.* Los Angeles, CA: Institute of Pure and Applied Mathematics, UCLA.

Transforming Post-Secondary Education in Mathematics. (2015b). *Strategic Plan.* Retrieved from https://d3n8a8pro7vhmx.cloudfront.net/math/pages/1/attachments/original/1466617785/TPSE_Strategic_Plan_Exec_Summ.pdf?1466617785.

Treisman, U., & Taylor, M. (2015). *Collaboration opportunities for two-year and four-year colleges.* American Association of Community Colleges. Retrieved from Collaboration opportunities for two-year and four-year colleges.

U.S. Department of Education. (2015). National Center for Education Statistics, National Assessment of Educational Progress (NAEP), various years, 1992–2015 Mathematics Assessments.

Waterman, S. (2010). *Pathways report: Dead ends and wrong turns on the path through Algebra.* Noyce Foundation. Retrieved from http://www.noycefdn.org/documents/Pathways_Report.pdf.

Wei, C. C., & Horn, L. (2013). *Federal student loan debt burden of noncompleters.* (Stats in Brief). Washington, DC: National Center on Education Statistics.

Williams, T., Haertel, E., & Kirst, M. (2011). Improving middle grades math performance. *EdSource.* Retrieved from https://edsource.org/wp-content/publications/pub11-middle-grades-math.pdf.

Wlodkowski, R. J., Mauldin, J., & Campbell, S. (2002). *Early exit: Understanding adult attrition in accelerated and traditional postsecondary programs.* Indianapolis, IN: Lumina Foundation.

Zimmerman, B. J., Moylan, A., Hudesman, J., White, N., & Flugman, B. (2011). Enhancing self-reflection and mathematics achievement of at-risk urban technical college students. *Psychological Test and Assessment Modeling, 53*(1), 141–160.

12 Supporting College and Career Readiness through Social Psychological Interventions

Kathryn M. Kroeper and Mary C. Murphy

What abilities are necessary to succeed in school and in life? Proficiencies in mathematics and language are fundamental skill sets; however, these skills alone may not be enough for students to persist and succeed in their educational training. In addition to cognitive skills that boost college and career readiness, researchers find many noncognitive factors are highly influential (Aronson, Fried, & Good, 2002; Hulleman & Harackiewicz, 2009; Walton & Cohen, 2011). For example, students' beliefs about the nature of intelligence impact their motivation and persistence in the face of failure. Their construals[1] of social and academic hardships affect whether they perform well or flounder. Additionally, identifying personal relevance and value in what students are learning can influence their achievement. In this chapter, we address these topics by presenting several well-supported social psychological interventions that confer noncognitive skills and strengths by encouraging students to change their mindsets—their thoughts, feelings, and beliefs—and their construals of the local environment.

The social psychological interventions we review utilize a person-by-situation approach. According to this approach, personal factors (e.g., students' social identities, such as race, gender, or social class) interact with societal stereotypes and environmental cues (e.g., a bad grade, rejection by a peer) to affect students' thoughts, feelings, and behaviors. For example, Black and Latino students—whose intelligence is negatively stereotyped and who find themselves underrepresented in postsecondary settings—may construe a bad grade as a signal that they don't belong in college, while White students who do not contend with the same stereotypes may not draw the same conclusion. Because of the stereotypes tied to gender groups, a woman in a math class may interpret the fact that she was not invited to join a study group as a sign that others have low expectations of her, while a man in the same situation might think he was simply overlooked. Once personal and situational factors are identified, researchers create and test interventions that directly target these factors, while promoting more adaptive construals of the environment. As we will see, when these interventions are properly implemented, they can be a powerful force for boosting college and career readiness.

Identity Threat as a Psychological and Contextual Barrier to College and Career Readiness

One way students' social identities can interact with the broader academic context is by engendering social identity threat. Identity threat refers to the worries that people may have about being devalued or disrespected in settings, due to their social group membership(s). There are two necessary ingredients for identity threat to occur. First, an individual must belong to a stigmatized group (e.g., being a woman, older, an underrepresented person of color, gay, poor). Second, the individual must be engaged in a context where the situational cues suggest that one (or more) of their identities may be devalued or disrespected. Identity threat negatively affects college and career readiness, because it causes people to ruminate on the possibility that one could be disrespected, devalued, or discriminated against—taking up cognitive resources that could otherwise be put toward learning, while stoking anxiety and vigilance that disrupt attention (Schmader, Johns, & Forbes, 2008). Thus, the aim of many social psychological interventions is to alleviate identity threat by offering different, more productive, ways to think about the self and our relationship to our environments.

Probably, the most widely researched form of identity threat is stereotype threat (Steele & Aronson, 1995). Students from traditionally stigmatized groups often contend with negative stereotypes that impugn their intellectual abilities. Even when students do not believe these stereotypes themselves, simply being aware that others could perceive them stereotypically often leads stigmatized individuals to underperform (e.g., Steele, Spencer, & Aronson, 2002). Why? Increased attention to the possibility of stereotyping undermines attention to learning tasks and reduces executive functioning required to perform well on difficult tasks (Beilock, Rydell, & McConnell, 2007; Schmader et al., 2008). Moreover, because of their underrepresentation and stigmatized status, these students are more likely to feel uncertain about whether they belong in a setting, struggle with whether they can be their authentic selves, and worry about being discriminated against (see Murphy & Taylor, 2012 for a review of identity threat concerns).

Because identity threat results from a feeling that the environment may not value stigmatized individuals, researchers have tried to alleviate threat by either offering new ways to think about the self to help students cope with a challenging environment or by changing the situation—removing identity-threatening cues, adding identity-safe cues, and providing more resources to support stigmatized people. The most effective interventions do both.

Chapter Overview

The goal of this chapter is to review examples of social psychological interventions that improve the readiness, persistence, and success of students and professionals—with a particular emphasis on the mechanisms by which these interventions effectively address social identity threat concerns and improve outcomes for stigmatized people. First, we will discuss one of the most popular person-focused interventions—the growth mindset intervention—that communicates that people can grow their intelligence and abilities. Next, we turn to interventions that confer adaptive construals of the social environment and its relationship to the self. We examine how social belonging and utility value interventions change students' relationships with their social context. Finally, we discuss how insights from these interventions can be used to improve college and career readiness.

Growth Mindset Interventions

People's mindsets are the beliefs they have about how the social world operates, and they are incredibly powerful. In academic and employment settings, the fundamental beliefs that we have about the nature of intelligence—what intelligence is and where it comes from—exert tremendous influence over our perception, judgment, motivation, and behavior (e.g., Dweck, Chiu, & Hong, 1995; Molden & Dweck, 2006). Researchers have predominantly examined the consequences of endorsing one of two mindsets. People who endorse a fixed mindset think intelligence is a relatively unchangeable trait that a person either has or doesn't have. People who endorse a growth mindset think intelligence is a quality that can be developed over time by sustained effort, flexibly adopting new strategies, and persisting through challenges. These often unspoken, yet influential mindsets serve as a framework for drawing meaning about success and failure in academic and career contexts (Molden & Dweck, 2006). That is, students' mindsets affect how they interpret and act on feedback from peers, teachers, and employers.

Because students who endorse a fixed mindset believe intelligence cannot change, they are motivated to demonstrate their intellectual prowess. This motivation, however, is a double-edged sword, because it also means that students will avoid challenges and actively hide their vulnerabilities and mistakes so as not to appear unintelligent to others (Dweck & Sorich, 1999; Nussbaum & Dweck, 2008). In the face of challenges or failures, fixed mindset students are more likely to interpret negative feedback as a signal that they have reached the limit of their natural ability. In consequence, when these students face intellectual challenges (e.g., criticism from a teacher), they give up (Hong, Chiu, Dweck, Lin, & Wan, 1999; Molden & Dweck, 2006).

Students who endorse a growth mindset believe that by putting in effort and persisting through challenges, they can grow their intelligence (Dweck et al., 1995). These students are motivated to constantly develop themselves and their skills, even if it means failing sometimes along the way. Individuals with a growth mindset therefore tend to approach academic and employment challenges as learning opportunities that identify places for improvement and growth. To them, intellectual challenges are not indicative of a lack of ability; they simply indicate that a particular area needs more attention or a new strategy. Of course, failures may still sting for growth-minded students, but they also motivate them to work harder and seek help, rather than withdraw. Thus, in the face of failure or setbacks, growth mindsets motivate greater effort and persistence (Hong et al., 1999; Molden & Dweck, 2006).

Interventions That Encourage Individuals to Adopt a Growth Mindset

Can students be encouraged to adopt a growth mindset? Will such changes boost college and career readiness? In short, yes. Efforts to promote growth mindset beliefs among students are gaining popularity in educational contexts. Several randomized controlled trials demonstrated that students who learned to adopt a growth mindset through social psychological interventions—especially students from stigmatized groups who contend with identity threat—engaged in more adaptive learning strategies and showed improved academic performance compared to control group students (Aronson et al., 2002; Blackwell, Trzesniewski, & Dweck, 2007; Good, Aronson, & Inzlicht, 2003).

For example, in a field experiment, middle-school students participated in an eight-week workshop led by a trained college student. Students in the growth mindset treatment condition learned about insights from neuroscience studies that demonstrated the brain's ability to grow new connections—providing scientific evidence that intelligence and skills develop over time through practice and new strategies. In the control condition, students learned about the mechanics of human memory, along with tips to improve it. Although teachers did not know which students received the growth mindset treatment, results revealed that students who did showed greater classroom motivation and effort. Moreover, these students earned higher math grades at the end of the term compared to students in the control group. While the grades of students in the control condition actually declined over the course of the year, this downward trend was halted and reversed among students in the growth mindset treatment condition (Blackwell et al., 2007).

Growth mindset interventions seem to be especially beneficial for students from underrepresented and stigmatized groups. Because these students contend with negative cultural stereotypes suggesting their groups' intellectual inferiority, communicating that intelligence is expandable with effort and motivation refutes these negative stereotypes. For example, another field experiment demonstrated how African-American students particularly benefited from a growth mindset intervention. African-American and Caucasian undergraduates were randomly assigned to one of three groups. One group of students joined a pen pal program and was encouraged to learn about and share growth mindset messages with their pal (treatment);

a second group joined the pen pal program, but did not share growth-oriented messages (control group 1); and a third group of students did not participate in the pen pal program at all (control group 2). African-American students who communicated growth mindset messages to a pen pal reported greater enjoyment of the educational process (e.g., studying, going to class, taking tests), placed more value on their academics, and earned higher grades than their African-American peers in either of the two control groups. Communicating the growth mindset message also had positive, but more modest, effects on the enjoyment and academic achievement of Caucasian students (Aronson et al., 2002). These results suggest that growth mindset interventions can increase academic motivation, persistence, and performance, especially for students from underrepresented and stigmatized backgrounds.

Social Belonging Interventions

In the previous section, we reviewed a person-focused intervention emphasizing the malleability of intelligence. Now, we turn to two context-focused interventions that confer adaptive construals of the social environment. The first of these targets belonging uncertainty as a barrier to college and career readiness.

Feeling that one belongs and is valued is fundamental to human flourishing. People are vigilant to cues that signal social acceptance and rejection (Leary, 2010). Whereas cues that bolster belonging tend to have positive implications, cues that threaten our sense of belonging are often accompanied by negative consequences. For instance, cues that signal a lack of belonging are associated with lowered self-esteem (Leary & Baumeister, 2000), hurt feelings (Buckley, Winkel, & Leary, 2004), increased loneliness (Leary, 2010), and a reduced sense of control (Zadro, Williams, & Richardson, 2004). Indeed, people's sense of belonging is critical to their college and career success. For example, feeling uncertain about whether one belongs in college is associated with lower grades, poorer physical health, and lower life satisfaction (Walton & Cohen, 2011).

Negative cultural stereotypes and underrepresentation in postsecondary settings are two powerful factors that shape people's sense of belonging. People from stigmatized and underrepresented backgrounds are more likely to experience belonging uncertainty than people from majority groups (Walton & Cohen, 2007). For racial and ethnic minorities, women in STEM fields, low-income, and first-generation college students, social and academic adversities can be particularly painful, because a plausible explanation is that the adversities could be due to their group membership, stereotyping, or discrimination (e.g., "Is it because I'm Black? Is my professor racist? Or are they just having a bad day?"). This attributional ambiguity means that stigmatized people may interpret these adversities as evidence of non-belonging (Crocker & Major, 1989). For example, an African-American college student may be enrolled at a university, but for many reasons (e.g., peer exclusion, concerns about being negatively stereotyped, and so forth) feel unaccepted at college. These identity-threatening attributions about adversity, while sometimes protective of health and well-being (Crocker, Voelkl, Testa, & Major, 1991), may simultaneously undermine motivation and achievement.

Fortifying Sense of Belonging through Social Psychological Intervention

If one of the barriers to college and career success is the meaning that people make of adversity, then interventions that provide strategies for connection may support people's sense of belonging and their achievement. Social belonging interventions harness classic social psychological principles to help people see that they are not alone in questioning their fit with the school and provide strategies to reduce academic and social hardships by bolstering connection with others.

Put differently, when people encounter identity-threatening cues—like critical feedback from a professor or sitting alone in the cafeteria—they can view these cues as evidence that they may not belong. Social belonging interventions help people respond to these threatening cues by sharing stories from both stigmatized and non-stigmatized peers that communicate (a) students are not alone in their uncertainty, and (b) there are strategies that have worked for others to increase connection and manage adversity. For example, if a first-year college student performs poorly on an exam, the student can interpret it to mean that he or she doesn't belong. Alternatively, the student could see it as a relatively common negative experience that happens to many students who are still learning to master college material and test taking. The student can see that other students found it helpful to talk with a professor, join a study group, or seek tutoring. By addressing the identity-threatening meaning of adversity, negative thoughts are challenged and people are better equipped to manage and overcome adversities.

Across several randomized controlled trials, social belonging interventions improved academic persistence and performance among racial and ethnic minority college students and college women in STEM majors (Walton & Cohen, 2007, 2011; Walton, Logel, Peach, Spencer, & Zanna, 2015). For example, African-American and Caucasian freshmen were randomly assigned to a social belonging treatment or a control group (Walton & Cohen, 2011). Students in the treatment group read short stories, ostensibly written by upperclassmen from racially diverse backgrounds, which framed adversities and the resulting feelings of belonging uncertainty as common to many students and due to the challenging nature of the college transition. To help students draw connections between their own experiences and the intervention's message, students were asked to write essays about how their experiences transitioning to college were similar to the stories they read. Students believed their essays would be shared with future college students to help ease these incoming students' transitions to college. This process turned students into benefactors—rather than beneficiaries—bestowing a helpful and hopeful message to younger peers. Researchers then tracked students' college grades and sent them a brief survey to follow up on their psychological well-being and health.

Compared to African-American students in the control group, African-American students in the treatment group reported less belonging uncertainty, better health and well-being, and significantly improved academic performance—an effect sustained throughout college. Whereas African-American students in the control group showed no improvement in GPA from their freshman year through their senior year, African Americans in the treatment group showed significant improvement in GPA throughout their college years. By students' senior years, the achievement gap between African-American students and Caucasian students was narrowed by 52% in the treatment group. Researchers found that while the social belonging intervention had no consequences for Caucasian students, it significantly improved academic, social, and health outcomes for African-American students.

A similar field experiment addressed the unique belonging concerns of first-generation college students (Stephens, Hamedani, & Destin, 2014). These students tend to have more academic difficulties—completing fewer credit hours and earning lower grades—than their continuing-generation peers (Pascarella, Pierson, Wolniak, & Terenzini, 2004). Many colleges assume that these difficulties are due to greater financial struggle and poorer academic preparation; however, the increased feelings of belonging uncertainty that these students experience are another powerful factor contributing to achievement disparities (Stephens et al.). To address the belonging uncertainty of first-generation students, Stephens and colleagues randomly assigned incoming first-generation and continuing-generation college students to participate in one of two discussion panels about the transition to college. Students assigned to the first discussion panel listened to a diverse group of upperclassmen discussing how their social class backgrounds could be both a challenge and a source of strength at college (treatment).

For example, one of the panelists described the unique struggles she encountered as a first-generation student, as well as the strategies she employed to overcome that adversity:

> Because my parents didn't go to college, they weren't always able to provide me the advice I needed. So it was sometimes hard to figure out which classes to take and what I wanted to do in the future. But there are other people who can provide that advice, and I learned that I needed to rely on my adviser more than other students.

> (p. 3)

Students assigned to the second panel also listened to the same group of upperclassmen discuss their transitions to college, but their stories did not reference how social class backgrounds can be a source of challenge and strength (control group). After participating in one of the two discussion panels, all students (a) completed brief surveys assessing their well-being and tendency to seek campus resources and (b) created a video testimonial describing what they learned from the panel. This speaking exercise encouraged students to think critically about the intervention message and personalize it to fit within their own experiences.

First-generation students in the treatment group earned higher cumulative GPAs than their first-generation peers in the control group. Moreover, the intervention reduced the achievement gap between first-generation and continuing-generation students in the treatment group by 63%. Further analyses revealed that this achievement gap reduction was driven by the increased resource-seeking behavior of first-generation students in the treatment group. Put differently, first-generation students who learned that their social class background can sometimes make college more challenging, but can also be harnessed as a source of strength, took greater advantage of campus resources than their first-generation peers in the control group. This increased resource-seeking bolstered first-generation students' academic performance. These results suggest that tailoring the social belonging message to fit the local context can robustly boost academic achievement outcomes.

Utility Value Interventions

Another barrier to college and career readiness is the "why does it matter" question. Feeling that something (like learning or performance) is pointless can sap motivation. Indeed, research reveals that cultivating meaning and interest in a topic enhances cognitive functioning, increases students' learning motivation, and is critical to school success (Hidi & Harackiewicz, 2000; Hulleman & Harackiewicz, 2009). This is the goal of utility value interventions.

To illustrate, let's imagine students are learning a mental math technique. At first, many students may not see the point. Utility value interventions nudge students to think about the value of mental math—how and when it could come in handy. Examples could include situations when we find ourselves without a calculator, phone, pen, or paper; contexts when using mental math will be faster than using a calculator (e.g., calculating tip at a restaurant); or the competitive edge provided in time-pressured standardized testing where strong performance will help them get into a good college. When students see the personal relevance and value in a topic or task, research suggests they will become more motivated and interested, which should, in turn, boost performance (Hulleman & Harackiewicz, 2009).

Indeed, discovering the value of what one is learning increases task interest (Hulleman, Godes, Hendricks, & Harackiewicz, 2010), learning motivation (Simons, Dewitte, & Lens, 2003), and task-related performance (Hulleman & Harackiewicz, 2009; Hulleman et al., 2010). By contrast, when the value of what students are learning is unclear, students are more likely to believe that the task is pointless and disengage from the lesson or, worse yet, the entire subject (e.g., math or science).

When the utility value of topics or assignments is unclear, it can have a disparately negative effect on students who are insecure about their academic abilities. Researchers found that students with lower confidence in their academic abilities had more difficulty drawing personal relevance from their coursework (Hulleman & Harackiewicz, 2009), suggesting that these students may need additional support to find value in their work.

Furthermore, racial minorities, low-income students, and first-generation college students often perceive a mismatch between their personal values—which tend to prize collective, interdependent, group-focused goals—and the values of schools and coursework—which tend to prize independent, self-focused goals (Stephens, Fryberg, Markus, Johnson, & Covarrubias, 2012). Therefore, stigmatized students may especially benefit from interventions that help them identify ways in which their coursework is relevant to and serves their interdependent values (Harackiewicz, Canning, Tibbetts, Priniski, & Hyde, 2015).

Interventions Helping Students Find the Value in Learning

Utility value interventions encourage students to identify the relevance and worth of their coursework. While there are many ways utility value interventions are delivered, in most, students are prompted by researchers, teachers, advisors, or parents to think about the ways in which their learning and coursework matter. That is, students are challenged to apply course-related concepts to their daily life and describe how learning particular topics is applicable and supportive of their future plans (Hulleman & Harackiewicz, 2009). Similar to social belonging interventions, utility value interventions often encourage students to personalize the intervention message and make it relevant to their own experiences.

A field experiment conducted by Hulleman and Harackiewicz (2009) examined the effectiveness of a utility value intervention among high- and low-confidence students. In this study, researchers asked high school students to write essays in one of their science classes. Half of the students were randomly assigned to write about how science topics in class were useful (treatment), whereas the remaining students wrote summaries of what they had learned in class (control). Results revealed that low-confidence students in the treatment group (i.e., those who expected to be less successful in their science class before the intervention) reported greater interest in science and earned higher grades than their low-confidence peers in the control group. The intervention had no effect on high-confidence students, whose interest and grades were already relatively high.

In another study, researchers asked college students to learn a four-step technique for solving two-digit multiplication problems in their head—a task that could easily be dismissed as arcane and irrelevant to daily life (Hulleman et al., 2010). After learning the technique, students were randomly assigned to either write an essay about the relevance of the technique for themselves and other college students (treatment) or to write an essay about the objects they saw in two pictures that hung on the walls of the experimental room (control). Students in the treatment group reported greater interest in the technique and reported an increased likelihood of using the technique in the future compared to their control group peers. Moreover, the intervention especially benefitted the interest and performance expectations of low-confidence students.

Utility value interventions may also address achievement gaps. Because racial minority and first-generation students often perceive a mismatch between their personal values (collective, interdependent) and the values of their schools and coursework (self-focused, independent), researchers hypothesized that racial minority and first-generation students would benefit from a utility value intervention that helped students see how their coursework could serve their interdependent values and goals (Harackiewicz et al., 2015). To test this hypothesis, undergraduate college students in an introductory biology course were randomly assigned to complete writing assignments that either focused on the personal relevance and usefulness of course topics to students' interdependent goals and values (treatment) or that summarized the topics they learned in class (control group). The utility value intervention improved the performance of all students in the treatment group, while having a particularly positive effect on first-generation racial minority students. Moreover, the intervention reduced the racial achievement gap in the treatment group by 40%.

Implications for Policy, Practice, and Research

In this chapter, we've reviewed several social psychological interventions that confer noncognitive skills and strengths to students, which, in turn, boost their college and career readiness. These interventions promote learning, persistence, and performance by alleviating identity threat. Researchers alleviate threat by offering new ways to think about the self in order to help students cope with a challenging environment, by changing the situation—removing identity-threatening cues, adding identity-safe cues, providing resources to help meet the needs of stigmatized people—or by a combination of both.

We discussed how teaching people about the malleability of intelligence engenders greater zest for learning and improved performance. This appears to be especially true for individuals from groups that are stereotyped as intellectually inferior and traditionally underrepresented in postsecondary settings. Classroom teachers and administrators are particularly influential, as they can use their positions to transform a fixed mindset culture—focused on proving and performing—into a growth mindset culture—focused on learning and developing (Emerson & Murphy, 2014).

Leaders can cultivate growth mindsets in several ways. First, they can directly express growth values to their students, employees, and colleagues. Noticing and pointing to others' development, praising them for persisting and adopting different strategies in the face of challenge, and providing constructive feedback are all strategies that foster a growth mindset culture. In addition, how people think about, and respond to, failure may be equally critical in communicating a growth mindset. For example, parents' "failure mindsets"—their beliefs about the meaning of failure—predicted whether their children adopted fixed or growth mindsets about intelligence (Haimovitz & Dweck, 2016). Parents who endorsed the idea that failure is debilitating and detrimental to learning expressed higher levels of worry, pity, and doubt about their children's abilities, which, in turn, led their children to adopt fixed mindsets about intelligence. Conversely, when teachers and leaders greet failures and setbacks as beneficial to learning, it is likely to encourage growth mindsets.

We also described how belonging is fundamental to human flourishing. Social belonging interventions show people that they are not alone and provide strategies for connection that help them manage academic and social hardships. These interventions normalize social and academic frustrations and boost health, well-being, and performance outcomes (Walton & Cohen, 2007, 2011; Walton et al., 2015).

What can teachers and faculty do to create a culture that normalizes adversity and emphasizes belonging? The message that adversity is common and does not necessarily signal nonbelonging is the core of social belonging interventions. Telling diverse stories of adversity while shining a light on successful strategies for overcoming those adversities will help guide people who are struggling to adopt productive strategies. When people are transitioning to new settings—beginning college or starting a new job—it is especially important to address uncertainty with inclusive messages and behaviors that explicitly value people from diverse backgrounds and help them connect with others.

Finally, we reviewed how developing interest in a topic boosts cognitive functioning, motivation, and achievement (Hulleman & Harackiewicz, 2009). Utility value interventions help people identify the relevance and worth of their work. Practitioners who read about utility value interventions may come away with the idea that implementing these interventions is easy and straightforward. However, a close reading of successful utility interventions will reveal that each intervention asked students to self-generate the reasons that topics or coursework was personally relevant and useful.

Indeed, studies that directly examine different methods of delivery have found that when authorities (e.g., teachers) directly communicate the usefulness of a topic or task, it may backfire—especially among low-confidence individuals (Canning & Harackiewicz, 2015). When authorities explain why something is relevant, it may undermine interest by ramping up the pressure to perform, increasing the level of threat for low-confidence students and causing them to disengage. Practitioners can mitigate this threat by offering students opportunities to self-generate reasons that topics and tasks matter to them and by asking authorities to focus on lower-stakes examples (e.g., calculating tip), rather than higher-stakes examples (e.g., setting students up to get into a good college).

These interventions are powerful, yet they are not magic (Yeager & Walton, 2011), and there are important limits to their efficacy. To the extent that institutional, academic, and social barriers exist in an environment (e.g., prejudice and discrimination, lack of funding, few social-support structures), social psychological interventions are less likely to be effective. These interventions are most likely to be successful in places where resources support the intervention message: in organizations that have cultivated a growth-mindset culture; where others experience belonging uncertainty and where people are open to attempts to forge connection; and where topics and tasks are relevant and useful to people's lives. In these places, interventions represent an effective lever—mitigating identity threat and helping all people thrive at school and work.

Note

1 The term "construal" refers to the way that people understand, interpret, and make meaning of an experience.

References

Aronson, J., Fried, C., & Good, C. (2002). Reducing the effects of stereotype threat on African American college students by shaping theories of intelligence. *Journal of Experimental Social Psychology, 38*, 113–125.

Beilock, S. L., Rydell, R. J., & McConnell, A. R. (2007). Stereotype threat and working memory: Mechanisms, alleviation, and spillover. *Journal of Experimental Psychology: General, 136*(2), 256–276.

Blackwell, L. B., Trzesniewski K. H., & Dweck, C. S. (2007). Implicit theories of intelligence predict achievement across an adolescent transition: A longitudinal study and an intervention. *Child Development, 78*(1), 246–263.

Buckley, K. E., Winkel, R. E., & Leary, M. R. (2004). Reactions to acceptance and rejection: Effects of level and sequence of relational evaluation. *Journal of Experimental Social Psychology, 40*(1), 14–28.

Canning, E. A., & Harackiewicz, J. M. (2015). Teach it, don't preach it: The differential effects of directly communicated and self-generated utility-value information. *Motivation Science, 1*(1), 47–71.

Crocker, J., & Major, B. (1989). Social stigma and self-esteem: The self-protective properties of stigma. *Psychological Review, 96*, 608–630.

Crocker, J., Voelkl, K., Testa, M., & Major, B. (1991). Social stigma: The affective consequences of attributional ambiguity. *Journal of Personality and Social Psychology, 60*(2), 218–228.

Dweck, C. S., Chiu, C., & Hong, Y. (1995). Implicit theories and their role in judgments and reactions: A world from two perspectives, *Psychological Inquiry, 6*(4), 267–285.

Dweck, C. S., & Sorich, L. A. (1999). Mastery-oriented thinking. In C. R. Snyder (Ed.), *Coping* (pp. 232–251). New York: Oxford University Press.

Emerson, K. T. U., & Murphy, M. C. (2014). Identity threat at work: How social identity threat and situational cues contribute to racial and ethnic disparities in the workplace. *Cultural Diversity and Ethnic Minority Psychology, 20*(4), 508–520.

Good, C., Aronson, J., & Inzlicht, M. (2003). Improving adolescents' standardized test performance: An intervention to reduce the effects of stereotype threat. *Applied Developmental Psychology, 24*(6), 645–662.

Haimovitz, K., & Dweck, C. S. (2016). Growth intelligence mind-sets? Not their parents' views of intelligence but their parents' views of failure. *Psychological Science, 27*(6), 859–869.

Harackiewicz, J. M., Canning, E. A., Tibbetts, Y., Priniski, S. J., & Hyde, J. S. (2015). Closing achievement gaps with a utility-value intervention: Disentangling race and social class. *Journal of Personality and Social Psychology, 111*(5), 745.

Hidi, S., & Harackiewicz, J. M. (2000). Motivating the academically unmotivated: A critical issue for the 21st century. *Review of Educational Research, 70*(2), 151–171.

Hong, Y., Chiu, C., Dweck, C. S., Lin, D. M. S., & Wan, W. (1999). Implicit theories, attributions, and coping: A meaning system approach. *Journal of Personality and Social Psychology, 77*(3), 588–599.

Hulleman, C. S., Godes, O., Hendricks, B. L., & Harackiewicz, J. M. (2010). Enhancing interest and performance with a utility value intervention. *Journal of Educational Psychology, 102*(4), 880–895.

Hulleman, C. S., & Harackiewicz, J. M. (2009). Promoting interest and performance in high school science classes. *Science, 326*, 1410–1412.

Leary, M. R. (2010). Affiliation, acceptance, and belonging: The pursuit of interpersonal connection. In S. T. Fiske, D. T. Gilbert, & G. Lindzey (Eds.), *Handbook of Social Psychology* (5th ed., pp. 864–897). Hoboken, NJ: John Wiley & Sons, Inc.

Leary, M. R., & Baumeister, R. F. (2000). The nature and function of self-esteem: Sociometer theory. In M. P. Zanna (Ed.), *Advances in experimental social psychology* (Vol. 32, pp. 1–62). San Diego, CA: Academic Press.

Molden, D. C., & Dweck, C. S. (2006). Finding "meaning" in psychology: A lay theories approach to self regulation, social perception, and social development. *American Psychologist, 61*(3), 192–203.

Murphy, M. C., & Taylor, V. J. (2012). The role of situational cues in signaling and maintaining stereotype threat. In M. Inzlicht & T. Schmader (Eds.), *Stereotype threat: Theory, process, and applications* (pp. 17–33). New York: Oxford University Press.

Nussbaum, A. D., & Dweck, C. S. (2008). Defensiveness versus remediation: Self-theories and modes of self-esteem maintenance. *Personality and Social Psychology Bulletin, 34*(5), 599–612.

Pascarella, E., Pierson, C., Wolniak, G., & Terenzini, P. (2004). First-generation college students: Additional evidence on college experiences and outcomes. *Journal of Higher Education, 75*, 249–284.

Schmader, T., Johns, M., & Forbes, C. (2008). An integrated process model of stereotype threat effects on performance. *Psychological Review, 115*(2), 336–356.

Simons, J., Dewitte, S., & Lens, W. (2003). "Don't do it for me. Do it for yourself!" Stressing the personal relevance enhances motivation in physical education. *Journal of Sport & Exercise Psychology, 25*, 145–160.

Steele, C. M., & Aronson, J. (1995). Stereotype threat and the intellectual test performance of African Americans. *Journal of Personality and Social Psychology, 69*(5), 797–811.

Steele, C. M., Spencer, S. J., & Aronson, J. (2002). Contending with group image: The psychology of stereotype and social identity threat. *Advances in Experimental Social Psychology, 34*, 379–440.

Stephens, N. M., Fryberg, S. A., Markus, H. R., Johnson, C. S., & Covarrubias, R. (2012). Unseen disadvantage: How American universities' focus on independence undermines the academic performance of first-generation college students. *Journal of Personality and Social Psychology, 102*(6), 1178–1197.

Stephens, N. M., Hamedani, M. G., & Destin, M. (2014). Closing the social-class achievement gap: A difference-education intervention improves first-generation students' academic performance and all students' college transition. *Psychological Science, 25*(4), 943–953.

Walton, G. M., & Cohen, G. L. (2007). A question of belonging: Race, social fit, and achievement. *Journal of Personality and Social Psychology, 92*(1), 82–96.

Walton, G. M., & Cohen, G. L. (2011). A brief social-belonging intervention improves academic and health outcomes of minority students. *Science, 331*, 1447–1451.

Walton, G. M., Logel, C., Peach, J. M., Spencer, S. J., & Zanna, M. P. (2015). Two brief interventions to mitigate a "chilly climate" transform women's experience, relationships, and achievement in engineering. *Journal of Educational Psychology, 107*(2), 468–485.

Yeager, D. S., & Walton, G. M. (2011). Social-psychological interventions in education: They're not magic. *Review of Educational Research, 81*(2), 267–301.

Zadro, L., Williams, K. D., & Richardson, R. (2004). How low can you go? Ostracism by a computer is sufficient to lower self-reported levels of belonging, control, self-esteem, and meaningful existence. *Journal of Experimental Social Psychology, 40*(4), 560–567.

13 Changing the Assessment Relationship to Empower Teachers and Students

Margaret Heritage

Introduction

The thesis of this chapter is that college- and career-ready students must be active agents in their own learning. Skills related to student agency are developed in assessment contexts, specifically through formative assessment practices, modeled at first in teacher-student interactions, and subsequently applied by students themselves in self-regulation and peer-to-peer feedback (Clark, 2012; Cowie, 2012). Agentive self-regulation is developed in classrooms where the skill is valued by teachers, time is set aside for its development, and a classroom culture is created that forwards its emergence (Paris & Paris, 2001).

Assessment has two fundamental purposes: summative and formative (National Research Council [NRC], 2001). The key difference between them is how assessment information is used—either to guide and advance learning during the process of learning or to obtain evidence of what students have learned after a period of teaching and learning, typically after several weeks, at the end of a semester, or annually. While results of assessment for summative purposes are often used beyond the classroom (e.g., accountability, making decisions about student placement, certification, curriculum, and programs), formative assessment rests entirely with teachers and students in order to advance learning day by day in their classrooms (Heritage, 2010, 2013; Klenowski, 2009; Swaffield, 2011).

Notably, formative assessment is not just for teachers; students are actively involved in the assessment process. A key practice in formative assessment is for students to monitor their progress against established learning goals and performance criteria, to compare a current learning state with the goal and criteria, and then to make judgments about how they can attain their goals (Hattie & Timperley, 2007; Sadler, 1989).

The student role in formative assessment is consistent with contemporary perspectives on learning that acknowledge the importance of learner agency, understood as the ability to actively manage one's own learning through setting goals, monitoring progress toward those goals, and adapting learning approaches to optimize learning (Zimmerman & Schunk, 2011). If learner agency is to be supported, the assessment relationship between teacher and students must change from vertical to horizontal. Most often, assessment operates in a vertical relationship, as for example, when students take a test at the end of a period of instruction and are just informed of their results, or when they are assigned a grade. In formative assessment, the relationship becomes a horizontal one, where students receive feedback about their learning from teachers, peers, and their own self-monitoring process, so that they can make judgments about the actions they need to take to advance learning.

This chapter examines how, when the assessment relationship is changed in formative assessment, students can be empowered to be active agents in their own learning. The first section provides background on formative assessment, which is followed by a discussion of the "spirit" and the "letter" of formative assessment that has direct bearing on student agency. The chapter then addresses feedback as a core practice of formative assessment and of student agency, describes a learning culture to support student agency, and concludes with a section on implications for policy, practice, and research.

Background

Formative assessment or assessment for learning (AfL)[1] was first promoted in the 1980s (Crooks, 1988; Natriello, 1987; Sadler, 1989) as a way to connect the two assessment activities of making judgments about student learning and providing feedback to students that is intended to move learning forward. A major landmark in establishing formative assessment as an explicit domain of practice was Paul Black and Dylan Wiliam's research synthesis (Black & Wiliam, 1998), which encompassed "diverse bodies of research, including studies addressing: teachers' assessment practices, students' self-perception and achievement motivation, classroom discourse practices, quality of assessment tasks and teacher questioning, and the quality of feedback" (Shepard, 2009, p. 32). Since then, research, research reviews, and theory have reinforced Black and Wiliam's claims that formative assessment, when well implemented, is a powerful engine for promoting learning (e.g., Bell & Cowie, 2001; Birenbaum, 2007; Black, Harrison, Lee, Marshall, & Wiliam, 2003; Hattie & Timperley, 2007; Torrance & Pryor, 2001).

The practical implementation of formative assessment includes sharing learning goals and success criteria with students, obtaining evidence of learning while learning is taking place, self-assessment, and timely feedback from teachers and peers (Absolum, 2010; Black et al., 2003; Heritage, 2010, 2013; Wiliam, 2011). These practices have been increasingly embedded worldwide into policy and the language of quality teacher practices (OECD, 2013).

Successfully engaging students in formative assessment is a hallmark of higher levels of expertise. Teachers who are expert practitioners in formative assessment share responsibility for moving learning forward with their students; learning is recognized as a social process and becomes a joint responsibility (Cowie, Harrison, & Willis, 2016). This perspective is echoed in a recent National Research Council (NRC) report, which identified three broad and interrelated domains of competence for deeper learning required to meet college- and career-ready standards: cognitive (e.g., critical thinking, reasoning, argumentation); interpersonal (e.g., collaboration, negotiation, cooperation); and intrapersonal (e.g., metacognition, self-monitoring, self-direction) (NRC, 2012).

Figure 13.1 illustrates how effectively formative assessment practices form a substrate for developing these skills.

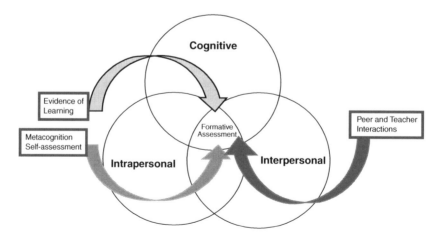

Figure 13.1 Formative Assessment Practices and College and Career Ready Skills

Cognitive competencies are supported through the evidence of learning that is elicited and acted upon by teachers and students during the learning process; feedback is a focus of peers and teacher in their interactions; students assess their own learning and learn to be self-directing, setting goals and adapting their learning strategies.

The principles of learning that underlie and are implemented in formative assessment practices are well established and firmly supported by cognitive research. Simply put, these principles are:

1   start from a learner's existing understanding;
2   involve the learner actively in the learning process;
3   develop the learner's overview (i.e., metacognition, which requires that students have a view of purpose; understanding of criteria of quality of achievement; and self-assessment, which is essential for student agency); and
4   emphasize the social aspects of learning (e.g., learning through discussion, collaboration) (Black, Wilson, & Yao, 2011).

The Spirit and the Letter of Formative Assessment

Starting with the hypothesis that AfL is built on an underlying principle that promotes student autonomy, Marshall and Drummond (2006) analyzed videos of lessons and teacher interviews to focus on the ways that teachers enact this principle in their classrooms. From their analysis, they drew a distinction between lessons that embody the "spirit" of AfL and those that conform only to the "letter" (Marshall & Drummond, 2006). The "spirit" of AfL is instantiated in the ways that teachers conceptualize and sequence tasks to reflect a progression of learning and in the way that they value student agency. In contrast, the "letter" of AfL is represented through a fixed view of what happens in a lesson with only the procedures of AfL in place. For example, the "letter" of AfL is evident when teachers consider feedback as any comments given to students informally in an unplanned way or are given to the class as a general statement that does not relate to any individual student. The "spirit" is evident when teachers provide feedback that is closely tied to the task at hand and to the problems the students are experiencing in their learning (Earl & Timperly, 2014).

The differences reflected in the "spirit" and the "letter" echo Perrenoud (1998), who characterizes AfL as the regulation of learning. For Perrenoud, the nature of the tasks planned for a lesson significantly impacts the potential for interaction and feedback as the lesson progresses. He differentiates between "traditional" sequences of activities within lessons that merely allow remediation of prescribed concepts and those lessons where the tasks are not "imposed on learning but [adjusted] once they have been initiated" (Perrenoud, 1998, cited in Marshall & Drummond, 2006, p. 134).

To illustrate, a National Council of Teachers of Mathematics (NCTM) publication describes the traditional lesson paradigm as featuring "review, demonstration and practice" (NCTM, 2014, p. 9). This approach can be considered a fixed sequence of tasks, focused on correctness and accuracy, and which prescribe the learning. Such an approach leads to the implementation of formative assessment as a set of procedures and reinforces the notion of formative assessment as "got it, didn't get it" (Otero, 2006), with remediation as the primary pedagogical response and little to no room for student agency. The NCTM publication describes the change in approaches to teaching and learning needed to achieve college- and career-ready standards. These changes are much more likely to embody the "spirit" of AfL. For example, "using and connecting mathematical representations" involves teachers in "selecting tasks that allow students to decide which representations to use in making sense of the problem; and allocating substantial instructional time for students to use, discuss, and make connections among representations" and involves students in "using multiple forms of representations to make sense of and understand mathematics; and describing and justifying their mathematical understanding and reasoning with drawings, diagrams, and other representations" (NCTM, 2014, p. 29). The context established for mathematics learning not only affords rich opportunities for deeper learning but also for "adjustments" to be made by both teachers and students after the tasks have been initiated. In this situation, the lesson progresses in response to learning, rather than in loose contact with it as in a more "prescribed" approach. Moreover, learner agency can be promoted by engaging students in self-assessment and peer feedback about their representations, descriptions, and justifications, and by providing the opportunity for them to revise goals, act on feedback, or change their learning strategies to enhance their learning.

The nature and sequence of the learning opportunities a teacher offers in a lesson affects all subsequent interactions in the class, including how the relationships in the class develop and the role of student agency. The design of learning is a critical element for formative assessment and especially student agency and is one that, all too often, is overlooked. While the implementation of college- and career-ready standards has resulted in considerable efforts to shift pedagogical practice to align with cognitive research, years of calcified current teaching practices are hard to change. Until they do, the effective implementation of formative assessment that promotes student agency will continue to be challenging.

The Role of Feedback

Feedback from Teachers

In his foundational model of formative assessment, D. Royce Sadler identified feedback as the decisive element to assist learning (1989). Beginning from a systems perspective of feedback (Ramaprasad, 1983), Sadler conceived of formative assessment as a feedback loop to close the gap between the learner's current status and desired goals. More recently, Hattie and Timperley's (2007) review of the research on feedback concluded that, "feedback is among the most critical influences on student learning" (p. 102). Additionally, John Hattie's synthesis of over 800 meta-analyses relating to achievement emphasizes programs with effect sizes above 0.4 as worth having and those below 0.4 needing further consideration. The influence of feedback has an effect size of 0.73, slightly greater than teacher-student relations (0.72), whereas class size and ability grouping influences have an effect size of 0.21 and 0.12, respectively (Hattie, 2008).

While feedback can have a strong influence on learning, not all feedback is effective (Kluger & DeNisi, 1996). Feedback that is effective is related to the learning goals and focused on the learning; is not ego involving (i.e., not focused on the individual); is of the right kind (e.g., detailed, narrative, and actionable—not graded); and is delivered in the right way (constructive and supportive), at the right time (sooner for low-level knowledge; later for complex tasks), and to the right person (who is in a receptive mood and has reasonably high self-efficacy—the belief that one can succeed in a particular situation) (Andrade, 2010). Of course, it is incumbent upon teachers to set the conditions for students to be open to receiving feedback. When students understand the purpose of feedback, they see teachers model feedback, and they are taught the skills of giving peer feedback, they are more inclined to find feedback worthwhile and useful, rather than perceive it as a criticism or something negative (Heritage, 2013).

When teachers plan lessons that instantiate the "spirit" of AfL with their view of learning as an evolution with room for adjustments along the way, feedback becomes a natural part of ongoing teaching. Given the research on the influence of feedback on learning, teacher feedback to students cannot be a sporadic event. Rather, it must be an integral component of effective teaching. With clear goals and success criteria in mind, teachers can intentionally observe and elicit evidence of learning through what students say, do, make, or write in the course of the lesson (Griffin, 2007). Using the goals and criteria as an interpretive framework, teachers can decide on feedback intended to move learning forward. Critically, students must be given time to consider the feedback and decide if and how to use it to make progress in closing the gap between their current learning status and desired goals. If this use of feedback does not become an essential part of the learning process, then students are precluded from agentive action—and an opportunity to maximize learning will likely be lost.

As Black and Wiliam emphasized in their research synthesis,

> The core of the activity of formative assessment lies in the sequence of two actions. The first is the perception by the learner of a gap between a desired goal and his or her present state (of knowledge, and/or understanding, and/or skill). The second is the action taken by the learner to close that gap in order to attain the desired goal.
>
> (1998, p. 20)

Both of these center on actions taken by the learner. Teachers can provide feedback, but in the end, it is the student who actually does the learning. Students' own self-generated feedback is a significant component of the learning process and of student agency.

Student Feedback from Self-Assessment

Self-assessment involves students in monitoring their learning and making judgments about their progress in relation to goals and criteria. When they perceive a discrepancy between their current learning status and desired goals, they take action to move forward.

A key outcome of students engaging in self-assessment is the promotion of self-regulated learning (SRL). SRL is defined as the degree to which students are metacognitively, motivationally, and behaviorally active participants in their own learning processes (Zimmerman, 2008). Metacognitive processes involve learners in setting goals and monitoring their progress toward goals and evaluating how well they are achieving those goals. In light of their progress evaluation, they reflect on their learning approaches and adapt current and future methods. When students do this, they become aware of their learning and can make conscious decisions about how to manage it.

These behaviors are emblematic of the intrapersonal skills associated with college and career readiness (NRC, 2012). Being metacognitive distinguishes stronger learners from less competent ones (NRC, 2012). For example, when students are metacognitive, they can explain the strategies they used to solve a problem and why, whereas less competent students monitor their learning sporadically and ineffectively and provide incomplete explanations (Chi, Bassok, Lewis, Reimann, & Glaser, 1989). If students are to be successful in achieving college- and career-ready standards, they will need to be strong learners who are able to monitor their learning and adapt learning strategies to secure progress. Not only is metacognitive ability a key ingredient in meeting standards, but it is also an intrapersonal skill that students will need to sustain for success in college and the workplace (NRC, 2012).

The result of engaging in metacognitive processes is that students' motivation and feelings of self-efficacy are increased. Highly motivated students are more attentive to their learning processes than poorly motivated ones (Boekaerts & Corno, 2005; Bouffard-Bouchard, Parent, & Larivee, 1991), and they expend extra effort to learn something difficult (Schunk & Hanson, 1985). Students' SRL processes and feelings of self-efficacy are reciprocally interactive (Zimmerman & Schunk, 2008). Behaviorally active students are those who are able to manage their own learning, including time management, and as a result of self-monitoring, take actions leading to improvement. These actions range from adapting a learning strategy, to seeking help or information, or to finding a less distracting place to work.

The positive benefits that come from self-assessment mean that it is cannot be left to chance; rather, it is a skill that takes time to develop and requires teaching and dedicated time in lessons. To engage in effective self-assessment, students need:

1   awareness of the value of self-assessment;
2   access to clear criteria on which to base the assessment;
3   a specific task or performance to assess;
4   models of self-assessment;
5   direct instruction in and assistance with self-assessment, including feedback;
6   practice;
7   cues regarding when it is appropriate to self-assess;
8   and opportunities to revise and improve the task or performance (Goodrich, 1996).

Moreover, students should be asked about what self-assessment strategies they use; as how and when they are used; or how they would describe what they do before, during, and after a task (Zimmerman, 2002). All of the attributes that contribute to self-assessment require constant attention on the part of both teachers and students.

As with teacher feedback to students, feedback about learning that students generate through self-assessment must be used—otherwise, self-assessment is of no consequence in terms of learning. Therefore, time to act on self-assessment should be included in the flow of a lesson. Teachers may provide specific structures, such as templates or protocols for self-assessment, especially as students are beginning to develop these skills, and then build time into the lesson for students to use their own feedback to revise their work or adjust their learning strategies. However, once students have acquired skills in self-assessment, the process will become embedded in teaching and learning. Students will be making real-time decisions about courses of action they need to take based on their judgments of progress. For this reason, lesson design characterized by the "spirit" of formative assessment, throughout which learning is evolving and adjusting, is conducive to the student agency that self-assessment rests on.

Teachers will need to attend to the quality of the student-generated feedback and the actions they take in response. Part of the changing assessment relationship in the classroom is signaled when teachers and students take joint responsibility for learning. In this context, teachers will not leave students to their own devices, but will discuss with students the evidence from which they derived their own feedback, how it relates to the goal and criteria, and their justifications for taking the action they have in mind. At the highest level of self-assessment, the teacher should have sufficient information from the student to encourage the student in taking the proposed next steps in learning and factor this information into future teaching plans.

The skills of self-assessment contribute to the development of learning dispositions, habits, attitudes, and identities that enable students to become lifelong learners. Today's students will find themselves in a fast-paced and ever-changing world of work. Take just one example: 65% of the jobs that today's entering kindergarten children will occupy have not yet been invented (Ross, 2016). In addition to meeting the content requirements of college- and career-ready standards, students will need workplace skills related to self-assessment, such as reflective judgment and decision making. Self-assessment is a vital disposition and core skill for lifelong learners (Dawson, 2008). Consequently, if self-assessment does not become part of the fabric of learning in the classroom, students are deprived of access to an important lifelong skill. Moreover, they remain reliant on teachers and may transfer this reliance on external authorities to other contexts later in life.

Peer Feedback

Up to this point, the focus has centered on teacher feedback to students and students own self-generated feedback loops. However, another aspect of student empowerment through horizontal relationships in the classroom is peer feedback. Peer feedback has been defined as "a communication process through which learners enter into dialogues related to performance and standards" (Liu & Carless, 2006, p. 280). Research indicates that there are learning benefits of providing both high school and college students with opportunities to give and receive feedback (Falchikov, 2001; Liu & Carless, 2006; Miller, 2008; Topping, 2003).

Just as self-assessment needs to be taught, so too do skills in peer feedback. The models that teachers provide in their own feedback to students and the scaffolds they provide for the next step in learning will influence the quality and uptake of peer feedback, as will specific teaching on how to provide constructive feedback to classmates (Gielen, Peeters, Dochy, Onghena, & Struyven, 2010). Equally important is providing structures and time in the classroom that allow peers to reflect on each other's learning with respect to goals and criteria and to make suggestions about improving work products or advancing learning.

In classrooms where the assessment relationship is a horizontal one, feedback from teachers, peers, and from individual students' own feedback loops will be seen by everyone as "just the way we do business."

A Learning Culture

Lessons that are characterized by the "spirit" of formative assessment contribute to the possibilities for feedback, but the culture of the classroom is also an important enabling factor. The way that assessment—formative and summative—is incorporated into the learning process has a significant impact on classroom culture. Assessments determine both the character and quality of education, setting the actual on-the-ground goals for learning, and the limits of the learning opportunities provided (Shepard, 2013). Previously, Shepard wrote about the role of assessment in a learning culture in an effort to get at the "underlying fabric, linking meanings and classroom interaction patterns that have created a 'testing' culture and think instead about the profound shifts that would need to occur to establish a learning culture" (Shepard, 2013, p. xix).

Recognition of the importance of interactional patterns for student agency is founded in the sociocultural learning theory developed by Vygotsky (1962). Vygotsky viewed learning as a social process in which learners collaborate with more knowledgeable others—including teachers and peers. Consequently, he understood learning to be a process in which responsibility for outcomes is a shared one. Effective feedback from teachers, peers, and student self-assessment acts as a scaffold for the next step in learning, intended to move students from the edge of their current learning to a more advanced state.

When teachers and students work together to use information about each student's learning status to advance all participants' learning, they are forming a community of practice (Wenger, 1998). Inherent in the idea of a community of practice is that when individuals participate in the community the collective practices of the community are the product of actions by its individual members. When group members mutually codetermine their collective practices in support of student agency, they are shaping their identities as effective learners who are independent, self-directing, and can act as a learner among other learners (Heritage, 2013). These participant behaviors have implications for the workplace. Increasingly, there is a demand for complex communication competencies, such as interacting with people to acquire information, understanding what the information means, and persuading others of its implications for action (Levy & Murnane, 2004). These competencies need to be fostered throughout K–12 education, and classrooms conceived of as a communities of practice can provide an effective context for their development.

Creating learning cultures that reflect a community of practice involves establishing routines and behaviors that support student participation in learning and assessment. In addition to learning the requisite skills for self-assessment and peer feedback, structures in the classroom must orient students to careful listening to peers and to understanding the value that peers bring to the learning context (Heritage, 2013). Other structures and routines must provide opportunities for self-reflection, discussion among students about their respective learning, and the chance to use feedback for themselves.

The competencies for deeper learning and transferable knowledge and skills that are the aspirations of college- and career-ready standards can be fostered through a learning culture in which student agency in assessment and horizontal relationships are hallmarks.

Implications for Policy, Practice, and Research

There are two main implications that arise from the foregoing discussion: (1) professional learning for teachers and (2) federal and state education policies.

Professional Learning for Teachers

Cowie (2016) refers to the expertise that teachers need to practice high levels of formative assessment as *connoisseurship*—a level of skill that enables them to access information on student learning, orchestrate an extraordinary number of complex judgments in the course of a lesson, and implement appropriate and immediate actions in response to evidence. These actions, when combined with students' willingness to engage in learning, move that learning forward. This orchestration stands in contrast to a much simpler version of formative assessment. Teachers teach the content, and assessment is carried out at the end of a sequence of instruction to determine students' level of achievement "in order to fix their failings" and target the next objective (Klenowski, 2009, p. 263).

Undergirding a high level of orchestration are several competencies:

1   Strong, flexible disciplinary knowledge;
2   The ability to prioritize content to focus on key learning targets;
3   An understanding of which formative assessment strategies are most effective for the subject learning at hand;
4   Knowledge of how student learning of that content develops; and
5   Understanding what the students in their specific context know and care about, as well as what would be the students' priority, given what students know and care about.

These competencies are also required for teaching college- and career-ready standards with their emphasis on rigorous, challenging content. Without significant disciplinary knowledge and knowledge of how students learn in that specific discipline, teachers remain disadvantaged in planning learning opportunities to meet the standards.

Developing *connoisseurship* requires initial and ongoing professional learning for teachers.[2] However, this kind of professional learning is still in short supply. In their efforts to promote formative assessment, some states in the United States have explicitly included formative assessment as part of a balanced assessment system with accompanying professional learning provided by the state (e.g., Iowa, Michigan, Maryland). A few of the obstacles to sustained professional learning for effective formative assessment at the district and school levels include too many competing priorities that don't focus on the real work of schools (i.e., teaching and learning), leaders who see themselves as managers instead of instructional leaders, and district policies and mandates that vitiate formative assessment efforts. And, for the most part, teacher education remains within the purview of faculty who can decide whether formative assessment is worth focusing on.

Educational Policies

In the United States, education policy at both the state and the federal level has provided little or no support for formative assessment. By way of illustration, it is instructive to examine the three references to formative assessment in the Every Student Succeeds Act (ESSA):

1   **Literacy Education for All, Results for the Nation**
    …uses age-appropriate, valid, and reliable screening assessments, diagnostic assessments, *formative assessment processes*, and summative assessments to identify a child's learning needs, to inform instruction, and to monitor the child's progress and the effects of instruction. (Emphases added).

2   **Grants for State Assessments and Related Activities**
    …developing or improving balanced assessment systems that include summative, interim, and *formative assessments*, including supporting local educational agencies in developing or improving *such assessments*. (Emphases added).

3   **Supporting Effective Instruction**
    … providing training, technical assistance, and capacity building in local educational agencies to assist teachers, principals, or other school leaders *with selecting and implementing formative assessments*, designing classroom-based assessments, and using *data from such assessments* to improve instruction and student academic achievement, which *may include providing additional time for teachers to review student data* and respond, as appropriate. (Emphases added).

The first example refers to "formative assessment processes," but does not specify what they are. Furthermore, the use of these processes is unidirectional, from teacher to student, with no role for the student included. The next two examples squarely place formative assessment as a tool, an assessment event, for adult use only (i.e., not student use). Notwithstanding references to evidence-based practices in ESSA, of which formative assessment is one, when such misconceptions of formative assessment are enshrined in legislation, it is hard to conceive of a less conducive policy environment for effective formative assessment implementation and sustained professional learning.

In other countries where formative assessment—including an emphasis on student agency—has taken hold, government policy has led the way. For example, New Zealand's Ministry of Education (1994) provides clear guidance about formative assessment: "Formative assessment is an integral part of the teaching and learning process. It is used to provide feedback [to students] to enhance learning and to help the teacher understand students' learning" (p. 8). More recently, the Ministry (2011) emphasized the "importance of building student assessment capability so that students become autonomous learners and lead their own learning" (p. 10). Through its Quality System Assurance Agency, the Chilean Ministry of Education has created policy that makes formative assessment part of a balanced assessment system and is producing national professional learning for teachers on formative assessment (personal communication, Carolina Vidal Leyton).

Some US states have engaged in the same kind of policy creation and capacity building among their teacher population for formative assessment. However, these states largely remain a minority, and much greater emphasis on policy and practice is needed to fulfill the promise of formative assessment and student agency in achieving college- and career-ready standards.

This chapter has affirmed the view that the fundamental practices of formative assessment constitute a powerful basis for the development of college- and career-ready competencies and the development of students as lifelong learners. In particular, the assessment practices enabled through the implementation of formative assessment provide a new model for the assessment relationship—one in which vertical relationships are reshaped into horizontal ones and in which authority is transformed into collaboration. These new assessment relationships are prototypical of the relationships that students will encounter in college and beyond. Students' exposure to, and acquisition of, the skills necessary to manage such relationships early in life can serve as the foundation for a lifetime of successful learning.

Notes

1 In this chapter, the terms "formative assessment" and "AfL" are used interchangeably.
2 Expert opinion suggests that the time taken to develop real expertise in formative assessment is between three and five years (Cowie et al., 2016).

References

Absolum, M. (2010). *Clarity in the classroom: Using formative assessment to build relationships.* Winnipeg: Portage and Main Press.

Andrade, H. L. (2010). Students as the definitive source of formative assessment: Academic self-assessment and the regulation of learning. In H. L. Andrade & G. J. Cizek (Eds.), *Handbook of formative assessment* (pp. 90–105). New York: Routledge.

Bell, B., & Cowie, B. (2001). *Formative assessment and science education.* Dordrecht, The Netherlands: Kluwer.

Birenbaum, M. (2007). Evaluating the assessment: Sources of evidence for quality assurance. *Studies in Educational Evaluation, 33*(1), 29–49.

Black, P., Harrison, C., Lee, C., Marshall, B., & Wiliam, D. (2003). *Assessment for learning: Putting it into practice.* Berkshire: Open University Press.

Black, P., & Wiliam, D. (1998). Assessment and classroom learning. *Assessment in Education: Principles Policy and Practice, 5,* 7–73.

Black, P., Wilson M., & Yao, S-S. (2011). Roadmaps for learning: A guide to the navigation of learning progressions. *Measurement: Interdisciplinary Research and Perspectives, 9*(2–3), 71–123.

Boekaerts, M., & Corno, L. (2005). Self-regulation in the classroom: A perspective on assessment and intervention. *Applied Psychology, 54*(2), 199–231.

Bouffard-Bouchard, T., Parent, S., & Larivee, S. (1991). Influence of self-efficacy on self-regulation and performance among junior and senior high-school students. *International Journal of Behavioral Development, 14,* 153–164.

Chi, M. T., Bassok, M., Lewis, M. W., Reimann, P., & Glaser, R. (1989). Self-explanations: How students study and use examples in learning to solve problems. *Cognitive Science, 13*(2), 145–182.

Clark, I. (2012). Formative assessment: Assessment is for self-regulated learning. *Educational Psychology Review, 24*(2), 205–249.

Cowie, B. (2012). Focusing on the classroom: Assessment for learning. In B. Fraser, K. Tobin, & C. J. McRobbie (Eds.), *Second international handbook of science education* (Vol. 24), 679–690. New York: Springer.

Cowie, B. (2016, April). *Connoisseurship in formative assessment.* Presentation at the FAST SCASS Conference, Portland, OR.

Cowie, B., Harrison, C., & Willis, J. (2016, April). *Student agency in formative assessment.* Presentation at the FAST SCASS Conference, Portland, OR.

Crooks, T. J. (1988). The impact of classroom evaluation practices on students. *Review of Educational Research, 58,* 438–481.

Dawson, T. L. (2008). *Metacognition and learning in adulthood.* Northampton, MA: Developmental Testing Service.

Earl, L. M., & Timperley, H. (2014). Challenging conceptions of assessment. In C. Wyatt-Smith, V. Klenowski, & P. Colbert (Eds.), *Designing assessment for quality learning* (Vol. 1), 325–336. Dordrecht: Springer.

Falchikov, N. (2002). 'Unpacking' peer assessment. In P. Schwartz & G. Webb (Eds.), *Assessment (Case studies of teaching in higher education series): Case studies, experience and practice from higher education* (pp. 70–77). London: Kogan Page Stylus Publishing.

Gielen, S., Peeters, E., Dochy, F., Onghena, P., & Struyven, K. (2010). Improving the effectiveness of peer feedback for learning. *Learning and Instruction, 20*(4), 304–315.

Goodrich, H. (1996). Student self-assessment: At the intersection of metacognition and authentic assessment. *Unpublished doctoral dissertation.* Cambridge, MA: Harvard University.

Griffin, P. (2007). The comfort of competence and the uncertainty of assessment. *Studies in Educational Evaluation, 33,* 87–99.

Hattie, J. (2008). *Visible learning: A synthesis of over 800 meta-analyses relating to achievement.* Oxford: Routledge.

Hattie, J., & Timperley, H. (2007). The power of feedback. *Review of Educational Research, 77,* 81–112.

Heritage, M. (2010). *Formative assessment: Making it happen in the classroom.* Thousand Oaks, CA: Corwin Press.

Heritage, M. (2013). *Formative assessment: A process of inquiry and action.* Cambridge, MA: Harvard Education Press.

Klenowski, V. (2009). Assessment for learning revisited: An Asia-Pacific perspective. *Assessment in Education: Principles, Policy, & Practice, 16*(3), 263–268.

Kluger, A. N., & DeNisi, A. (1996). The effects of feedback interventions on performance: A historical review, a meta-analysis, and a preliminary feedback intervention theory. *Psychological Bulletin, 119,* 254–284.

Levy, F., & Murnane, R. J. (2004). *The new division of labor: How computers are creating the next job market.* Princeton, NJ: Princeton University Press.

Liu, N., & Carless, D. (2006). Peer feedback: The learning element of peer assessment. *Teaching in Higher Education, 11*(3), 279–290.

Marshall, B., & Drummond, M. J. (2006). How teachers engage with assessment for learning: Lessons from the classroom. *Research Papers in Education, 18*(4), 119–132.

Miller, V. (2008). The incorporation of peer assisted study sessions (PASS) into the core curriculum of a first year chemistry module. In A. Irons (Ed.), *Enhancing learning through formative assessment and feedback.* London: Routledge.

National Council of Teachers of Mathematics. (2014). *Principles into actions: Ensuring mathematical success for all.* Reston, VA: Author.

National Research Council. (2001). *Knowing what students know: The science of design and educational assessment.* Washington, DC: National Academies Press.

National Research Council. (2012). *Education for life and work: Developing transferable knowledge and skills in the 21st century.* Washington, DC: National Academies Press.

Natriello, G. (1987). The impact of evaluation processes on students. *Educational Psychologist, 22,* 155–175.

New Zealand Ministry of Education. (1994). *Assessment: Policy to practice.* Wellington: Learning Media.

New Zealand Ministry of Education. (2011). *Ministry of Education position paper: Assessment.* Wellington: Learning Media.

OECD. (2013). *Synergies for better learning: An international perspective on evaluation and assessment. OECD reviews and assessment in education.* Paris: OECD Publishing.

Otero, V. (2006). Moving beyond the "get it or don't" conception of formative assessment. *Journal of Teacher Education, 57*(3), 247–255.

Paris, S. G., & Paris, A. H. (2001). Classroom applications of research on self-regulated learning. *Educational Psychologist, 36*(2), 89–101.

Perrenoud, P. (1998). From formative evaluation to a controlled regulation of learning. Towards a wider conceptual field. *Assessment in Education: Principles Policy and Practice, 5*(1), 85–102.

Ramaprasad, A. (1983). On the definition of feedback. *Behavioral Science, 28*(1), 4–13.

Ross, A. (2016). *Industries of the future*. New York: Simon & Schuster.

Sadler, D. (1989). Formative assessment and the design of instructional systems. *Instructional Science, 18*, 119–144.

Schunk, K. H., & Hanson, A. R. (1985). Peer models: Influence of children's self-efficacy and achievement. *Journal of Educational Psychology, 77*, 313–322.

Shepard, L. A. (2009). Commentary: Evaluating the validity of formative and interim assessment. *Educational Measurement: Issues and Practice, 28*(3), 32–37.

Shepard, L. A. (2013). Foreword. In J. McMillan (Ed.), *Sage handbook of research on classroom assessment* (pp. xix–xxii). Thousand Oaks, CA: Sage.

Swaffield, S. (2011). Getting to the heart of authentic assessment for learning. *Assessment in Education: Principles, Policy & Practice, 18*(4), 433–449.

Topping, K. (2003). Self and peer assessment in school and university: Reliability, utility and validity. In M. Segers, F. Dochy, & E. Cascallar (Eds.), *Optimising new modes of assessment: In search of qualities and standards* (pp. 57–87). The Netherlands: Kluwer Academic Publishers.

Torrance, H., & Pryor, J. (2001). Developing formative assessment in the classroom: Using action research to explore and modify theory. *British Educational Research Journal, 27*, 615–631.

Vygotsky, L. S. (1962). *Thought and language*. Cambridge, MA: MIT Press.

Wenger, E. (1998). *Communities of practice: Learning, meaning, and identity*. New York: Cambridge University Press.

Wiliam, D. (2011). *Embedded formative assessment*. Bloomington, IN: Solution Tree Press.

Zimmerman, B. J. (2002). Becoming a self-regulated learner: An overview. *Theory into Practice, 41*(2), 64–70.

Zimmerman, B. J. (2008). Investigating self-regulation and motivation: Historical background, methodological developments, and future prospects. *American Educational Research Journal, 45*(1), 166–183.

Zimmerman, B. J., & Schunk, D. H. (2008). Motivation: An essential dimension of self-regulated learning. In B. J. Zimmerman & D. H. Schunk (Eds.), *Motivation and self-regulated learning: Theory, research and applications* (pp. 1–30). New York: Lawrence Earlbaum Associates.

Zimmerman, B., & Schunk, D. (2011). *Handbook of self-regulation of learning and performance*. New York: Routledge.

Conclusion

Future Directions for College- and Career-Readiness Research: Where Do We Go from Here?

Krista D. Mattern, Matthew N. Gaertner, and Katie Larsen McClarty

When Katie, Matt, and I first sat down to brainstorm ideas for a book prospectus on college and career readiness, we articulated our hopes for what *another* book on the topic could contribute to the literature. College and career readiness had been generating substantial interest and enthusiasm among educators, researchers, policymakers, and the general public, but there were already quite a few books on the topic. How could this book be different, and what could we contribute to the dialogue?

We set out to produce an edited book on college and career readiness that was grounded in scientific research. That is, we felt the college- and career-readiness discourse could benefit from more systematic empirical evidence. Debates too often hinge on anecdotes or case studies that have not been replicated or generalized, so we wanted a volume with a balance of theory, research, and practice, supported by rigorous scientific research findings. It quickly became apparent that there were three questions the book would need to address:

1   How should we define and measure college and career readiness?
2   What are some best practices for validating college- and career-readiness performance levels and uses?
3   What interventions show the most promise for improving college and career readiness among students?

These questions dictated the structure of the book and the information conveyed within. As authors began to submit their chapters, themes began to emerge within each section as well as some themes that spanned the entire book. We will use this closing chapter to summarize some of those themes. We believe that in doing so, we can highlight current issues and trends in college- and career-readiness research as well as elucidate future directions for research and practice.

Part 1 Themes: Defining and Measuring College and Career Readiness

Part 1 focuses on identifying the knowledge, skills, and attributes associated with college and career readiness as well as how those constructs are measured. As we reviewed the four chapters in this section, we noticed several key issues repeatedly surfacing. The major themes include: (1) Multidimensional definitions, (2) Improved prediction, (3) Malleability, and (4) Personalized feedback and improved decision-making.

Multidimensional Definitions of College and Career Readiness

Research clearly suggests that definitions of college and career readiness focusing solely on English language arts and mathematics do not sufficiently represent what a student needs to know to be able to succeed in college and beyond. Even McCallum and Pellegrino point out that to fully understand one's level of mathematics mastery, assessment of not only knowledge and skills but also mathematical practice and durability is essential. Conley eloquently takes this point further and highlights some forward-thinking models of college and career readiness that take a more holistic view. Gaertner and Roberts focus their chapter on the importance of noncognitive factors and make a compelling case for why these attributes should be included in definitions of college and career readiness. Taking a slightly different angle, Wai, Worrell, and Chabris argue that general cognitive ability often does not get the attention it deserves in definitions of college and career readiness. That is, many definitions stipulate the knowledge and skills students need to succeed, but often fail to underscore the importance of general cognitive ability. Given the plethora of research showing a relationship between general cognitive ability and important outcomes later in life, ignoring such information may result in unrealistic expectations about future endeavors and, ultimately, poor decision-making.

It is pretty clear that current definitions of college and career readiness need to expand to include a broader set of knowledge, skills, abilities, and personal attributes. We still lack consensus, however, on exactly which knowledge, skills, abilities, and personal attributes should be included. We also lack consensus on the appropriate grain size for these constructs, given the tradeoffs between improved measurement and limited time and instructional resources for new content areas. This is a topic McCallum and Pellegrino articulate with clarity. We will revisit the idea of a common model of college and career readiness when discussing future directions for research.

Improved Prediction

One benefit of including more dimensions in models of college and career readiness is better power to explain variance in key outcomes. If success is multidimensional, it follows that success predictors should be multidimensional too. All four chapters discuss the importance of validity evidence for informing definitions of college and career readiness. For example, Conley discusses the need to move from an "eligibility model," which focuses on who will be admitted to college, to a "readiness model," which focuses on who will be successful once in college. Though their focus is on readiness in mathematics, McCallum and Pellegrino's point that it is imperative to validate assumptions about predictive validity applies to any construct and assessment being used for college- and career-readiness diagnoses. Likewise, one of the central theses of Gaertner and Roberts's chapter is improved prediction by the inclusion of noncognitive traits. On this point, the research is unambiguous; noncognitive factors, like conscientiousness and motivation, add incremental validity to the prediction of educational and workplace outcomes above and beyond traditional cognitive measures. Finally, given the independent predictive power of cognitive measures, Wai et al. rightly caution against excluding such measures in models of college and career readiness.

In general, we have witnessed a shift in the type of evidence needed to support measures of college and career readiness. College- and career-readiness definitions used to rely solely on content claims developed by subject matter experts (SMEs). There is now a push to tie college- and career-readiness standards and performance levels to college success, so predictive claims have become central to validity arguments. Reliability and concurrent validity are no longer enough; test developers must now demonstrate that a student's performance on a state's measure of college and career readiness provides a precise and accurate forecast of his or her likelihood of future success. In principle, predicting distal student outcomes demands longitudinal data, and collecting these data requires careful planning, strong partnerships, and ongoing monitoring.

Malleability

Another reoccurring theme across the chapters was acknowledgment that some constructs are more malleable than others. Conley takes a strong stance that the feedback we give students should be actionable. Constructs that students can't change (say, socioeconomic status) should not be included in definitions of college and career readiness. Gaertner and Roberts also give a good deal of attention to this topic and generally agree with Conley that by focusing on constructs that are most malleable, we are more likely to impact college- and career-readiness rates. They do argue, however, that for reasons both statistical and political, less malleable constructs (e.g., cognitive ability) should not be ignored; however, we may be better served by developing interventions that focus on areas that students can develop and improve upon. Because of the immutability of general cognitive ability, Wai et al. argue that it is often excluded from definitions of college and career readiness, despite its importance for determining success later in life. Whether or not interventions can actually boost intelligence, Wai et al. make a compelling case for keeping cognitive ability in definitions of college and career readiness. Wai et al. and Gaertner and Roberts agree: underspecified models or an omitted variable problem will bias regression results and could result in spurious findings. Clearly, some of the most important factors that predict college and career readiness may be relatively fixed. Rather than ignoring this concern, we would be better served using this information to develop tailored interventions or deliver instruction that maximizes learning. As such, we see personalized learning as an area that holds significant promise.

Personalized Feedback and Improved Decision-Making

College- and career-readiness diagnoses and feedback should be personalized and nuanced, because personalization improves decision-making. In particular, Conley emphasizes the benefits of providing feedback in terms of students' profiles of strengths and weaknesses rather than focusing on single data points in isolation. Nuanced profile data can support better decision-making (for both students and postsecondary institutions) by spotlighting the majors or career pathways that fit best with students' skills and interests. Gaertner and Roberts also argue that we can provide more nuanced diagnoses and more tailored interventions by considering students' varied strengths and weaknesses, particularly when constructs are measured at a finer grain size. McCallum and Pellegrino make a similar case by highlighting the utility of learning progressions to understand exactly what content a student has and has not mastered. Another use of improved decision-making based on personalized feedback is choosing colleges based on academic fit, as Wai et al. point out. Put simply, more information—thoughtfully organized—begets more informed decisions. So, what stands in the way? First, we need more research validating new measures and multidimensional models of college and career readiness by linking student performance to postsecondary (i.e., academic and workplace) outcome data. We also need to reconcile operational constraints, including the collection and storage of longitudinal student data across a multitude of constructs and feasible mechanisms for providing interactive and holistic reports.

Part 2 Themes: Validating College- and Career-Readiness Performance Levels and Uses

Part 2 focuses on research validating the use of college- and career-readiness measures, standards, and benchmarks. Specifically, the first two chapters describe some common approaches for setting college- and career-readiness benchmarks and standards; the next two chapters focus on the use and implications of college- and career-readiness performance levels for institutions of higher education and for diverse student populations; and the final chapter addresses the challenge of mixed messages that attend the widespread adoption of many different college-readiness measures. Themes identified in Part 2 include: (1) college readiness versus career readiness, (2) content-empirical evidence continuum, (3) equity concerns over misclassification, and (4) coherence of feedback.

College Readiness versus Career Readiness

Several chapters in Part 2—including McClarty, Loomis, and Pitoniak's chapter, Camara, Allen, and Moore's chapter, and Zwick's chapter, as well as Conley's and McCallum and Pellegrino's chapters in Part 1—discuss the issue of whether college readiness and career readiness are the same or different. This is a persistent and fundamental consideration; before one can evaluate the evidence of intended interpretations and claims of readiness diagnoses, the intended interpretations need to be clearly articulated. Do readiness cut scores indicate college readiness? Career readiness? Both? Though the term "college and career readiness" is ubiquitous, most college- and career-readiness benchmarks are derived based only on the relationship between test scores and college success. Empirical studies focused on evaluating whether college readiness and career readiness are the same or different are scant. Based on the handful of studies addressing this issue, some researchers have concluded that the terms are the same, whereas others argue there are meaningful differences between being college ready versus career ready. In sum, the jury is still out.

There are several reasons that this remains an open question. First, there is no consensus on the correct criteria to use to evaluate career readiness. Whereas college success is a fairly straightforward concept (e.g., course grades), it is not clear whether career success should be defined in terms of performance in career technical education courses, successful completion of a job training program, or on-the-job performance. Even if there were consensus on career success criteria, career readiness benchmarks remain elusive, given the lack of workforce outcome data linked to traditional college- and career-readiness assessments. We obviously need more research before the "college versus career" debate can be settled definitively. Studies should evaluate not only whether the same constructs (e.g., reading, math, teamwork) are relevant for college readiness and career readiness but also whether the same performance levels (e.g., cut scores) are appropriate for readiness in both domains.

One commonly cited barrier to progress in defining career readiness is the fact that different occupations require different knowledge, skills, abilities, and personal characteristics. Therefore, there can't be a single definition of career readiness. However, the same difficulties arise when defining college readiness, as different college majors require different knowledge, skills, abilities, and personal characteristics. College-readiness benchmarks represent the typical level of knowledge that students need to succeed at a typical institution. A similar approach could be taken to define career readiness: the typical level of knowledge, skills, abilities, and personal characteristics to be successful at a typical job or occupation. For both college and career readiness, more personalized diagnoses could be provided as they relate to a student's goals and aspirations. However, for monitoring readiness across students, states, and time, a single, general definition of readiness is a more pragmatic solution.

Content-Empirical Evidence Continuum

Both McClarty et al. and Camara et al. discuss different standard-setting approaches by highlighting the fact that the evidence to set college- and career-readiness performance levels can run the gamut from strictly content-based approaches, at one end, to strictly empirical approaches, at the other. Each approach has its strengths and drawbacks, and McClarty et al. make a compelling case for blending them. In fact, McClarty et al. and Camara et al. both discuss the importance of empirical (or predictive) claims and content claims. However, McClarty et al. describe a process where SMEs would define both predictive and content claims, which could result in disagreement between the two types of claims. On the other hand, Camara et al. describe a process where SMEs define the predictive claims (outcome, success criteria, probability of success). Then, based on the empirically derived cut score, performance level descriptors can be developed to indicate what students know and are able to do at each performance level.

Predictive claims and content claims are not necessarily at odds with each other, but it does seem like there should be a prespecified order to how the two types of claims are defined. Camara et al. describe an approach where the predictive claims are first defined, which then drives the performance level descriptions. Alternatively, one could first set cut scores based on what students should know and be able to do (content claims). Based on those cut scores, the likelihood that students who meet those thresholds will be successful once in college can be estimated. Whether one chooses to set predictive claims first or content claims first, it seems like this should be an iterative process, where the criteria is continually updated until the SMEs are satisfied with both claims. For example, SMEs may choose a content claim that results in an unreasonably low likelihood of success. Given the predictive evidence, they may want to revise their content claims to a more rigorous level, which would produce a predictive claim that a student has a higher likelihood of success.

Equity Concerns over Misclassification

The chapters by Barnett and Reddy and Zwick both comment on classification errors associated with using narrowly defined measures of college and career readiness to label students as not ready or in need of remediation and in particular the potential ramifications for underserved, minority populations. Zwick makes the point that "not ready" diagnoses may have the unintended consequence of lowering both teacher and student expectations and ultimately, student achievement; research suggests that this effect may be larger for minority students. Both Barnett and Reddy and Zwick argue that classification accuracy would be improved with inclusion of high school grades and caution against overreliance on a single test score. Barnett and Reddy also discuss supplemental measures one may wish to consider for placement purposes, such as career interest inventories and noncognitive traits. Zwick, however, cautions against including noncognitive measures in college- and career-readiness diagnoses, as their use may exacerbate social inequality—especially if such factors are not uniformly taught at school. Camara et al. and McClarty et al. note the importance of examining and communicating impact data (i.e., projected pass rates) during the standard-setting process for this very reason.

Coherence of Feedback

Camara et al. and Mattern and Gaertner stress the importance of providing coherent feedback to students over time and from different sources. Camara et al. weigh different methodologies and approaches to providing students with valid "on track" forecasts in earlier grades. Ideally, earlier cut scores would be estimated based on data tracking students longitudinally from elementary school through college enrollment. In reality, cut scores usually can't wait for longitudinal data to accrue, and Camara et al. describe different approaches to estimating cut scores when complete longitudinal data are not available. Mattern and Gaertner also stress the importance of providing coherent feedback to students and the ramifications inherent in "mixed messages"—ranging from a distrust of test scores to widespread confusion in trying to compare college- and career-readiness rates meaningfully over time and across states. Given the Every Student Succeeds Act's commitment to decentralization, mixed messages will continue to threaten large-scale evaluations of educational progress without proactive coordination across research groups and educational agencies.

Part 3 Themes: Improving College and Career Readiness

The third and final section of this book includes four chapters focused on college- and career-readiness interventions. Our decision to include research on educational interventions in a National Council on Measurement in Education (NCME) volume was unorthodox, but quite purposeful. Put simply, we are interested in not only how to define and measure college and career readiness but also how to improve it. The book's final section therefore highlights interventions that have shown promise, and across its four chapters, four common themes emerge: (1) improving access, (2) implementing noncognitive interventions to improve cognitive performance, (3) contextualized instruction, and (4) personal agency.

Improving Access

If the United States is ever going to reach the goal of all students graduating high school college and career ready, access to high-quality education must be broadened. This argument is the centerpiece of both the Tillery and Duckor chapter, as well as the Leahy and Landel chapter. In fact, Tillery and Duckor begin their chapter with statistics highlighting the disparity in college enrollment rates between low- and high-income students. Such inequities motivated development of the GEAR UP program as a way to improve college access for low-income students. By providing both cognitive and noncognitive services, GEAR UP has had a positive impact on a variety of educational outcomes, including college and career readiness. Likewise, Leahy and Landel discuss the importance of equal access to a high-quality education for all, with a particular focus on effective math course sequencing. Schools, teachers, and educational resources are not all created equal; however, finding ways to level the playing field so that all students have access to a high-quality education should be a national priority. This is not a new argument, but at a time when cultural and class divides have been brought into sharp relief, it bears repetition with emphasis.

Implementing Noncognitive Interventions to Improve Cognitive Performance

All four chapters in Part 3 discuss the key role of noncognitive factors for improving college and career readiness. Tillery and Duckor highlight some of GEAR UP's noncognitive domains, such as college fit and parent engagement, in its holistic approach to preparing students for college. Similarly, Leahy and Landel indicate that one of the New Mathways project's four main principles is intentional use of strategies—such as self-regulated learning, motivational beliefs, and growth mindset—to help students develop skills as learners. Heritage also notes the importance of self-regulated learning as an essential ingredient to promote academic progress within the framework of formative assessments. Likewise, Kroeper and Murphy stress the importance of noncognitive and contextual factors, such as growth mindset, social belongingness, and utility value, and discuss ways to improve learning through social psychological interventions. Perhaps contrary to conventional wisdom, this collection of chapters makes a strong case for developing noncognitive skills, not just because they supplement cognitive skills but also because noncognitive skill-building actually helps boost cognitive outcomes.

Contextualized Instruction

In order to engage students in their course material, Leahy and Landel, along with Kroeper and Murphy, point to the benefit of students understanding the value and relevance of the curriculum being delivered. Many students fail to see the connection between what they are learning in the classroom and the world of work. In response, Kroeper and Murphy suggest utility value interventions where students articulate the value of their coursework, which in turn promotes better performance, in particular for minority students. In a similar vein, providing more experiential learning opportunities to students—strengthening the link between school and work—would boost engagement and encourage career exploration, as noted by Conley.

Personal Agency

Academic progress depends on students taking an active role in their learning and development; students cannot be passive players in the learning experience. Heritage discusses this issue in depth. In particular, to successfully implement a horizontal relationship in the classroom where the student, the teacher, and peers all provide feedback and take an active role in the learning process, personal agency must be cultivated and reinforced. Leahy and Landel also note the ineffectiveness of (and present overreliance upon) traditional teacher-centered and lecture-oriented practices in the classroom, where student-centered practices are too rarely implemented. This is a key insight. Although the discourse on student intervention revolves around what we should be doing to students, it is equally important to help students take ownership of their own educational careers, so they know what to do for themselves to best prepare for a happy and prosperous future.

Future Directions for Defining and Measuring College and Career Readiness

Based on the themes we have identified throughout the book, we next highlight areas where more research is needed to advance college and career readiness research and practice. The areas we have identified are: (1) common model of college and career readiness, (2) new constructs and measurement models, (3) personalized learning, and (4) personalized feedback.

Common Model of College and Career Readiness

Many different frameworks and models of college and career readiness have been put forth, each with its own unique features. Though none of the models are identical, there is considerable overlap in terms of the constructs identified as important for college and career readiness. To move the field and science behind college and career readiness forward, these various models need to be compared empirically in order to identify the constructs that are most important for college and career readiness and success and thereby drive the development of a unified model. This line of research should include testing whether the same model applies for college versus career readiness. Our reluctance to state a definitive conclusion may be frustrating, but it is appropriately conservative; we need more evidence before we can say with confidence whether college readiness and career readiness are the same or different.

The development and adoption of a common model is critical to effectively track and monitor college- and career-readiness rates over time and across state borders, as Mattern and Gaertner mention. A common college- and career-readiness model must also align assiduously with what is taught in school. As both Conley and McCallum and Pellegrino point out, if readiness definitions are used for accountability, then it is imperative that readiness constructs are plainly visible in the curriculum and in the classroom.

New Constructs and Measurement Models

Depending on which constructs are ultimately included in a common model of college and career readiness, new assessments will need to be developed. Given the research underscoring the importance of noncognitive factors for educational and workplace success, we suspect that many of these assessments will need to measure noncognitive constructs. This is an area where much work is needed. Compared to a cognitive assessment—say, an assessment of algebra mastery where there are clearly correct answers—noncognitive item development is a bit trickier. Moreover, traditional measurement models that assume higher levels of a trait are best may not be appropriate for noncognitive measures. Additional measurement approaches should be considered.

One of the biggest hurdles facing the implementation of noncognitive assessments, particularly for high-stakes uses such as accountability, is the issue of fakability and coaching. It is clear that when asked if one works hard or shows up on time, the desirable answer is "Yes!" To combat this issue, novel item types (e.g., forced-choice formats) are currently being developed and researched. Along these lines, alternative assessment types such as serious games may address a critical need and will therefore demand an ongoing program of rigorous research.

Personalized Learning

Another area we believe holds much promise is personalized learning and formative assessment. Although research indicates that students learn at different rates, K–12 education tends to be incompatibly rigid. Students progress through the system in yearly intervals, even though some are advancing to the next grade level without successfully mastering the content, while others learn the material well before year's end and could benefit from more advanced content. Research on how to craft and deliver curriculum (1) that is tailored to the individual, (2) at scale, and (3) that maximizes learning could revolutionize education. When content is appropriate to what kids know and are able to do, deficiencies can be identified early and remedied before students falls too far behind. Thus, personalized learning is a potentially viable way to address stagnant college- and career-readiness rates, though there is a large disparity between personalized learning's current and ideal states.

Personalized Feedback

In line with the Gestalt psychology principle that "the whole is other than the sum of its parts," we firmly believe that taking a holistic view of student preparedness will provide insights that are not apparent when looking at each construct in isolation. To fully realize the potential of new models of college and career readiness, attention and resources should be devoted to creating formal structures to seamlessly collect and store data on individuals across a multitude of constructs and develop interactive and holistic reporting mechanisms that provide personalized and timely feedback. By personalized feedback, it is not enough to tell students how they are doing across a variety of constructs. They need to understand the implications of their strengths and weakness as they relate to future success. By providing feedback relative to a student's unique configuration of skills, abilities, and interests, we can offer actionable diagnoses that assist in decision-making, such as selecting a well-fitting college major or career pathway. In order to provide more personalized feedback, much more research is needed building and validating statistical models focused on a variety of outcomes to better understand whether key readiness predictors are compensatory, conjunctive, additive, and/or interactive.

Research on college and career readiness has advanced considerably in the last couple of decades. The chapters in this book make that clear. The measurement field is expanding in an abundance of new and exciting directions, many of which hold great promise for college and career readiness. Our hope is that this book serves as both a useful register of where we are now and a provoking stimulus for future inquiry.

Contributors

Jeff M. Allen is a statistician in the Statistical and Applied Research department at ACT. He specializes in research linking test scores to educational outcomes, and he contributed to the development of the ACT College Readiness Benchmarks. Other research interests include growth model methodology and the relationship of psychosocial factors to high school and college success. Jeff earned his PhD in biostatistics from the University of Iowa and a BS in mathematics from Wartburg College.

Elisabeth Barnett is a senior research associate at the Community College Research Center (CCRC) at Teachers College, Columbia University and also serves as associate director of the National Center for Education, Schools and Teaching (NCREST) at Teachers College. She leads a USDOE funded evaluation of a data analytics approach to assessment under the auspices of the Center for the Analysis of Postsecondary Readiness. Dr. Barnett's research interests relate to high school to college transition, assessment and placement, community colleges, and workforce education. Dr. Barnett received her PhD from the University of Illinois at Urbana-Champaign in Educational Organization and Leadership.

Wayne J. Camara is the senior vice president of research at ACT. Before coming to ACT, Wayne served as associate executive director at the American Psychological Association (APA) and as vice president for research and development at College Board. Wayne has served as president or chair of the Association of Test Publishers (ATP), National Council on Measurement in Education (NCME) and divisions of the APA and American Educational Research Association (AERA). Wayne has a PhD in organizational psychology from the University of Illinois at Champaign-Urbana and degrees from Rhode Island College and the University of Massachusetts at Dartmouth.

Christopher F. Chabris is a professor at Geisinger Health System in Pennsylvania and Visiting Fellow at the Institute for Advanced Study in Toulouse, France. He received his PhD in psychology and AB in computer science from Harvard University. His research focuses on attention, intelligence (individual, collective, and social), behavioral genetics, and decision-making. His scholarly work has been published in leading journals including *Science, Nature, PNAS, Psychological Science, Perception,* and *Cognitive Science.* Chris is also the coauthor of *The Invisible Gorilla: How Our Intuitions Deceive Us,* which has been published in 19 languages.

Mitchell D. Chester has served as Massachusetts Commissioner of Elementary and Secondary Education since 2008. He began his career as an elementary school teacher. He oversaw curriculum and instructional programs for the Connecticut State Education Department in the 1990s. In 1997, Chester was appointed the executive director for Accountability and Assessment for the School District of Philadelphia. In 2001, he moved to Ohio, where he served as the Ohio Department of Education's Senior Associate State Superintendent for Policy and

Accountability. He was responsible for Ohio's implementation of the *No Child Left Behind Act*. Chester holds a doctorate in education from Harvard University.

David T. Conley is a professor of Educational Policy and Leadership in the College of Education at the University of Oregon, where he directs the Center for Educational Policy Research. He is the founder and president of EdImagine, an educational strategy consulting company. He is the founder and served for 12 years as CEO of the Educational Policy Improvement Center, EPIC. He recently completed an appointment as Senior Fellow for Deeper Learning with the Hewlett Foundation. Dr. Conley is a national thought leader on college and career readiness, student ownership of learning, systems of assessment, and new models of educational accountability.

Brent Duckor is an associate professor at the Lurie College of Education at San Jose State University. Dr. Duckor's research interests include teachers' understanding and use of formative assessment in the K–12 classroom; validation of teacher licensure exams and certification in state, national, and international contexts; and measuring noncognitive outcomes for program evaluation and school improvement to better serve historically disadvantaged, low-income youth. He has served as a measurement consultant to SJSU's GEAR UP program and is an advisory committee member of NCCEP's College and Career Readiness Evaluation Consortium. He holds a PhD in quantitative methods and evaluation from U.C. Berkeley.

Matthew N. Gaertner is a principal research scientist in SRI International's Center for Education Policy. His research focuses on college and career readiness and the effects of educational policies and reforms on disadvantaged students' access, persistence, and achievement. Gaertner's work has been published in Harvard Law & Policy Review, Harvard Educational Review, Educational Evaluation and Policy Analysis, Research in Higher Education, Educational Measurement: Issues and Practice and the Journal of College Admission. Gaertner earned a BA from Georgetown University and a PhD in research and evaluation methodology from the University of Colorado, Boulder.

Margaret Heritage joined WestEd as senior scientist in October 2014 after 22 years at UCLA, where she served as principal of the laboratory school of the Graduate School of Education and Information Studies, then as an assistant director at the National Center for Research on Evaluation, Standards and Student Testing (CRESST) UCLA. Before joining UCLA, she worked for many years in schools in the United Kingdom, including a period as an Inspector of Schools. She taught in the Department of Education at the University of Warwick, England and has taught in the Departments of Education at UCLA and Stanford University.

Kathryn M. Kroeper is a doctoral student in Psychological and Brain Sciences at Indiana University and a National Science Foundation Graduate Research Fellow. She and her advisor, Mary Murphy, design, implement, and evaluate educational interventions intended to improve the academic outcomes of students, especially members of groups that have been historically underrepresented and disadvantaged in postsecondary settings. Kathryn earned a BA from Rutgers University in 2012.

Carolyn Landel, PhD is the managing director of the Charles A. Dana Center at The University of Texas at Austin. Dr. Carolyn Landel works alongside the executive director to establish long-term strategic goals in programmatic and partnership development. She directs the day-to-day mobilization of personnel and programs to achieve these goals. Before joining the Center, Dr. Landel was chief program officer for Washington STEM, a nonprofit organization dedicated to advancing excellence, equity, and innovation in science, technology, engineering, and math education in Washington state. In this role, she created innovative partnerships with districts, higher education institutions, and state and national STEM education organizations and agencies.

Francesca Fraga Leahy, EdM assists the Dana Center's executive director with research and communications related to students' successful transitions to postsecondary education. She works with Center teams to transmit clear messages to constituents, collaborators, and funders related to the Center's work in redesigning pathways to upward mobility in higher education. Before joining the Center, Ms. Leahy taught for five years in the Rio Grande Valley and Central Texas to majority low-income and English language learner students. Her graduate work at Harvard University focused on state education policy and applied data analysis.

Susan Cooper Loomis served as assistant director for Psychometrics with the National Assessment Governing Board 2004–2012 and currently serves as a consultant for standard setting projects. She has held leadership roles in standard setting procedures for the National Assessment of Educational Progress (NAEP) in all subjects since 1991. She was also a leader in the design and implementation of the NAEP grade 12 preparedness research program. Dr. Loomis worked with ACT, Inc. for 18 years, directing development of K–12 assessments and conducting and reporting research in a variety of educational issue areas. She held postsecondary faculty positions in both political science and geography and professional research positions at the University of Michigan, the Norwegian Data Commission in Oslo, Norway, and the University of Iowa.

Krista D. Mattern is a director of ACT's Statistical and Applied Research Department. Her research focuses on evaluating the validity and fairness of both cognitive and noncognitive measures for predicting student success. She is also interested in higher education issues such as college choice, major selection, and college completion. Her work has been published in journals such as the *Journal of Applied Psychology, Educational Measurement: Issues and Practice, Educational and Psychological Measurement,* and the *Journal of College Student Development.* Dr. Mattern received her PhD in industrial and organizational psychology with a minor in quantitative psychology from the University of Illinois, Urbana-Champaign.

William McCallum is a professor of Mathematics at the University of Arizona. He received his PhD in Mathematics from Harvard University in 1984. His professional interests include arithmetical algebraic geometry and mathematics education. He is a member of the Harvard calculus consortium and is the lead author of the consortium's multivariable calculus and college algebra texts. In 2009–2010, he was one of the lead writers for the Common Core State Standards in Mathematics. In 2013, he founded Illustrative Mathematics, a nonprofit dedicated to creating a world where learners know, use, and enjoy mathematics.

Katie Larsen McClarty, chief assessment officer at Questar Assessments, oversees item and test development, publishing, psychometrics, and research. Her own research centers on assessment design, college readiness, standard setting, and gifted education with publications in journals such as the *American Psychologist, Gifted Child Quarterly, Educational Measurement: Issues and Practice,* and *Educational Researcher.* She is a recipient of the 2013 Charles F. Elton Best Paper Award from the Association of Institutional Research and the 2015 Best Paper Award from the National Association of Gifted Children. McClarty earned her PhD in social and personality psychology from the University of Texas at Austin.

Joann L. Moore is a research scientist in the Statistical and Applied Research Department at ACT, specializing in the prediction of secondary and postsecondary outcomes from academic and noncognitive factors. She has conducted empirically based standard setting for states using the ACT for accountability purposes. She has a PhD in educational measurement and statistics from the University of Iowa, a MS in Psychology from Montana State University, Bozeman, and a BA in psychology from Coe College in Cedar Rapids, Iowa.

Mary C. Murphy is an associate professor of Psychological and Brain Sciences at Indiana University and a cofounder of the College Transition Collaborative. Her research illuminates the situational cues that influence students' academic motivation and achievement with an emphasis on understanding when those processes are similar and different for majority and minority students. She develops, implements, and evaluates social psychological interventions that reduce identity threat for students and examines their effects on students' motivation, persistence, and performance. Dr. Murphy earned a BA from the University of Texas at Austin and a PhD from Stanford University. She completed an NSF postdoctoral fellowship at Northwestern University.

James W. Pellegrino is Liberal Arts and Sciences Distinguished Professor and Codirector of the *Learning Sciences Research Institute* at the University of Illinois at Chicago. His research and development interests focus on children's and adults' thinking and learning and the implications for assessment and instructional practice. He has published over 300 books, chapters, and articles in the areas of cognition, instruction, and assessment and has chaired several National Academy of Sciences study committees, including the *Foundations of Assessment, Defining Deeper Learning and 21st Century Skills,* and *Developing Assessments of Science Proficiency in K–12*. He is a past member of the Board on Testing and Assessment of the National Research Council.

Mary J. Pitoniak is a senior strategic advisor in the Office of the Vice President of Research within the Research and Development division at Educational Testing Service (ETS). Dr. Pitoniak is an internationally known expert in standard setting, having published, conducted research, and provided training in this area in the United States and worldwide. She is the coauthor of the standard setting chapters in the fourth edition of *Educational Measurement*. She has served on the Technical Advisory Committee on Standard Setting for NAEP since 2004. She has also done work in the area of testing accommodations for students with disabilities and English language learners.

Vikash Reddy is a postdoctoral research associate at the Community College Research Center at Teachers College, Columbia University. Dr. Reddy researches developmental education through his affiliation with the Center for the Analysis of Postsecondary Readiness. His previous research at CCRC examined the impacts of performance funding programs on public colleges and universities. Reddy received his PhD in education policy from Teachers College, Columbia University in 2016. Prior to enrolling at Teachers College, Reddy taught third grade in East New York, the first two of those years as a member of Teach For America.

Richard D. Roberts, PhD is vice president and chief scientist, Center for Innovative Assessments, ProExam, New York. His main area of specialization is measurement, with a special emphasis on developing and researching innovative new items types for the assessment of both cognitive and noncognitive factors. Dr. Roberts has published over a dozen books and about 200 peer-review articles/book chapters on these topics in diverse subdisciplines, with nearly 400 presentations across the globe. He has recently developed a new noncognitive assessment system for students—Tessera™—which includes student, teacher, and school-level reporting.

Chrissy Tillery, EdD, is the director of evaluation at the National Council for Community and Education Partnerships in Washington, DC, where she leads Gaining Early Awareness and Readiness for Undergraduate Programs (GEAR UP) research and evaluation, including the College and Career Readiness Evaluation Consortium, a multistate evaluation focused on evidence-based outcomes of college access and success. Dr. Tillery works with national constituents to promote best practices in research and evaluation focused on students in low-income schools as they pursue their college dreams. Dr. Tillery has provided research and evaluation leadership on US Department of Education grants for two decades.

Jonathan Wai is a research fellow at Geisinger Health System in the Autism & Developmental Medicine Institute and a visiting researcher at Case Western Reserve University in the department of Psychology. Dr. Wai studies how individual talents, education, and contextual factors collectively impact the development of achievement and expertise across a variety of domains. He's used historical, longitudinal, and experimental approaches to examine the multiple factors that contribute and take away from human capital development and how they are connected to policies and conversations on enhancing education, creativity, and innovation. His work has won multiple international Mensa Awards for Research Excellence and has been discussed broadly in the global press.

Frank C. Worrell is a professor of School Psychology at the University of California, Berkeley, where he serves as Faculty Director of the School Psychology Program, the Academic Talent Development Program, and the California College Preparatory Academy. Dr. Worrell's research interests include the role of psychosocial variables in educational and psychological functioning, cultural identities, scale development, and translation of psychological research into school-based practice. He is a fellow of the Association for Psychological Science, the American Educational Research Association, and five divisions of the American Psychological Association. He concluded a term as Editor of *Review of Educational Research* in 2016.

Rebecca Zwick is a distinguished presidential appointee at Educational Testing Service and a professor emerita at the University of California, Santa Barbara. Her most recent research has focused on college admissions, test validity and fairness, and score reporting. She is the author of *Who Gets In? Strategies for Fair and Effective College Admissions* (2017).

Index